KEEPER of STORIES

CRITICAL READINGS OF EASTERINE KIRE'S NOVELS

With the visible growth of scholarship on the Northeast of India across disciplines, there is also an increasing need for critical materials. And adding to the wide range of research interests on the region, literary studies, borderland studies and inter-disciplinary studies have gained momentum. The present volume makes an obvious and a modest attempt at exploring the emerging literary and cultural studies. However, given the enormity of the literary tradition, a singular focus on the works of Easterine Kire has been considered, that too, only on her novels. Among the many contemporary writers of the region, she stands as a pioneer of writings in English, and, of late, her works have gained substantial academic attention from different universities across the country. This, of course, is partly propelled by the growing fascination in the Anglophone literatures from the region and the fresh perspectives that one derives from these writings because they offer a reimagination of the Northeast beyond the much-hyped issues of conflict and violence.

K.B. Veio Pou is Associate Professor in the Department of English, University of Delhi. He is the author of Literary Cultures of India's Northeast: Naga Writings in English (2015) and debut novel, Waiting for the Dust to Settle (2020). Winner of the Gordon Graham Prize for Naga Literature (Fiction) in 2021, his current research interests include studies on the Northeast of India, the oral/written interface, and cultural studies. Besides his academic engagements, he also likes to discuss issues on society, life, and faith at the popular level.

KEEPER of STORIES

CRITICAL READINGS OF EASTERINE KIRE'S NOVELS

Edited by
K.B. Veio Pou

 Highlander

Highlander

http://www.highlanderpress.org

Highlander Press
11 Main St Hill
Dexter, Maine 04930
United States of America

ISBN: 979-8-987-93390-9
Library of Congress Control Number: 2023935062

Cover image by Harshad Marathe
Design and layout by Alina Ronghangpi & Rokovor Vihienuo
Typeset in Gaudy Old Style by Prepress Plus

To the growing tribe of scholars in/on India's Northeast.
May your tribe increase!

CONTENTS

CONTRIBUTORS

Achingliu Kamei is a short story writer, poet, haikuist and creative writer. She teaches Literature at the University of Delhi. She has a Ph.D. from Jawaharlal University. Some of her publications include *Naga Tales: Dawn* (2017), *Songs of Raengdailu* (2021), and *Liangtuang Pu: Illustrated Novella for Children* (2021), *Headspace: The Mind's Realm* (2022), *Naga Tales: Morning Blush* (2023). *Bluest Water at the River Crossing* and *Roots and Wings* (a book of Haiku, Senryu, and Haibun) are forthcoming in 2023. Her works have been published in several journals and anthologies in the USA, Canada, Singapore, and India. She is also a passionate Ultra-Trail runner, having participated in official marathons and ultra-running events across India.

Adenuo Shirat Luikham is an Assistant Professor in the Department of English, Don Bosco College Kohima. She holds a PhD in English Literature from The English and Foreign Languages University, Hyderabad. Her research interests are Women's Writings, Writings in English from the North-East of India, and American literature. Her first collection of poems was titled *Luna. Bisous. Poesy.* (2019).

Avinuo Kire is a writer and teacher from Kohima, Nagaland. She has authored five books- two short story collections, *The Last Light of Glory Days: Stories from Nagaland* (2021), *The Power to Forgive & Other Stories* (2015), a collection of poetry titled *Where Wildflowers Grow* (2015). She has also co-authored an anthology of oral narratives, *Naga Heritage Centre: People Stories* (2016). Her latest book is a novel, *Where the Cobbled Path Leads* (2022).

Bendangrenla S Longkumer is currently working as an Assistant Professor at Fazl Ali College under Nagaland University. She is also doing her PhD at the Centre for English Studies, Jawaharlal Nehru University on the topic "Being Free for Others: Dietrich Bonhoeffer's Theology of Sociality". Her research interest areas include Political Theology, Public Theology,

Postcolonial Literatures, Northeast Indian Literature, Subaltern Literature and theory, Nationalism Studies and Translation studies.

Boniface Gaiguilung Kamei is a doctoral student in the Department of English, University of Hyderabad. He is currently working on a doctoral thesis on the relationship between law, sovereignty, and literature. He also has an MPhil degree from the University of Hyderabad.

Emisenla Jamir is a writer and educator from Kohima, Nagaland. She completed her Ph.D. from Nagaland University and has authored two collections of poetry, *Loneliness is an Orange* (2018) and *This Is How We Disappear* (2022). Her short stories have also been published in the Zubaan anthology, *The Many that I Am* (2019).

K.B. Veio Pou is Associate Professor in the Department of English, University of Delhi. He is the author of *Literary Cultures of India's Northeast: Naga Writings in English* (2015) and debut novel, *Waiting for the Dust to Settle* (2020). Winner of the Gordon Graham Prize for Naga Literature (Fiction) in 2021, his current research interests include studies on the Northeast of India, the oral/written interface, and cultural studies. Besides his academic engagements, he also likes to discuss issues on society, life, and faith at the popular level.

Lalthansangi Ralte is an Assistant Professor in the Department of English, Govt. J. Thankima College, Mizoram University. She finished her M. Phil and PhD from the Center for English Studies at JNU, New Delhi. Her areas of interest are Writings from Northeast India, Indian Writings in English, Translation Studies and Gender Studies.

Limayangla Pongener is an Assistant Professor at Kohima College, Kohima. She is currently pursuing Ph.D. in English Literature from North-Eastern Hill University, Shillong. Her areas of interest are writings in English from North-East India and Postcolonial literature.

Maisnam Arnapal is a doctoral student at University of California, Santa Barbara. Prior to this, he taught at Gargi College, University of Delhi. His areas of interest are Gender and Sexuality, Indigenous and Northeast India Studies.

Neikehienuo Mepfhuo is from Kohima, Nagaland. She completed her Ph.D from Assam Don Bosco University, Gauhati on Comparative literature of Naga and Native American literature. She authored the book *My Mother's*

Daughter (2019) and also contributed to Zubaan published anthology, *The Many that I am*. She currently teaches Functional English at Kohima College, Kohima. Her latest novel *Out of the Woods* was published in 2022.

Rengleen Kongsong is an Assistant Professor in the Department of English at Hindu College, University of Delhi. He is also a member of Chiru Literature Committee (CLC), Manipur and Assam, which is currently working on translation and language research projects of the Chiru tribal community. His research interests and publications include Northeast and Naga writings and is currently working on his doctoral research on Easterine Kire and other Naga writings at Jawaharlal Nehru University.

Rhelo Kenye teaches at the Centre for Comparative Literature, University of Hyderabad, as a Guest Faculty. He has submitted his PhD thesis at the Department of Cultural Studies, English and Foreign Languages University, Hyderabad. His doctoral research was on the cultural practice of music, its impact, and implications in contemporary Naga society. His areas of interest include intersection(s) of cultures and traditional lifeworld, politics and identity in Naga society, and Naga Writings in English. He is the co-editor of *Discoursing the Shifts of the Naga Society in Northeast India* (2022) and is also the coordinator of Naga Research Scholars' Forum, Hyderabad.

Roderick Wijunamai is a PhD student in the Department of Anthropology, Cornell University. His PhD research focuses on economy formation and ecological transformations in India's Northeast. Roderick is also a Fellow at The Highland Institute, Kohima. He holds an English Literature degree, and an MA in Development Studies.

Shelmi Sankhil is Assistant Professor of Comparative Literature and Translation Studies, School of Letters, Ambedkar University Delhi. His research interests include myth and fantasy, Indian writing in English, hermeneutics, and translation studies. Sankhil is also an occasional poet, singer-songwriter and author of *Flame on a Hill: A Collection of Stories* (2021).

Vizovono Elizabeth is an independent researcher and freelance editor from Kohima, Nagaland. She holds a PhD in English literature from University of Pune. She is the co-author of *Insider Perspectives: Critical Essays on Literature from Nagaland* (2017), and co-editor of *Sharing Stories* (2019). She has contributed to various literary platforms and journals and has a chapter in the book *Northeast India: Readings in Cultural Life* (2021). Her latest work is a co-edited volume of contemporary Naga writings entitled *Homegrown: Anthology of New Writings from Nagaland* (forthcoming, 2023).

ACKNOWLEDGEMENTS

Every book is a journey – one that always takes unexpected detours before it reaches its final form. This book project started a few years back and initially I thought it wouldn't take long, but alas it did. I know that the contributors at various points along the way wondered whether this would ever materialize. Well, here it is, friends! But I begin by acknowledging you all for your patience. Thank you for waiting!

My appreciation and thanks to Michael Heneise and Highlander Press for taking this up. Thank you, Michael, for investing in the quality of the production. A special thanks also to Catriona Child for the meticulous copy-editing work, and the host of anonymous reviewers for taking time and providing critical insights to improve the chapters.

Thanks to Harshad Marathe for the amazing cover art, Alina Ronghangpi for the design, Deepak Sharma and team for the typesetting and layout, and Rokovor Vihienuo for managing production.

My gratefulness also to Ashuni for sharing ideas and encouragement along the way, and to so many of my friends for constantly asking me about this project – you really helped push me along.

My gratitude, of course, to Easterine Kire for always being so kind and encouraging. This is just a small way to honour you and your immense literary contribution. Thank you for lighting the way.

Finally, and above all, my honour and glory to *El Shaddai* – from whom all blessings, creativity, and wisdom flow!

01

INTRODUCTION: KEEPER OF STORIES

K.B. Veio Pou

The idea for this book was shaped by recent conversations around the emerging Anglophone literature from the Northeast[1] of India. Like a newfound interest that captivates the discoverer, literary works based on the region and/or by writers whose roots are there have garnered sensible curiosity from different corners. However, unlike former times, when the region's people and culture were largely regarded as "exotic" subjects, there now seems to be a genuine effort to understand the complexities of the unique geographical landscape. Perhaps the interest is augmented by the fact that the erstwhile subjects are now the storytellers. With the turn of the century ushering in a flurry of literary outputs from the region, it may be fair to say that this new movement is aiding the re-imagination of the

---

[1] For want of a better word, the term 'Northeast' has emerged as a viable reference to the geographical area that is linked to the rest of India through a narrow strip of land north of West Bengal. There are different usages of the term, like, 'Northeast', 'North-East', 'North East', 'northeast', 'north-east', etc., but the compound word 'Northeast' has been preferred here. The states of Arunachal Pradesh, Assam, Manipur, Meghalaya, Mizoram, Nagaland, and Tripura were popularly known as the 'seven sister states' until Sikkim was added as the 'eighth' state in 2003.

Northeast people's culture and history. Moreover, the growing visibility of Northeasterners in other parts of India pursuing educational and employment opportunities facilitated by economic liberalization is helping to bridge the mainland/periphery divide.

The literary landscape of the region reflects the heterogeneous cultural environment. While the tradition of writing in the vernacular dates back several centuries, the recent trend of writing in English owes much to the English-medium schools instituted by the Christian missionaries in the nineteenth century (Misra 2011). And, although the vernacular literature remains vibrant within the specific linguistic communities, the writings in English, or translations into English, have gained a wider readership. Arguably, the region's linguistic diversity, with over four hundred spoken languages and no viable common language, has somehow enabled English to evolve as the dominant *lingua franca*, especially among the English-medium-educated generation that makes up the literary scene today. Like any literary tradition rooted in its culture, the literature that emerges from here shows a confluence of written and oral traditions, an element observable in many of the writings. Temsula Ao, a prominent Naga writer, defines this development as "writing orality" because the authors derive metaphors and "elements from the oral traditions", which in turn engender a new form of creative expression by synthesizing the oral and the written (106-9). And so we see a sort of shamanistic invocation in the works of Mamang Dai, mythic recovery in Easterine Kire, and folkloristic lyricism in Kynpham Singh Nongkynrih, just to take a few examples. The myriad storytelling traditions, replete with myths, legends and folklore, enable the writers to indulge in metaphors fed by their oral cultures. Besides, the post-colonial and post-independence experiences contribute a host of simultaneously compelling and complex narratives.

This volume makes a modest attempt at meeting the increasing need for critical materials on literary and cultural studies from the region. However, given the wide scale of the literary tradition, a singular focus on the works of Easterine Kire is given here while recognizing the need to undertake similar academic exercises on the works of other prominent writers. Among the many contemporary writers of the region, she stands as a pioneer of writings in English, and, of late, her work has gained much academic attention from different universities across the country. This is partly propelled by the growing interest in the literature from the region and also the introduction of Northeast studies centres in various central universities. Perhaps, this academic development fits into Victor Hugo's idiomatic expression, "an idea whose time has come". Or, as the writer under discussion, Easterine Kire, also put it, "it was a matter of timing... they had reached a level of maturity, so that the literature was rich and confident, not amateur, not hesitant. So the timing was right for it, was perfect for it" (2020).

EASTERINE KIRE: THE MAKING OF A STORY KEEPER

Born on March 29, 1959, an Easter Sunday, Easterine was named after the auspicious day. Now in her early sixties, she has a large body of work covering a wide range of subjects and genres, reflecting her varied life experiences. Because she grew up during the troubled times of the sixties and seventies in Nagaland, she has often talked about witnessing many changes. Her early years of education were spent at the Baptist English School, Kohima, while her two years of pre-university were spent at Kohima College. Later, she moved to Shillong for her graduation at Lady Keane College under North East Hill University (NEHU) and then went on to complete her post-graduate diploma in journalism from the University of Delhi in 1979. In the autumn of the same year, she joined the Kohima campus of NEHU for an MA in English. Her professional career began in 1981 when she joined the Department of Publicity, Government of Nagaland, as an Editor and worked there till 1983. From 1985 to 1988, she was a Lecturer in English Literature at Kohima College and from 1988 to 2005 was a Lecturer and, subsequently, Reader in the Department of English, NEHU – Kohima campus, before eventually joining Nagaland University. Midway through her university teaching, she completed her PhD in English Literature from the University of Poona (now The Savitribai Phule Pune University). From 2005 to 2007, she was a guest writer hosted by the University of Tromsø, Norwegian PEN, the County and the Municipality of Tromsø. She also taught post-colonial poetry briefly at the Arctic University of Tromsø in 2008, and from 2010 to 2014, she was ICORN (International Cities of Refuge Network) coordinator, Tromsø Kommune.

Easterine Kire's colourful career as a writer began at the young age of twenty-two when she published her first book of poetry titled *Kelhoukevira* (1982). Her first novel *A Naga Village Remembered* (2003), now re-issued as *Sky is My Father: A Naga Village Remembered* (2018), also happens to be the first novel in English written by a Naga. Besides poetry books and novels, she has written a number of short-story collections and children's books in English, as well as one in Norwegian. She also translates from Tenyidie (her native language) into English. Today, she has over thirty books to her credit. In 2011, she was awarded the Governor's Award for Excellence in Naga Literature, and in 2013 she won the Catalan PEN International Free

Voice Award, a recognition of her writings internationally. Her first major recognition in India came in 2015 when her novel *When the River Sleeps* was awarded The Hindu Prize. Earlier, in 2013, *Bitter Wormwood* was also nominated for the same prize. In 2017, *Son of the Thundercloud* won the Tata Literature Live Award for Book of the Year Award, and the same novel was awarded the Bal Sahitya Puraskar by Sahitya Akademi in 2018. She is also the first recipient of the Gordon Graham Prize for Naga Literature (fiction category) in 2018 for her novel *When the River Sleeps*. These national and international awards are a testament to her credentials as a storyteller par excellence. Besides her writing career, she also enjoys performing jazz poetry, a blend of jazz and poetry, and occasionally writing for Nagaland dailies.

One may wonder how all this was possible! In a sense, it is not a surprise that, given her profusely creative life, she is lauded as a "one-woman cultural renaissance" who has transformed the literary landscape of the Nagas as well as "establishing herself in the front line of contemporary indigenous literature" (Menezes). Perhaps, some insights into the influences on her life might be helpful in this aspect. In an interview, she told me, "We grew up enriched by stories". She went on to explain how being with grandparents added to this – "Every night, one grandparent would take on the delightful duty of telling stories". At the same time, she also said, "I liked to read and probably my interest in reading has much to do with me taking up writing in later life" (Kire 2020). Or perhaps, a combination of the two, "enriched by stories" and "interest in reading", has made Easterine Kire the person she is today! Even a cursory look at her work reveals the kind of reach she has in terms of her literary production. She began with poetry, and it remains one of her fortes. However, it is her fiction, mainly her novels, that has given her a readership from far and wide. At the same time, she has done exceptionally well writing for children and translating folktales too. Her books *Once in Faraway Dorg* (2011) and *Dinkypu* (2012) quickly became favourites with children, who loved the friendly new creatures introduced to their imagination. Yet, it was the publication of *The Log-drummer Boy* (2013) and *The Dancing Village* (2015) that drew the attention of Naga readers, young and old. The culture-specific motifs and symbols appealed to the sentiments of the Nagas, who have long felt a sense of disconnection from their culture due to encounters with the agents of modernity. On being asked about writing for children, she says, "It is increasingly important to write for children, because it gives them a sense of roots and a good sense of identity from childhood. If all that they read is from other cultures, they may be affected adversely. What I mean is that books with Naga characters and Naga situations build in Naga children a sense of pride in their traditions and a healthy curiosity to learn more" (Kire 2020).

In this sense, one can see Easterine Kire's conscious effort to find value in her own culture and tradition. She often says that her primary audience is the Nagas "because I write things that are familiar to them: we have shared memories, shared story-banks from the past, both from the natural world and the spiritual world" (*ibid*). And this, I must say, says a lot about her investment in the project called "peoplestories", initiated by Barkweaver Publications, a publishing house she helped establish to promote Naga art and storytelling. She explains that these stories are an important way of transmitting "shared memories, shared story-banks". "Peoplestories", she said, "are not mythical tales but the accounts of ordinary people and their lives" (Kire 2014, 99). She believes that "people need to tell their stories, and they deserve to be given the opportunity to share their stories" (*ibid*). With that aim in mind, *Forest Song* (2011) was published to record "the stories of real people". It places value on the extraordinary stories of ordinary people and offers them a platform to tell their story (3).

Earlier, the first volume of folktales titled *Naga Folktales Retold* (2009) was published in order to "encourage young children to spend time with their grandparents, collecting folktales and peoplestories in order to imbibe the rich teachings of culture that is passed on in folktale narration" (Kire 2014, 99). "Culture lives on if its practisers can reinvent it", she said sensibly (*ibid*, 101). The reinvention of tradition is at work at various levels in every culture; translation is just another way of doing it. Interestingly, she has also been actively translating texts from her native language Tenyidie (Angami) into English, especially folk poems, some of which were published in the *Anthology of Contemporary Poetry from the Northeast* (2003). But she gives us a different understanding of the performance of translation when she says that it is a continuous process: "For those of us writing in English, remembering the fact that English is not our mother tongue, we are always translating" (2020). Talking of her creations, she said she had to "constantly translate the thought patterns of my characters" and by "translating in this way is one way of retaining the uniqueness of their thought life and the authenticity of their speech patterns". This is evident throughout her work.

There are a number of expressions common to most Naga languages, and when one reads Easterine Kire, there is a sense of nativized English – a distinctive literary craftsmanship. One of the concepts that recur in her storytelling is the idea of "story keepers" in reference to the storytellers of old. In Naga society, as in many oral cultures, the place of a storyteller is venerated because she or he does not merely tell to entertain but tells with a sense of responsibility and honour. It is in stories and songs, along with other material entities, that the cultural heritage is passed on to the next generation. Therefore, the forgetting of the stories and songs and the destruction of cultural objects both constitute a huge loss for the community. Nagas have felt this loss in many ways due to the different waves of change that have swept through their land since the early nineteenth century. But of late, there has been a sense of awakening of the need to preserve and reconstruct culture and history. Recreating the environment for storytelling is one way to encourage the present generation to do this. Through all her writings, Easterine Kire carries forward the storytelling legacy by vividly reimagining the beauty of the Naga culture and history. She is, in that context and in the truest sense, the keeper of stories. She shoulders this legacy with respect. And, as one reads her works, especially her historical novels, one sees an important thematic outline – the chronological writing of stories.

WRITING HISTORICAL NOVELS CHRONOLOGICALLY

In many instances, especially in her interviews, Easterine Kire has categorically stated the importance of writing historical novels chronologically. In an interview she categorically puts it, "I have been writing my novels chronologically in order to give the historical background of my people and their lives. Therefore, the first novels I wrote were historical fiction, centring on historical events. I felt this was important, to chronicle our history in the form of a novel" (Kire 2016). And she finds this important "because the insider's voice was silent in all the historical narratives on us"; thus, by writing about significant historical events, she is "documenting unwritten history" (Kire 2019). This makes for an interesting discussion. It is not that historical accounts are not available. In fact, the colonial period saw a lot of works on the Nagas, mainly anthropological and ethnographic in nature, and designed to meet the needs of Western administrators. Thus, writings on the Nagas have mostly been for outside audience, largely western. Unfortunately, this exercise continued well into the late twentieth century in the hands of many non-Naga writers.

Therefore, the requirement for "the insider's voice", is due to the fact that the native voice has largely been silent. This is particularly true for communities that are historically oral, like the Nagas. Although writing was introduced to the Nagas sometime in the later part of the nineteenth century, primarily through the advent of a Western mode of education, orality continued to hold sway as the most important medium of engagement in the public realm. A conscious effort to write about one's own culture and history is a more recent development. Yet, by now, there is a substantial body of works by Nagas in different disciplines and genres. This has expanded the contours of storytelling, which has always thrived in the Naga society.

For Easterine Kire, interestingly, her decision to write historical novels chronologically springs from her desire to accurately present an insider's account of the Naga people's historical background alongside a discussion of their socio-cultural and political legacy.

At the same time, when we talk of things "chronologically", we tend to imagine numbers on the calendar, as is the practice in many societies. However, in the Naga imagination, chronology is recorded by a different kind of mind map, often relating to events that loom large in community memory. For instance, the Second World War is a clear marker delimited by phrases such as "before the War" and "after the War". It constitutes a useful reference point because of the enormous changes that the War brought. In Kire's books, we find documentation of some important events that shaped the identity of the Nagas. Her first novel A Naga Village Remembered (2003), describes the resilient spirit of the Khonoma warriors who resisted the British invasion of the Naga territory in the latter part of the nineteenth century. After several bitter clashes, a peace treaty was signed in 1880. In the recent history of the Nagas, this would be chronicled as a major event that transformed the political landscape. That this Angami village later produced some of the most important Naga leaders in the nationalist movement is no coincidence. Mari (2010), set during the Second World War, covers this major historical event. Based on a true story of a girl who kept a diary during the war period, the novelist made sure that it is also the story of Kohima and its people. The Second World War, although not of their making, deeply affected the imagination of the Nagas because one of the decisive battles was fought on their land. Today it is referred to as the Great War or the Japanese War, literally translated. Another novel, A Respectable Woman (2019), chronicles the aftermath of the War. Using the resource of memory, the novel allows the daughter, Kevinuo, to see the impact of the War through the eyes of her mother, Khonuo.

Remarkably, these two novels feature some of Kire's strongest female characters. Both novels highlight women as active witnesses of war, and thus, "Women are now at the heart of acts of remembrance... women as well as men now construct the story, disseminate it, and consume it" (Winter 6). However, while much of A Respectable Woman reminisces about the War, the experiences of the daughter and the primary narrator take us through the later decades that saw radical changes in Naga society. Another important novel covering the crucial decades of the 1960s and 70s is A Terrible Matriarchy (2007). With the wind of modernizing forces engulfing various facets of Naga society, many changes occurred, including the spread of education. Nevertheless, despite the various opportunities ushered in by the new waves, the old patriarchal structure was still lurking and imposing male privileges. Ironically, patriarchy was sometimes promoted by the society's matriarchs, as the novel cleverly exposes. More importantly, it succinctly bares the fact that any ideology can condition the social mindset that it appears normative over a sustained period. Considered one of the most realistic depictions of Naga society in transition, the novel also incorporates the challenges that came with change, including alcoholism, domestic violence, and other ills.

The protracted political problem of the Nagas forms the core plot of *Bitter Wormwood* (2011). This novel gives a poignant insight into the struggle of a people whose romantic idea for independence got entangled in bloodshed and violence. While chronicling the early decades of the 1950s and 60s when fervent nationalism gripped the Naga masses, the novel shows what it meant to live through the turbulent phase of the crackdown by the Indian armed forces and presents the challenges faced by the later generations. *Bitter Wormwood* was closely followed by the novella *Life on Hold* (2011), which thematically covers the troubles that marred the Naga movement, especially with the rise of factional violence, and seemingly speaks directly to the Nagas, highlighting the need to introspect. Given the unresolved struggle of more than seven decades, the political conflict has somehow defined the present reality for the Nagas. The fact that it also lingers in the backdrop of other novels like *A Terrible Matriarchy* and *A Respectable Woman* suggests the inability of the Nagas to move on as a society unless the political crisis is resolved. However, to end the political imbroglio, reconciliation and forgiveness are required to bring healing to the wounded people. "Bitter wormwood", therefore, is a critical metaphor.

TRAVERSING THE NAGA COSMOLOGY

When Easterine Kire was awarded The Hindu Prize in 2015 for her novel *When the River Sleeps* (2014), the citation said that the book was a "tender philosophical novel" and one of the judges described it as "a sample of how the mythopoeic imagination can work in our times" (Hamid). I think that is a commendable recognition of her work. It is certainly philosophical because it explores the spiritual universe of the Nagas, and the mythopoeic elements are drawn from the rich oral culture replete with myths and legends. In Easterine Kire's fiction, one encounters a supernatural realm that easily overlaps with the human world. For many, it may seem like a fantasy world created by an imaginative mind. However, many Naga beliefs rest on an understanding of overlaps between the seen and the unseen worlds. Coincidentally, such semblances could be found in works of other writers originating from oral cultures. In an interview, Kire describes the feeling of recognition derived from reading writers from "formerly marginalized literary areas" and talking of the "writings of Edward Ahenakew, a Cree from Canada", she said, "I immediately felt at home with his narratives, as they are reminiscent of Naga storytelling and their moral and didactic tones behind each story" (Longkumer 4). And this gives us a clue as to how to approach works too.

The Naga worldview held that the worlds of spirits, animals and human beings intersected quite effortlessly. Perhaps, the existence of myths like the ancient mother who gave birth to the three entities continues to hold sway in their perception of the universe. Or the frequent appearance of weretiger men in the stories forges an understanding of such existential realities. In *When the River Sleeps*, Kire enlightens us with the story of a man's quest for the heart stone that promises to give him untold powers. But the protagonist's hunt for the mythical stone could not be straightforward because both natural and supernatural beings were on his trail! The novel ends on an anticlimactic and physically violent note. However, the protagonist, Vilie, is awakened to make another voyage in *Journey of the Stone* (2021). This time, he travels in spirit form and again encounters the supernatural.

In her other award-winning novel *Son of the Thundercloud* (2016), we see an invocation of ancient Naga cosmology. The plot of the story is borrowed from the legend of a woman who was impregnated by a raindrop, and the son born to her would avenge the spirit tiger that had deprived her of her husband and several children. Remarkably, this novel also reads beautifully as an allegory of hope, akin to the biblical story of the miraculous birth of Jesus. But this scriptural parallelism was intentional, as she said in an interview, "I was very interested in the idea of the boy Jesus growing up as a Naga boy, and in combining scriptural prophecy and Naga folk wisdom" (Kire 2017). This idea of a nativized Christianity should interest the Nagas, as many find it hard to blend the two beliefs. Yet, as Easterine shows, there is no contradiction between the two. In fact, in her interview with me, she said, "*Son of the Thundercloud* is a story about love and forgiveness, and it points to the world beyond this, which is part of the Christian tradition and also has a place in Naga tradition" (2020). Such explorations on Christian themes are, in fact, not new to her. For example, in her first novel, she compares the chicken sacrifice to the sacrifice of Jesus.

Then there is *Don't Run, My Love* (2017), a story of a young tiger-man who falls in love with a maiden. But when his marriage proposal is turned down, things become menacing. Many of Easterine Kire's short stories deal with human encounters with non-human worlds. Furthermore, her works have also garnered attention because of their focus on human relationships with the world of nature. Scholars have analyzed her novels, especially those that explore Naga cosmology through the lenses of ecology or climate change. Certainly, the critical issues of climate change and environmental concerns have increased interest in her works.

CONTRIBUTIONS TO THE BOOK:

The divisions of this book are broad and the study on Easterine Kire's works should not be limited to the subheadings. Rather, these categorisation should at best be treated as suggestive in the scope of exploration. The **first section** – "Indigenizing the narrative: contextualizing the text" – largely introduces Easterine Kire's works from an insider perspective as a long-desired guide to understanding culture and tradition. The chapter "Unweaving an Alternative Home in Easterine Kire's *When the River Sleeps*" by Shelmi Sankhil looks at Velie's expedition as "an inward journey for self-discovery", and is, thus, a type of *bildungsroman*, although with a twist. His refusal to return to the village is because of the freedom he finds in the forest, his alternative home. Roderick Wijunamai's "Understanding Naga Cosmology through Easterine Kire's Fictional Narrative" studies *When the River Sleeps* as an "ethnographic novel" and explores three important elements – tiger-man, forest spirit, and dreams – as a way to understand as well as bring alive, the Naga lifeworld. At a time when there are attempts at appropriating indigenous cultures, the chapter argues that the novel offers a narrative of resistance. At the same time, at an interdisciplinary level, "her ethnographic fiction supplements the intent and limitations of ethnographic materials which social science scholars are routinely faced with". In "Weaving Dreams and Living Folklore: Narrative Structure in *A Terrible Matriarchy*", Vizovono Elizabeth presents Easterine Kire "as an indigenous postcolonial writer" who writes with concern for her own Naga people and culture. The "distinguishing feature", as the chapter would contend, is the use of "folkloristic elements" in the novel by elaborating on "the form of dreams, spirits, and foodways". This is an important study considering that, like many communities in the Northeast region, the Nagas are experiencing rapid changes in society. "Writing Memory: The Preservation of Intangible Heritage in Easterine Kire's *Sky is my Father: A Naga Village Remembered*" by Avinuo Kire deliberates on the "transition of the Nagas from the oral to the written" as signalled by Easterine Kire's first novel. At the same time, the author argues, using script "does not necessarily entail a completer break from the oral" but "only signifies a new delicate balance wherein script could aid the cause of preserving the oral narratives", thus safeguarding the "endangered intangible heritage". And

Neikiehienuo Mepfuo's "Homing and the Sense of Belonging in Easterine Kire's *Son of the Thundercloud*" discusses the notion of "home" through the protagonist's personal quest for one after losing his family. But although he was seen "fixing homes or building homes throughout the novel", the search for belonging takes him to different locations, only to realize that "home" isn't fixed but "evolves with the person".

The **second section** – "Sites of resistance: exploring collective memory" – brings together some themes on the everyday experiences of the ordinary folk – how memories play a major role in shaping our perception of history and thus evolve into sites of resistance and contestation. As a by-product of society, literature speaks volumes on how individuals see the dynamics of politics as it interacts with history, culture, and modernity. In "Narrativizing History through the Everyday in *Bitter Wormwood*" Bendangrenla S Longkumer focuses on an emerging literary study – the everyday narratives in understanding history. By looking at the lived realities of common people, such studies have provided a subaltern reading to history that is "not documented by dominant history", thus becoming a site of resistance. Limayangla Pongener's "Tracing Naga History: A study of Easterine Kire's historical novels" draws our attention to the historical novels by analyzing them chronologically. However, beyond merely chronicling Naga history, the chapter posits that Kire not only foregrounds oral history as another important source of history but provides the common man with a much-needed voice and representation through the stories. The chapter "Sovereignty and Bare Life in Easterine Kire's *Bitter Wormwood*" by Boniface Kamei explores the interface between the idea of sovereignty and literature. Examining the novel *Bitter Wormwood*, he argues that it "provides a counter narrative to nation building narrative" and, thus, belongs "to the convention of resistance literature". In "*Beyond the Frontline*: Locating Conflict and *Refigurative* Reading of *A Terrible Matriarchy*", Rengleen Kongsong Chiru contests the stereotypes that the Northeast, including its literature, garners from various corners. This chapter largely calls for a need to "find a balanced treading ground" wherein the contemporary representations are reimagined and refigured. And Maisnam Arnapal's chapter titled "Gender, Indigeneity and the Second World War: The Battle of Kohima in Easterine Kire's *Mari*" proposes "a way of reimagining feminist politics in the Northeast". Considering *Mari* as "a radical departure from conventional history writings", he postulates that the novel "opens up new possibilities of reading the intersectionality of gender and indigeneity in the context of Nagaland/ Northeast India".

The **third section** – "Individual and society – rethinking identities" – looks at the multiple ways of understanding the Naga culture and tradition through Easterine Kire's writings. Elsewhere she had referred to the common cultural background of the Nagas as "shared memories, shared story banks", and they are her "first audience" (Kire 2020). By extending that idea of sharedness, the chapters in this section explore various facets of culture and identity consciousness in her novels. In "Listening to Little People Inside the Box: Culture, Tradition and Identity through the Representation of the Radio in Easterine Kire", Rhelo Kenye offers a stimulating discourse on "the role and impact of the radio in the Naga milieu", something that has not previously caught the attention of many people. This chapter also examines how the radio, a symbol of modernity, contributed to the consciousness of the Naga self, especially during the formative period that novels like *Mari*, *Bitter Wormwood*, and *A Respectable Woman* cover. Adenuo Shirat Luikham's "Critical Insights on the Treatment of Death in Easterine Kire's *A Terrible Matriarchy*" delves into an interesting, and yet often neglected subject – the function of death in literature. Arguing that "the representation of death in literature and its treatment" varies according to cultures, the chapter explores how it is perceived in the Naga context and all the customs, rituals, and beliefs attached to it.

In "Oral-tradition, Christianity and Nature: A study of Easterine Kire's novels" Emisen Jamir examines the impact of Christianity and colonization on the Nagas, especially in "their interaction with the natural world". The chapter looks into the pre-Christian and pre-colonial periods and shows how there is "an imbalance in the environment" at present. While the reason for the imbalance could be more than simply a disregard for nature, as seen through the intervention of various forces of modernity, a closer examination of Easterine Kire's work shows the need "for a re-visitation of the past in order to reinstate oneself with the natural world". Closely connected to the previous chapter, "An Ecocritical study of Easterine Kire's *When the River Sleeps* and *Son of the Thundercloud*" by Achingliu Kamei, points out that there is a growing trend to study literature as "one of the sites of dialogue on ecology" and, as the author would argue, various writings from Northeast India draw our attention to the need to engage more critically with the relationship between the human and the non-human worlds. Studying two of Easterine Kire's novels, the chapter argues that there is a need "to pass down to the next generation the knowledge of living off nature". And Lalthansangi Ralte's "Myth, reality and re-telling: A study of Easterine Kire's fiction" explores the interface of myth in the present Naga reality while simultaneously problematizing the notion of "real" as it is understood. At the same time, the chapter presents storytellers as "memory-keepers" who often break new ground to let their stories speak of important realities that are seldom discussed.

CONCLUSION

In no way is this book an exhaustive study of the works of Easterine Kire, a writer who has defied categorization through her extraordinary ability to crisscross a broad range of literary genres. However, the fact that this project only focuses on some of her novels indicates the potential for undertaking similar literary exercises based on her work, including her poetry and children's books. Moreover, as the reader can see, the contributors to this book represent only a fraction of the scholars who have shown a keen interest in her writings and researched widely. I am blessed by their overwhelming response in sending their chapters without me having to press them! At the same time, I acknowledge that many more academics are engaged with Kire's works at the research level; however, for want of space, the invitation for entries couldn't be wide enough to accommodate many who would have contributed handsomely. Perhaps, a future venture would bring more names on board. Needless to say, it is hoped that this volume will stimulate more scholarship, not only on Easterine Kire but also on other literary figures and generally on the wider literary landscape of the Northeast. Moreover, another attempt like this would, hopefully, help meet the demand for academic materials on subjects relating to literary and cultural studies on the Northeast of India.

WORKS CITED

Ao, Temsula. "Writing Orality" in Soumen Sen & Desmond L. Kharmawphlang (eds) *Orality and Beyond: A North-East Indian Perspective*, New Delhi: Sahitya Akademi, 2007, pp. 99-112.

Hamid, Zubeda. "Lit for Life: The Hindu Prize for 2015 goes to Easterine Kire", *The Hindu*, 16 January, 2016, https://www.thehindu.com/features/lit-for-life/Lit-for-Life-The-Hindu-Prize-for-2015-goes-to-Easterine-Kire/article14003138.ece#:~:text=Easterine%20Kire%2C%20poet%2C%20novelist%20and,Ms.

Kire. Easterine. "Stories of Nagaland." Interview by Namrata Kolachalam. *Helter Skelter*, 11 March, 2019, https://helterskelter.in/2019/03/interview-easterine-kire-a-respectable-woman-nagaland/

Kire, Easterine. "Of the lesser known." Interview by Sangeeta Barooah Pisharoty. *NEZINE*, 11 February, 2016, https://www.nezine.com/info/UnYxbmJRQjVjSkVrWDRyUXJxMHJpdz09/of-the-lesser-known.html

Kire, Easterine. "Years of listening to stories grows a wealth of knowledge within your spirit". Interview by Veio Pou. *Scroll*, 23 August, 2020, https://scroll.in/article/971141/years-of-listening-to-stories-grows-a-wealth-of-knowledge-within-your-spirit-easterine-kire

Kire, Easterine. "Beyond the news and the headlines, Easterine talks of God's grace, discipline and humility". Interview by A. Sentiyula. *The Naga Republic*, 23 November, 2017, http://www.thenagarepublic.com/features/beyond-news-headlines-easterine-talks-gods-grace-discipline-humility/

Menezes, Vivek. "Naga writer Easterine Kire's clear bright sound over a sleeping world". *Scroll*, 20 May 2021, https://scroll.in/article/995300/naga-writer-easterine-kires-clear-bright-sound-over-a-sleeping-world

Misra, Tilottoma. *Oxford Anthology of Writings from North-East India*. 2 vols. New Delhi: Oxford University Press, 2011.

Nongkynrih, Kynpham Sing & Robin S Ngangom (Eds.). *Anthology of Contemporary Poetry from the Northeast*, Shillong: NEHU, 2003.

Pou, KB Veio. "Of People and their Stories: Writings in English from India's Northeast" in Lipok Dziivichii & Manjeet Baruah (eds) *Modern Practices in North East India: History, Culture, Representation*, New York & London: Routledge, 2018, pp. 225-249.

Winter, Jay. *Remembering War: The Great War between Memory and History in the 20th Century*. New Haven/London: Yale University Press, 2006.

Section 1

INDIGENIZING THE NARRATIVE: CONTEXTUALIZING THE TEXT

02

UNWEAVING AN ALTERNATIVE HOME IN EASTERINE KIRE'S *WHEN THE RIVER SLEEPS*

Shelmi Sankhil

Like most (if not all) societies in the world with a colonial past, the Nagas have become willing participants in today's emergent global order. This has naturally entailed cultural crossovers and large-scale movements of people, goods, and ideas, altering Naga society to a great extent. A casual tour of the Naga territories in India will confirm this. Going by personal experience, the dialectical process of change in Naga society is relatively harmonious and context-dependent. However, the changes are neither uniform nor homogeneous across the full spectrum of society. Despite the encompassing ethnic term 'Naga', the collective experience is far from homogeneous. There is no *one* Naga way of seeing and responding to situations specific to a given historical period. Public discourses can and do take on various hues and forms of persuasion in Naga society. However, the different views are all supposedly premised on the desire, either stated or implied, to guide the Naga people to the best course of action available in the present.

Easterine Kire's prize-winning novel, *When The River Sleeps* (2014: *WTRS* henceforth), is part of an ongoing public process that seeks to engage with the shifting realities affecting the Naga people. On one level, the novel is an exciting adventure story about the protagonist, Vilie, set in a time that is neither contemporaneous nor remote. Within this world, and against the normative cultural logic, certain themes are explored that directly speak to aspects of contemporary Naga experience. The notion of home is one such theme. In fact, it is one of the least visible themes of the novel, subsumed, as it were, by the adventure *spirit* of the narrative – what next? For instance, the Nepalis in the novel are portrayed as constantly relocating for economic reasons (13). And if their 'silences' can be taken as evidence of their resigned acceptance of their fate, they would appear to possess a mobile notion of home. In contrast, psychological and cultural factors are given as the main causes of relocation for the Naga characters. Vilie and Zote are unable to find relative contentment in their new surroundings. A certain lack of understanding, or stoic adherence to a particular notion of home, seems to be the main cause of their evident disquiet, anger, and subsequent actions. However, unlike Vilie and Zote, Ate is the anomalous Naga character portrayed as exemplifying a *different* idea of home. In other words, different notions of home affect and determine the conduct of the principal characters in the novel. The objective of this chapter is to show how the quest for the heart-stone is an essential part of Vilie's journey to resolve the home question. My argument is that the outcome of this process is the articulation of an alternative notion of home that is incommensurate with the traditional notion widely prevalent in Naga society. I will demonstrate this position by closely examining the actions of the principal characters, Vilie, Zote, and Ate. Moreover, except where it is essential, I will refrain from extra-textual citations. Instead, I will rely fundamentally on a close reading of the novel (but not as a *formalist*) and let the text speak for itself as much as it can.

VILIE'S DISLOCATION AND DISCONTENTMENT

When the River Sleeps is structured as a *Bildungsroman*[1] The main narrative revolves around the adventures of Vilie, the novel's protagonist. His adventures are not aimless; rather, they are meant to lead him, with the aid of the heart-stone,

---

[1] My reading of this novel as a *Bildungsroman* takes a more liberal view of the age-criterion of the protagonist in the genre. Vilie may be in his forties, but he lacks understanding and suffers because of it. And if "maturity" or "coming of age" in the *Bildungsroman* means the capacity of the protagonist to go through a series of trials and then become wise/wiser to be able to adequately redress their unhappy situation, then Vilie fits the profile.

to an enlightened awareness of his situation and make the most appropriate choice in a given situation. The plot of a *Bildungsroman* scheme typically has a point A to B developmental curve for the protagonist. Acquainting the reader with the protagonist's status quo when the novel opens is a necessary schematic detail for tracking the trajectory of character development. Typically, the protagonist's inadequacy of character or knowledge/wisdom is the stock reason for the journey or quest. Then, the actions, thought-process, and fortunes of the protagonist along the journey, perforce, help create the person intended by the narrative. Now, let us consider the life of Vilie within this scheme and explore its connection with the home question.

Very early in the novel, Kire introduces us to the physical location of her protagonist: "The forest was home to Vilie" (3). However, the location has both physical and psychological meanings in the text. We know from the text that the forest is not Vilie's natal home. He had relocated there at age twenty-five after a series of events that rendered the village space emotionally unviable for him. So, the story opens *in media res*, and in that sense, there has already been some movement in the protagonist's life. The quiet of the forest had provided temporary relief to Vilie for more than two decades. However, now it is no longer capable of calming his nerves. He must find a way to fix the psychological unrest that has begun to periodically disturb his sleep in the last two years (1-2).

At the physical level, Vilie's choice of the forest as home is an obvious deviation from the norm. It is an uncommon example of inversion of the locus of one's habitation with the field of one's operation. The home in the village is normally the starting point for activity in the world. It is the reference point for the Naga even when he is in the wild. Typically, the home in the village represents a sanitised and safe place from which human beings commence their activity in the world, in the Levinasian sense of dwelling or home (152). However, in Vilie's case, the forest, associated with ideas of the wild and the unpredictable, becomes the reference point from which he engages with society and culture. He visits the village and the marketplace only when he needs salt, oil, and other edible items not easily found in the forest and when his job as an employee of the Forest Department requires it. It is as if Vilie wants to return to life in its simplest form to avoid the emotional and psychological entanglements of human society.

At another significant level, Vilie's choice of the forest as home raises psychological questions about his past and present. What kind of experience or thinking led him to relocate from his natal village to the forest twenty-five years ago? Is his present situation related to that memory? If yes, what does it tell us about Vilie's psychological and emotional state? Even though the text is not explicit about Vilie's reasons for relocating to the forest, two events are implied as possible causes: the loss of his beloved Mechuseno to a forest spirit when he was eighteen (4-6) and the loss of his mother (141). Two women that he loved dearly left him one after the other. At the time of the novel's opening, these events had become memories from more than twenty years ago. However, despite the passage of time, Vilie has not been able to find lasting closure for these wounds. The relocation to the forest only mitigated the pain without real healing. Therefore, he continues to suffer internally, as this passage suggests:

> And you buried your mother in that village and made the forest your home, but you always think of that village where your mother is buried as home, your real home, and you long to go back, at least in your dreams if not in your waking moments (141).

Vilie's move away from the site of pain, the village, is both symptomatic and necessary. The notion that moving away from the place of pain can facilitate slow but effective healing is understandable. However, the decision also reflects Vilie's inability to master his own grief as an adult: the grief from losing Mechuseno and his dear mother in quick succession. His lack of romantic interest in any woman even twenty-five years after Mechuseno passed away is symptomatic of a condition arising from a lack of closure of an event in which he was emotionally invested.. The unhappiness arising from these events places him in a position suitable for the novel's *bildung* scheme: how to redress it in a way that is both meaningful and self-enhancing. From the preliminary introduction of Vilie in the early pages of the novel, the nature of his crisis is characterised not so much as *material* as it is emotional and cognitive.[2] The resolution of his problem depends primarily on how he balances the two dimensions, and here the heart-stone, as a catalyst for the acquisition of wisdom, contributes to the plot.

Within the *bildung* scheme, Vilie has to journey from point A to B. Currently, he is beset with a gnawing existential crisis that has disturbed his sleep in the form of a recurring dream for two straight years. So, even though the narrator tells us that Vilie was relatively "content with how things were" (4), the textual evidence says otherwise. The opening paragraph of the novel tells us that Vilie is bothered by something that he is unable to articulate:

> Vilie plunged his hand into the river. It was cold – close to freezing – and perfectly still. It was just the way it should be.

[2] Kire seems to prefer the word 'spiritual' as an inclusive substitute to mean both, as Vilie's crisis has both emotional and cognitive (wisdom) dimensions.

> The river had gone to sleep. Everything was just as the seer had
> told him. Almost imperceptibly, he slid forward and entered
> the water and plucked a smooth stone from the bottom of the
> river. In a similar motion, he pulled his arm out of the water
> and stood still. But it was too late. He felt through the soles of
> his feet that a great force had awakened. Before he could reach
> the shore, the water had swelled above his waist – the river had
> come alive! In an instant, the great torrents had tethered his
> legs in its twisting undercurrents, dragging him down forcibly
> into its depths. Vilie's struggles were feeble against the force
> of the rushing water. Unable to reach the surface, his lungs
> began to burn for air and his mouth filled with water. He
> tried to shout, even as he felt himself being swallowed further
> into the darkness. Above his struggling form the river roared,
> drowning out his muffled screams. Then, in a final panicked
> outburst, he struck out against the power that was consuming
> him. His movements grew more frantic. A deep guttural
> sound escaped his throat. He flung out his hand and it hit
> the edge of the bed. It then dawned on him that he had been
> dreaming again (1-2).

The recurring dream of wresting a heart-stone from the mythical
sleeping river is a subconscious projection, in the Freudian sense, of Vilie's
desire to alleviate his present suffering, which a change of living space has
not fully remedied. Nevertheless, that desire is never articulated explicitly
in the text. Instead, it is vaguely implied and left to the reader to infer from
Vilie's emotional and physical circumstances. Nonetheless, the dream motif
is used to nudge the protagonist to undertake the adventurous journey to
the sleeping river. It is safe to presume that, like all Angamis, the tribe to
which he belongs, Vilie shares the belief that the heart-stone has a wide
range of powers:

> If you can wrest a stone from the heart of the sleeping river
> and take it home, it will grant you whatever it is empowered
> to grant you. It could be cattle, women, prowess in war, or
> success in the hunt. That is what is meant by catching the river
> when it is asleep. That way you can make its magic yours. The
> retrieved stone is a powerful charm called a heart-stone (3).

So, even if his intentions about the stone are unclear in the text, its
value is not unknown to him. It is also safe to presume that Vilie entertains
an undisclosed hope that success at the sleeping river would change his

present situation for the better. However, in Kire's reconfiguration of the stone, greater emphasis is given to the *immaterial* aspect of the stone, its capacity to give wisdom to the honest seeker in difficult situations, thereby alluding to the nature of Vilie's emotional problem as one that arises chiefly from spiritual bankruptcy.[3]

> The wisdom of the stone is more spiritual than physical. It helps us discover the spiritual identity that is within us, so we can use it to combat the dark forces that are always trying to control and suppress us. But men who are not initiated don't understand this about the stone, and they try to use it to gain wealth and other material things (228).

It is also worth noting that Kire also presents the stone as a neutral object whose real *value* depends on how and to what end its possessor uses it. This passive fact about the heart-stone returns agency to the possessor, making the characters the sites of moral and ethical actions.

Within the plot of the novel, Vilie's encounter with Subale and Kani marks the first significant moment in his personal development. His success in retrieving a heart-stone from the sleeping river depends on the knowledge about the sleeping river and its guardian spirits that the elderly couple impart. Subale and Kani are structural props meant to help the hero in his quest. However, the real challenge for Vilie begins after his success at the sleeping river. There is no obvious material change after he comes to possess the stone. However, he becomes more noticeable in a crowd, as an older man observes during an encounter at the Tuesday Market:

> You did not go after the beautiful river-spirits in the market yesterday as any other fool would have done. You sought neither to purchase nor possess the trinkets of the market. There was an otherness about you that I saw when I first spoke to you (125-26).

However, the culmination of Vilie's *spiritual* transformation comes via the chance encounter with the two sisters, Zote and Ate. After this encounter, he is able to articulate the answer to the nagging question of home.

---

[3] Kire's concept of "spiritual" is areligious, even though it is imbued with moral and ethical duties.

SAME SITUATION, DIFFERENT RESPONSES

In one of the stops on his return from the sleeping river, Vilie runs into the village of Kirhupfümia, where the sisters, Ate and Zote, dwell. Vilie is initially unaware that he has arrived at the village of the 'witches', an all-women village whose inhabitants were forced to live in isolation by their village of birth.[4] Ate promptly takes him under her 'protection'. However, because of their gifts in matters of the spirit, both sisters immediately perceive that Vilie has a heart-stone. While Ate does not covet the stone, Zote actively seeks it for herself in order to carry out an act of revenge that Kire underlines in the novel.

Within the scheme of the novel, Vilie's encounter with the sisters is the culminating point of the narrative. What makes this encounter central to the plot is that the said village does not fall along the path of Vilie's onward journey to the sleeping river. So, it is out of character for Vilie, who knows the forest like the back of his hand, to 'stray' into the Kirhupfümia village. However, Kire achieves two things by causing the protagonist to inhabit the same space as two other principal characters. First, she demonstrates the working of the stone and its range of powers, as Vilie and Zote employ it differently; secondly, the question of home is more directly addressed through their motives and actions. All three characters are estranged from their natal village and have different notions of home. However, the circumstances of their estrangement are not similar. Vilie chose to relocate to the forest of his own accord, but the two sisters were ostracised because they were considered to be witches. The stage is set for the two sisters to illustrate different notions of home through their motives and actions. Structurally, Kire uses this encounter to cause Vilie to grow and occupy a position of enlightened strength henceforth. So, if the wresting of the stone from the sleeping river is the apex moment of the narrative, then this encounter with the two sisters is the start of the resolution. Subsequently, Vilie becomes more precise and decisive in his thought and deeds.

Zote

Zote represents a *territorial* understanding of home, a very traditional idea in Naga *Lebenswelt*, where primacy is accorded to the physical space of one's

---

[4] "Kirhupfümia " is the Angami term for certain women believed to be born with poisonous powers.

natal village. Zote's relentless hatred for her village folks is fundamentally grounded in this psychosocial logic. Even though the narrative mentions that the village had mistreated Zote, it nonetheless portrays her as bitter, resentful, evil, and craving revenge (135-36). The narrative also gives the impression that Zote's reaction is the result of her giving in to the darker forces at play in the human heart. However, on closer examination of Zote's revenge motive, another factor emerges, displacing, or at least rivalling, righteous indignation, or even pure evil, as the fundamental driving force. In fact, this factor is not even obvious to Zote herself or to Ate or Vilie, for that matter. The surface manifestations of bitterness, rage, and desire for revenge disguise deeper psychological and cognitive issues, which, I would argue, are the cause of her destabilised actions.

Zote's actions result from emotional instability caused principally by inadequacy of cognition. She takes her ostracism from the village *personally* and refuses to move on. However, Zote is fully aware that the practice of expelling a known *kirhupfü* from the village is common among the Angami Nagas. She was not the first *kirhupfü* to be expelled in this way, nor would she be the last. As such, her extremely adverse reaction cannot be understood as arising entirely from moral indignation caused by injustice. Underneath the seemingly righteous indignation is Zote's inability to imagine home differently from the traditional, territorial model. Consequently, she is unable to move on and instead takes the folk belief personally as *her* fight. In that sense, Zote's fight is not only against her natal village; rather, it is against a custom in the Angami traditional belief system. Her death at the hands of the ancestor-spirits is suggestive of this view. The appearance of the ancestor-spirits to defend the village from Zote's revenge signifies the restoration of the disrupted status quo, wherein any known *kirhupfü* will continue to be expelled from the village. Zote's regret, rendered movingly towards the end of chapter thirty-nine, then is not so much about losing her life as about the manner in which she lost it and, with it, her sister and the *kirhupfümia* community. In the knowing words of Ate: "I know now for sure that she regretted doing what she did, and that she met her death through it. I know she grieves losing me"(167).

At another level of signification, Zote's premature end is not so much about the triumph of tradition as it is about Kire's subtle emphasis on the willingness to accept new realities and adjust the structures of meaning-making. Was a relatively normal life possible for Zote in a new village? The change in Ate's fortune is Kire's answer to the question. Should we then avoid confronting oppressive traditional practices? The text does not advocate an answer in the affirmative nor castigate folk beliefs in general. However, it would seem fair to say that adopting Zote's way of confronting oppressive folk beliefs should be avoided. Instead, a more delicate and circumspect manner of confronting is poignantly suggested through Ate's happy ending. One might argue that Zote is perhaps not the average Naga with a traditional notion of home, but she certainly represents one end of the home spectrum.

Ate

At the other end of the home spectrum is Zote's younger sister, Ate, who has accepted the arbitrary banishment from the village. She confesses to Vilie:

> This is my home. I feel home here where there are none to judge me or to spy on me and accuse me of things I am not guilty of. Here, there is no one to say that I caused a bad harvest or that I brought hail and lightning to destroy crops of my neighbours. I don't hanker to go back. I was quite young when I left. I have no pleasant memories of my ancestral village that I should want to go back to it (142-43).

At age nine, Ate was expelled from the village along with her sister Zote for being born as 'witches' – the Tenyidie/Angami word for it is *kirhupfü*. The passage quoted above indicates that Ate did have a rough childhood in her natal village. She attributes her lack of desire to return to the absence of "pleasant memories" about the natal village. Typically, regardless of the quality of life, a Naga village girl would have developed some form of attachment to her home and village by age nine. This is engendered by the fact that the *territoriality* of the village space is indispensable to the traditional Naga conception of home. So, even though the narrative suggests it, age is unlikely to be a significant contributory factor in Ate's indifference towards her natal village. Instead, what comes through as the cause of her peace in contrast to Zote's bitterness and anger is her attitude to *what* constitutes home. Compelled to live in the village of Kirhupfümia, Ate develops an attitude that allows her to find relative contentment in her new surroundings: "With time...she had embraced her new life in the village of the Kirhupfümia" (168). The hopeful acceptance of her new situation and the experience of relative happiness in limited circumstances combine to produce an unintentional effect: destabilise the Naga traditional notion that a home can be found only in a traditional village.[5] Instead, the affective aspects of home, like the quality of life, for instance, are given more

---

[5] 'Kirhupfümia' is called a village in the narrative; but there are no men and children in it. The women dwelling in it came from different villages and had no choice in

importance in the emerging home discourse in the novel. Consequently, Ate does not mind leaving her natal home, as it can never provide her with the dignity and freedom she now enjoys in the outcast-village of Kirhupfümia.

In abstract terms, Ate has now reconceived and rearranged the basic components of home according to their importance. Unlike Zote, the physical space of the village is not as important to her as the people who make up the community. Zote's attachment to the natal village is stronger than Ate's despite the greater scorn she faced there before their ostracism (132). However, to Ate, quality of experience is fundamental in thinking of home and belonging.[6] The physical house is an important component, for the spirit of home needs the body of the house, so to speak, but Ate represents a model of home that is moveable; a model that is more consistent with a mental concept, and essentially dependent on the effect produced by the place.[7] In short, Ate's notion of home is premised on the idea that the physical house is dispensable. So, when it became necessary, she has no trouble abandoning her second home in the village of Kirhupfümia as well. .

Generally, for a Naga, identity is tied to the village of birth and the tribe. These larger categories of selfhood tend to subsume individual subjectivities and influence one's perception of home and the world. So, Ate's capacity to feel at home wherever she is accepted breaks away from the traditional Naga conception of home, where the village space is sacrosanct. She also demonstrates an exemplary attitude of attachment to home that differs from the norm: "If I am going to start a new life, why should I take so much of the old with me? It would only hinder me from beginning my new existence" (170). Not only is Ate aware of the complication of looking back too often, symbolised by the material items she leaves behind, but she is also aware of the will required to make the new start possible. The new life will not be a *tabula rasa,* and memories of the old will continue to mark their presence in the fresh start, but a conception of life as a journey that passes through different points in time is underscored, and at each stop, there *is* a choice not be trapped in the past like Zote.

At this moment in the narrative, Ate's decision to follow Vilie to his village is crucial for resolving Vilie's problem. The grief that pushed our protagonist to relocate to the forest more than twenty years ago finds closure

---

coming to live there. They were ostracised for being 'witches' by their natal villages. Therefore, it is perceived as less of a village traditionally and in the text.

[6] See Peter Saunders' notion of "embodiment of the past memories", quoted in Somerville, 229. 1997.

[7] For mental concept of home, see Salman Rushdie's "Imaginary Homelands" in *Imaginary Homelands: Essays and Criticism 1981-1991.* 1991.

in the form of the actions of a young woman whose suffering is greater than his own. Ate's positivity amid gloom and uncertainty serves as a narratorial mirror to Vilie to put his own troubles in perspective: "Vilie marvelled at the wisdom of the young woman" (170).

IN THE END

Vilie's journey fulfils Gadamer's notion of 'double movement' encompassed in the complex term *bildung*, movement through time and space and inner transformation of the protagonist (8-17). Vilie's journey is physically circular, for he ends up where he started, but it is fundamentally an inward journey for self-discovery that brings out the plot motive of the heart-stone. Vilie's development is both a process and the result of a process: he goes through different stages of knowing and understanding. From being unable to deal with his own grief in chapter one, he grows into a man who can and wants to help those around him by the end of the novel. Redeeming Ate is a key example of his development as a person: calling the lie that she is cursed (136-39), helping her find her third home (223), and ultimately sacrificing his life for her (229-30). In fact, his sacrifice in the end to protect Ate and the Nepali child, both of whom share no blood ties with him, is not easily placeable within the circumscribed notion of kinship in traditional Naga culture. In that sense, Vilie can be said to have attained a level of humanism that diverges from the norm in the Naga lifeworld.

In the end, the status quo of the forest as the locus of Vilie's dwelling is retained. However, in contrast to the past, Vilie is now able to provide a clear reason for his choice not to live in the village: "I will not come back to live here. I am too used to the freedom that my forest life offers" (224). There is a paradigmatic shift in his articulation that was absent when the novel began. Vilie's initial relocation to the forest was more of a flight from unhappiness than the conscious decision of an adult. Now, his renewed choice of the forest as home is rooted in a teleology of home, in which freedom is both indispensable and the principal determinant. In other words, Vilie's choice to keep operating from his home in the forest, even though he now has parental duties towards Ate and the orphaned Nepali infant in the village, is not an escape from a situation that he cannot handle. Rather, it exemplifies the confidence and capability of a man who can meaningfully balance his individual life with his parental duties. Of course, the novel does not advocate a complete disavowal of the territory-centric traditional imagination of home among the Nagas. Nevertheless, in reiterating the *value* of freedom in the alternative conception of home, Kire draws attention to a commonly overlooked aspect of home in the Naga traditional conception. If home is where the heart is, surely the heart must be where freedom is most found. The physical house and the village, although important, are no longer *the* defining attributes of home.

WORKS CITED

Gadamer, Hans-Georg. *Truth and Method.* 1975. Translated by Joel Weinsheimer & Donald G. Marshall. Continuum, 2004. Print.

Kire, Easterine. *When the River Sleeps.* Zubaan, 2014. Print.

Levinas, Emmanuel. *Totality and Infinity: An Essay on Exteriority.* Translated by Alphonso Lingis. Kluwer Martinus Nijhoff Publishers, 1979. Print.

Rushdie, Salman. *Imaginary Homelands: Essays and Criticism 1981-1991.* Penguin Books, 1991. Print.

Somerville, Peter. "The Social Construction of Home." *Journal of Architectural and Planning Research.* vol. 14, no. 3, 1997, pp. 226-245. JSTOR, www.jstor.org/stable/43030210. Accessed 7 June 2020.

03

UNDERSTANDING NAGA COSMOLOGY THROUGH EASTERINE KIRE'S FICTIONAL NARRATIVE

Roderick Wijunamai

"Vilie was flung back like a bit of driftwood by the inrushing waters. His mouth and nostrils filled up with water as he felt himself being sucked down by the treacherous undercurrent. The river was almost human as it pushed him down and under, down and under, and the water rushed at him as though it would strangle him. He was shocked at the violence of the river. "I'm going to get out of this alive!" he swore as he fought back. At first he flailed his arms helplessly as he had in his nightmare-dreams of the river. But this was terrifyingly real. He would not wake up and cry with relief that it was only a dream. This was as real as real could be. Then he stopped struggling and concentrated instead on the spirit words he had learnt: "Sky is my father, Earth is my mother, stand aside death! Kepenuopfü fights for me, today is my day! I claim the wealth of the river because mine is the greater spirit. To him who has the greater spirit belongs the stone!" (Kire 105)

The anthropologists L.L. Langness and Gelya Frank remarked that ethnographic fictions, like standard anthropological ethnography, do the "conscious" and "integral" work of trying to accurately describe "another way of life" (8). The difference lies in the addition of plots and characters in fiction in ways that are not integral to standard ethnography. Ethnographic fiction in that sense, offers "a freedom in depicting or suggesting the thoughts and feelings... [of the native] impossible in a formal, scientific report" (Kroeber 13).

Ethnographic fiction has a long history in cultural anthropology. It emerged as a reaction to the "oft-shunned desire among some ethnographers to write lyrical prose" (Jacobson & Larsen 181). In resonance with what the archetypal literary social scientist Clifford Geertz calls "faction" (141), ethnographic fiction can be said to be an "imaginative writing about real people in real places"; it narrates or reports "events that actually happened, [but are] being shaped and dramatized using fictional techniques" (Sparkes 5). Plainly put, it is a form of literary fiction based on (anthropological) ethnographic research; a genre of writing that evokes cultural practices or lifeworlds "observed through fieldwork in a fictionalized account" (Jacobson & Larsen 181).

During the colonial period, Nagas attracted extensive ethnographic scholarship, mostly by administrators-cum-anthropologists, to the extent that Nagas were "arguably even a cradle of British Social Anthropology" (Wouters & Heneise 5). However, ethnographic research among the Nagas came to an abrupt halt with the difficult decolonization of the Naga-inhabited lands and the onset of the Naga Movement for sovereignty from the 1950s onward, which continues still. In academia, this resulted in a hiatus in ethnographic research of more than half a century. But it was also during this period that indigenous Naga writing, especially ethnographic and historical fiction writing, in English emerged alongside work from other Northeastern communities. Easterine Kire inaugurated this trend for the Nagas with her 2003 novel A *Village Remembered*. Since then, a sustained number of Naga historical and ethnographic fictional works have been published.

Kire's (2014) *When the River Sleeps* (subsequently *WRS*) is a rare ethnographic novel. It invites readers into an immersive tour of the Naga cosmology that suffers non-recognition because of the currently hegemonic creed and canons of Christianity and is, therefore, a world that risks being forgotten. It is rare, not only in its subject content but also in its prose style. The entire novel revolves around the journey of an Angami Naga hunter, Vilie, who sets off from his village to find a powerful stone from a "sleeping" river. In this way, Kire brings Naga folklore to the reading world in a very accessible form through creative infusions. She introduces her readers to the many other-than-human beings Vilie encounters on his journey, who are the same other-than-human beings that Nagas routinely encountered and acknowledged in their lifeworld in pre-Christian days.

In her poem, *The Speed of Darkness*, Muriel Rukeyser, the American poet, writes that "The universe is made of stories, not of atoms". As is the case for many indigenous communities across the globe, it is certainly true for the Nagas, whose culture is preserved, communicated, and disseminated through folklore and tall tales. Kire, with her many years of accumulated knowledge, from Naga elders as well as her contemporaries, introduces different spirits and beliefs from the Naga lifeworld in her novel *WRS*.

In this essay, I discuss three elements from this novel, namely, tiger-man, forest spirit, and dreams, all of which are mostly absent in the minds of an upcoming Naga generation – a generation that only knows what the Bible allows to be known. I use these three elements to argue that, apart from bringing alive the slowly disappearing Naga folklore, *WRS* is also an expression of the environmental humanities of the Nagas. Furthermore, her ethnographic novel compensates for the absence of fresh (anthropological) ethnography to understand the "just passed" Naga lives and lifeworlds.

TIGER-MAN

> There was yet another factor which now came to mind when he heard the tiger returning. This could very well be a weretiger, Vilie thought. As a rule, ordinary tigers kept their distance from man. This one had been scared off by a gunshot and yet he was coming back for more. Vilie was quite sure by now that it was a weretiger. The folk practice of certain men transforming their spirits into tigers was a closely guarded art. Despite the secrecy, most of the villagers knew who were the men who had become weretigers. He rapidly thought of the names of those men who had their tiger spirits in this region. Three names came to mind and he decided to use them all rather than use only one in case it was the wrong name. (Kire 34)

What the werewolf or wolf-person is to European folklore (Beresford 137; Blécourt 23; Otten 232) weretigers, colloquially known as tiger-men, is to the Naga folklore (Heneise "The Naga Tiger-man..." 91). In *The Angami Nagas*, Hutton (2) observed that tigers are very closely related to the Angamis and the Tenyimia Nagas in general. This stems from their belief that *terhuma* (the spirit), the tiger, and man were all born of the same mother. And so, "when a tiger is killed the village priest proclaims *penna*[1], a non-working day" (Hutton *Angami*[2] 92), as it is taken as the death of an older brother. Likewise, among the Semas, the dead body of a tiger is treated like a human enemy (Hutton *Sema*[3] 77), and their meat is considered sacred and it is forbidden to eat it.

To understand why [Naga] man and tiger parted ways and came to resent each other, the following Angami myth, as narrated by Hutton's (*Angami*) monograph, explains:

> [The] man, the tiger, and the spirit were three brothers, the sons of one woman, and whereas the man tended his mother carefully, washing her and bathing her, the tiger was always grumbling about the house, snarling at anything and giving everyone trouble. The man ate his food cooked, the tiger ate his raw, and the spirit just had his smoke-dried. One day the mother, who was tired of the family squabbles, made a grass mark and set it up in the jungle, and told the man and the tiger to race for it, saying, "Whoever touches it first shall go and live in villages, but the other must go and live in the dark jungles." Then the spirit said to the man, "I will shoot the mark over with an arrow when you call out, and then you can say you touched it first." So when they had run a little way in the jungle the man called out, "I have touched the mark," and at the same time the spirit drew his bow and struck the mark with an arrow, so that it trembled, and the tiger coming up while it was still shaking was deceived, and went away, angry, into the jungle.
>
> After this the man sent the cat from the village to say to the tiger, "After all, you are my brother; when you kill a deer, please put a leg on the wall for me," but the cat muddled the message and said, "When you kill a deer put it on the wall for the man," and the tiger, thinking that a whole deer was meant, was angry and hated the man. All the same they are brothers, and to this day, if a man kill a tiger, he will say in the village, "The gods have killed a tiger in the jungle," not "I have killed it." As if he did all other tigers would say, "This man has killed his

---

[1] Derived from the Tenyi word *kenna* (Kenyü in Tenyi spelling), meaning 'forbidden' in the Tenyimi Naga lifeways, *genna* (a super-category) has two abstentions: *kenna*, which is applied only to an individual, and *penna* (Penyü) which is applied to community (See: Hutton *The Angami Nagas* 192-93)

[2] Hereafter, I use *Angami* to refer to the monograph *The Angami Nagas*

[3] Hereafter, I use *Sema* to refer to the monograph *The Sema Nagas*

brother," and would go about to devour him. But the tiger is afraid of man because he (the tiger) cannot carry stones, while he sees the man take up stones as great as a basket. Therefore, thinking that man is very strong, he is afraid. (261-62)

Time and again in the colonial monographs, one finds accounts of the relationship between tiger and Naga that do not vary significantly between the tribes. These accounts, while sufficiently descriptive, are often read only by academics, particularly historians and cultural studies scholars. Moreover, they represent colonial ethnographers' "etic view", and were written for administrative purposes. In this regard, Kire's WRS, alongside her other novels, fulfils the function of what the Norwegian anthropologist Marit Melhuus calls "formidling" – "popularizing or mediating scientific knowledge to the general public...[through] research" (75).

In her earlier novel, *Don't Run, My Love*, the plot revolves around two protagonists, Visenuo and her daughter Atuonuo, running away from Kevi, a handsome young man, after finding out that the latter is a tiger-man (*tekhumevi*). It derails, in the words of Kire, their arduous yet peaceful life "in a well-knit community of wise elders and caring – though sometimes overbearing – neighbours and relatives".

Such human-animal relationships, or indigenous classification systems, are not unique to the Nagas. Interrogating "Why, to the Karam, is the cassowary not a bird", Ralph Bulmer, the twentieth-century British ethnobiologist, concluded that, "The cassowary is not a bird because it enjoys a unique relationship [with the Karam] man" (5). Among the Karam people, who live in the Kaironk Valley in the Schrader Mountains of New Guinea, cassowaries, large ostrich or emu-like birds, are distinguished from bats (which they categorize as birds) and are given a special taxonomic rank closer to humans. This stems from the Karam mythology, which recognizes cassowaries as sisters and cross-cousins to Karam men (i.e., father's sister's children) and restricts hunting them.

It should be mentioned here that, besides the tiger myths, there are also many other human-animal myths in Naga society. One is the belief about the trans-equatorial migratory bird, the Amur falcon, among the Rongmei Nagas. Known as *Akhuaipuina* in the vernacular, the Rongmeis believe that this bird species is sent by *Tingkao Ragwang* (The Supreme God) to herald a rich harvest and protect their land from famine. A Rongmei folk song has the following lyrics: *Chakaan pat munkazi ye, Khoipuina kaliap guang nga, Khokupuina san kangzang. Mei guai guang zao lo Rongmei khou khoipuina, Sam kangzami. Hei Raguang ta thuanna bam bu ye.* The translated folk song reads: "As the Amur falcon flaps its wing in the sky, it heralds winter, and the harvest is going to be plenty. Oh! Come everyone, and see the Amur falcon hovering and dancing in the sky. Hey! People are praising God" (Age-Old Lores of the Rongmeis…).

In terms of kinship terminology, like human siblings, the Karam men and cassowaries are perceived as mutually dependent, but the sister is under the brother's control. She is "married out (usually to the brother's advantage), and is in a sense dispossessed of much that she would have enjoyed if she had been a male" (Bulmer 18). However, in terms of such a relationship, what is different for the Naga people and their relationship with tigers is the expression of the relationship, which colonial ethnographers loosely call "lycanthropy" (Mills 228-29; Hutton *Angami* 243). Lycanthropy, in modern-day science, is classified as a psychiatric syndrome, characterized by "an unusual belief or delusion in which the patient thinks that he/she has been transformed into an animal…[and] in rare cases the patient believes that another person has been transformed into an animal" (Nasirian et al. 1).

Among the Nagas, it is believed that, under certain circumstances, the soul of a Naga person leaves the body temporarily and takes residence in the body of a tiger. Among most Naga tribes, these weretigers are traditional medicine experts or healers (called 'shamans' – as they can cure ailments by extracting 'dirt'). While there is little practical connection between being a medicine expert and a weretiger, there are, reportedly, discernible links between the two. For example, if the tiger (in whose body the medicine expert has taken residence) is wounded or killed, then a corresponding wound injury will occur on the weretiger's human body. Similarly, if the tiger is killed, the medicine expert also dies (Ovesen 10). Kire shows this in a particular twist to her tale, namely, the reluctance of the protagonist Vilie to kill the tiger he encounters:

> Vilie shouted and cocked his gun instantly. He ran to the door of the shed and peered into the darkness trying to catch a glimpse of his assailant. The light from the fire was so dim he could only just barely make out the dark shape lunging toward him. The tiger came at him fearlessly, throwing itself at the outline of the man. At the last second, Vilie sidestepped and the tiger crashed into the door, breaking it, and leaving torn fragments of wood hanging on the hinges. Vilie shot off a bullet above the animal's head. The sound was thunderous and the tiger sprung to its feet and leapt away into the night. The blinding flash from the shot lit up the darkness momentarily, and he saw that the tiger was much bigger than any he had ever seen. Its back was almost as wide as the door it had smashed. He had not wanted to kill the tiger if he could help it, and was pleased that the shot had had the right effect. (32)

Most of Kire's writings are "versions of lived reality [of the Nagas] that never make the headlines", but the book under review, in particular, is a departure from her previous ones[4] (Eriksen 3). This is because it inaugurates, for those interested in the environmental humanities of the Nagas, the indigenous discourse on "connectivity ontology" or "relational ontology". I perceive relational ontology as a convergence of multiple realities, a reality where the Nagas "conflate the abstract and immutable dualities of modernist ontologies" (Watts 1). By introducing her readers to the Nagas as a part of a larger living system, including humans and other-than-human entities, Kire lucidly ushers in an aspect that has been long due in Naga studies.

Environmental humanities, as a subject, has emerged over the last decade. Besides bridging the traditional divides between sciences and humanities, the field resists nature-culture as well as human-nonhuman binaries in the discussion of current ecological predicaments. In response to the latter, environmental humanities is "an effort to enrich environmental research with a more extensive conceptual vocabulary, whilst at the same time vitalising the humanities by rethinking the ontological exceptionality of the human" (Rose et al. 2). In other words, it recognizes the "diverse human understandings about, and activities in, the environment [as] critical factors in making sense of, and responsibly inhabiting, a dynamic more-than-human world" (O'Gorman et al. 428-29). Environmental humanities and Kire's WRS promote an understanding of the environment as being deeply entangled between humans and other-than-human persons, who co-evolve and co-become rather than exist in separate domains. It recognizes every place, point, and landscape as a "contact zone" (Haraway 216), or what Venessa Watts (2013) calls "place-thought" worlding.

FOREST SPIRIT

Men, especially when out hunting, swore they had seen beautiful long-haired girls playing and singing to each other in the forest. That was why they called them forest songs. A forest song was a spirit song sung very melodiously and could be heard by a lone hunter, and also by a group of people such as an age-group. The old men said that the spirits used forest

---

[4] With a lesser emphasis, Kire introduced Naga traditional cosmology in her debut novel, A Naga Village Remembered, and her 2016 novel, Son of the Thundercloud.

> songs to enchant humans, and draw them to the unclean forest
> so they would die and come to live with them there. Vilie had
> never heard a forest song but one of his age-mates had. He had
> recounted it to their mates in the age-group house at night
> when they were all sitting together by the fire. (Kire 82)

Steering away from anthropocentric views of the environment, Eduardo Kohn, in his book *How Forests Think*, indicates that trees (and other beings), indeed, have the ability to think, speak, and act. Denouncing the Cartesian divide between humans and nonhumans, as well as the idea of human exceptionalism, he annotates, "How other kinds (meaning, other-than-humans) of beings see us matters...[and] that seeing, representing, and perhaps knowing, even thinking, are not exclusively human affairs" (Kohn 1). Through the everyday lives of the Runa of Ecuador's Upper Amazon, Kohn demonstrates that living actors, not just humans, influence and are influenced by the living things around them. Nagas, for centuries, have lived within the loop of the same dialectic.

For any Naga, before Christianity arrived, the forest was not "just" an ecology or "resource" to be tapped. Nagas have culturally specific images, knowledge, and concepts of the physical landscape that affect how they interact with their landscape. Forest, or more broadly, nature, is an extension of the Nagas' social world, full of spirits (*terhuomia*) that influence their everyday lives. This concept resembles the Bhutanese belief system of place and space (Allison 268). For the Bhutanese, animated deities and spirits populate the lands they inhabit. These deities and spirits, they perceive, are the original owners of the Bhutanese landscape, predating even the arrival of Buddhism from Tibet, which leads the community to "express a relational ontology" vis-à-vis landscapes in their lifeways (Allison 268). As such, at a certain time of the year, the eastern part of Bhutan maintains *reedum* (or *ladam*), disallowing any human presence in the mountain forests, as a way of petitioning their protector deity (*tsen*).

From the start of the novel, Kire makes it clear that the forest, for Vilie, was not just "home", but his "wife"; Vilie asserts this time and again. Treating the forest as the "wife" of the hunter is not a common idea among Nagas. However, in the not-so-distant past, Nagas of every tribe acknowledged the presence of spirits in the forest; spirits of different kinds and personhood resided in the "wild" and the village. Stories were often told to characterize these spirits, which in turn shaped rules governing community behaviour. This being part and parcel of the Naga lifeworld, Kire dedicates a chapter to "Forest Etiquette" (87). The entire chapter is an exchange between Vilie and an angry forest spirit. Not only did Vilie know the cause of his affliction, but he was also well-versed in the responses he had to make. The angry forest spirit was after him because he had failed to abide by the "the rules of hospitality" his mother had taught him:

> If he took firewood or gathered herbs from the forest, he should acknowledge the owners. What was it his mother used to say when they had gathered herbs so many years ago? Terhuomia peziemu. Thanks be to the spirits. He knew what she meant by that. If he found an animal in his traps and brought it home, she would repeat that. Terhuomia pezie. It was her way of pronouncing a prayer of thanksgiving to the provider, to Ukepenuopfü. (85)

While "unquiet angry spirits", "vengeful sorcerers", and "demons", very much feature in the Naga cultural landscape, not all forests are shunned or viewed with fear and aversion. The Nayaka people in South India, who view the forest as their parent, have a somewhat similar perception (Bird-David 190). Vilie considered the forest area he lived in to be his home and his wife because of the providence of the forest and its spirit. And his loving and nurturing attitude towards the forest earned him the description "guardian of the forest" (Kire 48). It must be mentioned here that, for the Nagas, the referencing of land to their lifeways is not just a political strategy, but Nagas are "intrinsically and inseparably tied to land's intentionality" according to their indigenous como-visions (Watts 30).

DREAMS

> Vilie plunged his hand into the river. It was cold – close to freezing – and perfectly still. It was just the way it should be. The river had gone to sleep. Everything was as the seer had told him. Almost imperceptibly, he slid forward and entered the water and plucked a smooth stone from the bottom of the river. In a similar motion, he pulled his arm out of the water and stood still. But it was too late. He felt through the soles of his feet that a great force had awakened. Before he could reach the shore, the water had swelled above his waist – the river had come alive! In an instant, the great torrents had tethered his legs in its twisting undercurrents, dragging him down forcibly into its depths. Vilie"s struggles were feeble against the force of rushing water. Unable to reach the surface, his lungs began

to burn for air and his mouth filled with water. He tried to
shout, even as he felt himself being swallowed further into the
darkness. Above his struggling form the river roared, drowning
out his muffled screams. Then, in a final panicked outburst,
he struck out against the power that was consuming him. His
movements grew more frantic. A deep guttural sound escaped
his throat. He flung out his hand and it hit the edge of the
bed. It then dawned on him that he had been dreaming again.
(Kire 11)

Many cultures and/or religious traditions across the world, across
history, have regarded "dreams as profoundly meaningful and valuable
experiences" (Bulkeley 2). These dreams could be "revelations of the
sacred" (Merill 194) or a medium to come into contact with the dead,
particularly ancestors (Shaw 40-1). The American anthropologist Donald
Tuzin mentions the frequent encounters of the Ilahita Arapesh people,
from northern New Guinea, with the ghosts of their ancestors through their
dreams (565). What is more, dreams can also be means (mostly for shamans
and diviners) for knowing the causes of illness or suffering, as well as the
agency to gain insights on healing the same (Aristides 305). In the popular
understanding of indigenous communities – and in the orthodox Judeo-
Christian Abrahamic tradition – dreaming is a means to foresee the future.
It gives a "glimpse of the future, of destiny, of providence" with "a prophetic
meaning" (Bulkeley 4).

After the rather dramatic opening of the novel with a dream, the entire
narrative is Vilie's journey in pursuit of this dream. Ever since he heard
the story of the sleeping river, the dream of catching the "heart-stone" (a
powerful charm) haunted Vilie every month for the next two years until
he decided to go and retrieve it. If anything, this shows how the Nagas
"give great importance to dreams as sources of divine knowledge, especially
knowledge about the future" (Heneise "Making Dreams..." 67).

Here again, the British administrator-anthropologist John Henry
Hutton is noted as having said, "...of all forms of second sight dreaming
is the favourite and the best" (*Angami* 246). He goes on to talk about
different types of dreaming among the Angami Nagas, including dreaming
for someone else and charging fees for it. These dreams foretold the results
of hunting expeditions, trading ventures, decisions over marriage partners,
or even the choice of name for an infant. And so, "ignoring the dream was
believed foolish, and could lead to illness or even calamity for the wider
community" (Heneise "Making Dreams..." 68). This mitigates the potential
incredulity readers might have felt about why Vilie had to strive so hard to
pursue his dream.

The magnitude of the dream's influence on Vilie is obvious. It was a journey that nearly cost him his life, fighting all dangers and unforeseen circumstances, yet he braved them all. In Kire's depiction of how his dream haunted him and his sleep, Vilie was guided by a matrix of many small pointers and circumstances put together, but mostly by his conviction that his dreams foretold the significance of the stone. As Kire states, "[Vilie] didn't want to admit that he was not sure if he would find what he was searching for...Yet, when he thought of his dream, he had no doubt he was meant to find the river" (23).

As against the first two elements discussed above, recent scholarship suggests, despite the advent of Christianity, capitalism, and modern liberal democracy, "dreams and dreaming [in the Naga society] remain important avenues for negotiating uncertainty and dealing with the future" (Heneise "Agency and Knowledge..." 1). While dreams have to a great extent metamorphosed to have Christian connotations, they still constitute an important source of knowledge and continue to influence the everyday lives of the Nagas.

CONCLUSION

All in all, Kire's novel is an erudite treatise on a world that Naga elders will readily recognize. However, it is also a world that is now slowly being erased from the memory of Naga society. Through her novel, Kire takes us through the everyday life experiences of the Nagas before an ontological change. Before Christianity inundated Naga society, Nagas communicated and interacted with a host of nonhuman actors. These conversations came to an end with Christian conversion. Judeo-Christian epistemologies degraded agencies of autochthonous spirits, other-than-humans, and supernatural life forms. From being a part of an active body politic, this host of other-than-humans has been increasingly removed from the Naga landscape, and the latter has been made exclusive to humans. So, what Kire narrates in her novel is more than just an experience documented by colonial administrator-ethnographers with an exotifying gaze, which is now increasingly foreign also to Naga youth. Kire also reclaims the indigenous frame of understanding and interpreting the world. Along with other indigenous scholars, researchers, and writers, she reinstates the disrupted indigenous epistemologies.

Kire's WRS (and her other novels) constitute a bridge to new ethnographies of the contemporary historical period of the Nagas. More importantly, her writing brings alive the Naga lifeworld, not from the lens of the anthropological "other" but through her own embodied self as a Naga. More than just bridging the ethnographic lacunae, her ethnographic fiction also helps overcome the limitations of ethnographic materials that social science scholars are routinely faced with. Through rich plots and counter-plots in a flexible prose style, Kire's *WRS* combats the circumstantial forgetting of the Naga lifeways. In conclusion, it can be said that Kire's work balances the corrective of anthropological insights by accurately conveying the Naga lives and their onto-epistemologies.

WORKS CITED

"Age-Old Lores of the Rongmeis Believe Us to Be Heralds of a Rich Harvest That God Had Sent to Protect Their Land from Famine." *Paomi Post*, 27 Oct. 2020, www.facebook.com/paomipost/posts/160657665719658. Accessed 2 Dec. 2020.

Allison, Elizabeth. "Deity Citadels: Sacred Sites of Bio-Cultural Resistance and Resilience in Bhutan." *Religions*, 10.4, 2019, pp. 268.

Aristides, Aelius. *The Complete Works*. Translated by Charles A. Behr, Leiden: E.J. Brill, 1981.

Beresford, Matthew. *The White Devil: The Werewolf in European Culture*. Reaktion Books, 2013.

Bird-David, Nurit. "The giving environment: another perspective on the economic system of gatherer-hunters." *Current anthropology* 31.2, 1990, pp. 189-196.

Blécourt, Willem de. "I Would Have Eaten You Too": Werewolf Legends in the Flemish, Dutch and German Area." *Folklore*, 118.1, 2007, pp. 23-43.

Bulkeley, Kelly. "Dreaming as a Spiritual Practice." *Anthropology of Consciousness*, 7.2, 1996, pp. 1-15.

Bulmer, Ralph. "Why is the Cassowary Not a Bird? A Problem of Zoological Taxonomy Among the Karam of the New Guinea Highlands." *Man*, 2.1,1967, pp. 5-25.

Eriksen, Thomas Hylland. "The Young Rebel and the Dusty Professor: A Tale of Anthropologists and the Media in Norway." *Anthropology Today*, 19.1, 2003, pp. 3-5.

Geertz, Clifford. *Works and Lives: The Anthropologist as Author*. Stanford University Press, 1988.

Haraway, Donna J. *When species meet*. Minneapolis: University of Minnesota Press, 2013.

Heneise, Michael. *Agency and Knowledge in Northeast India: The Life and Landscapes of Dreams*. Routledge, 2018.

—. "Making Dreams, Making Relations: Dreaming in Angami Naga Society." *The South Asianist Journal*, 5.1, 2017, pp. 66-82.

—. "The Naga Tiger-man and the Modern Assemblage of a Myth." *Anthropology and Cryptozoology: Exploring Encounters with Mysterious Creatures*. 2017, pp. 91-106.

Hutton, John Henry. *The Angami Nagas*. Oxford University Press, 1921.

—. *The Sema Nagas*. Oxford University Press, 1921.

Jacobson, Matt, and Soren C. Larsen. "Ethnographic Fiction for Writing and Research in Cultural Geography." *Journal of Cultural Geography*, 31.2, 2014, pp. 179-193.

Kire, Easterine. *A Naga Village Remembered: A Novel*. Ura Academy, 2003.

—. *Don't Run, My Love*. Speaking Tiger, 2017.

—. Son of the Thundercloud *Speaking Tiger*, 2016

—. *When the River Sleeps*. Zubaan, 2014.

Kohn, Eduardo. *How Forests Think: Toward an Anthropology Beyond the Human*. University of California Press, 2013.

Kroeber, Alfred R. "Introduction." *AMERICAN INDIAN LIFE*, edited by Elsie Clews Parsons, New York: Viking Press, 1992, pp. 5–16.

Langness, L. L., and Gelya Frank. "Fact, Fiction and the Ethnographic Novel." *Anthropology and Humanism Quarterly*, 3.1⊡2, 1978, pp. 18-22.

Melhuus, Marit. "Anthropology and the Challenges of Cross-Cultural Comparison." *Anthropology, by Comparison*, 2002, pp.70.

Merrill, William. "The Rarámuri Stereotype of Dreams." *Dreaming. Anthropological and Psychological Interpretations*. 1987, pp. 194-219.

Mills, James Philip. *The Lhota Nagas*. Ams Press Inc, 1922.

Nasirian, Mansoureh, Nabi Banazadeh, and Ali Kheradmand. "Rare Variant of Lycanthropy and Ecstasy." *Addiction & Health*, 1.1, 2009, pp.53.

O'Gorman, Emily, et al. "Teaching the Environmental Humanities: International Perspectives and Practices." *Environmental Humanities*, 11.2, 2019, pp. 427-460.

Otten, Charlotte F., Ed. *The Lycanthropy Reader: Werewolves in Western Culture*. Syracuse University Press, 1986.

Ovesen, Jan. "Man or Beast? Lycanthropy in the Naga Hills." *Ethnos*, 48.1-2, 1983, pp. 5-25.

Rose, Deborah Bird, et al. "Thinking through the environment, unsettling the humanities." *Environmental Humanities* 1.1, 2012, pp. 1-5.

Rukeyser, Muriel. *Out of silence: Selected poems*. Northwestern University Press, 1994.

Shaw, Rosalind. "Dreaming as Accomplishment: Power, the Individual and Temne Divination." *Dreaming, Religion and Society in Africa*. 1992, pp. 36-54.

Sparkes, Andrew C. "Fictional Representations: On Difference, Choice, and Risk." *Sociology of Sport Journal*, 19.1, 2002, pp. 1-24.

Tuzin, Donald. "The Breath of a Ghost: Dreams and the Fear of the Dead." *Ethos*, 3.4, 1975, pp. 555-578.

Watts, Christopher. "Relational Archaeologies: Roots and Routes." *Relational Archaeologies: Humans, Animals, Things*, edited by Christopher Watts. New York: Routledge, 2014. 1-20.

Watts, Vanessa. "Indigenous place-thought and agency amongst humans and non-humans." *Decolonization: Indigeneity, Education & Society*. 2.1, 2013, pp. 20-34.

Wouters, Jelle JP, and Michael Heneise. "Introduction to Nagas in the 21st Century." *The South Asianist Journal*, 5.1, 2017. pp. 3-19.

04

WEAVING DREAMS AND LIVING FOLKLORE: NARRATIVE STRUCTURE IN *A TERRIBLE MATRIARCHY*

Vizovono Elizabeth

As a postcolonial indigenous writer, Easterine Kire has always situated herself in her cultural moorings, reflecting her concern with retrieving the unheard stories of her people and community and recording them in writing. This paper focuses on her use of living folklore in the form of dreams, spirits, and food-ways in the novel *A Terrible Matriarchy* by intermingling them in the narrative structure. It is framed on an interdisciplinary approach including concepts from folklore studies, anthropology and literary criticism. The aim is to highlight Kire's distinctive style of writing which she has developed through the use of folkloric forms. This is aptly demonstrated in the novel as she incorporates such elements not just in her themes and setting but also embeds them in the very structure of the narrative. This aspect deserves more critical attention as her writings have usually been read from a thematic aspect but not from a structural point of view. The paper contends that her narrative technique is in fact the distinguishing feature that establishes her style as an indigenous writer.

A Terrible Matriarchy (2007)is Easterine Kire's second novel. The 2nd edition was published in 2013 including a note from the author and the first reviews of the book, as a textbook edition, after it was prescribed for BA

English Honours course 'Writings in English from Nagaland' by Nagaland University. To supplement the insufficient critical readings of the book at the time, Kire herself also developed a study guide to accompany the book, which is also a first for an indigenous writer of the region. The novel has now achieved much critical attention over the years. The story is set in Kohima during the 1960s and 70s and presented through the eyes of the young protagonist Dielieno from her childhood through her young adulthood. But it is more than just a girl's story. As noted by Paul Pimomo, the novel is a "girl's coming of age story" set in the patriarchal Angami society through which the author also documents the Naga society coming of age (186). Set against the cultural landscape of a society in transition, the author presents how folklore functions in the everyday life of the characters.

THE SIGNIFICANCE OF FOLKLORE

The term "folklore" was coined in 1846 by William Thoms to signify 'the Lore of the People.' These include "the manners, customs, observances, superstitions, ballads, proverbs, etc., of the olden times" (qtd. in Haase 359). The significance of folklore was later expanded by American folklorist and anthropologist William Bascom in 1954, when he suggested that folklore has four functions in addition to entertainment: to validate culture, to educate, to maintain social control, and to provide a socially acceptable means of escape (362). Thus, according to Bascom, folklore has many cultural aspects, such as allowing for escape from societal consequences, serving to validate a culture and transmitting a culture's morals and values. Folklore portrays contemporary life, documents traditional behaviour, reinforces systems of belief, and provides safety-valves to release pent-up resentments.

Russian folklorist Vladimir Propp also states that "From the historical perspective, the entire creative output of people is folklore" (5). Historically, non-literate societies have depended on the use of myths, legends, and folk songs to maintain ethnic identity. This is particularly significant in the postcolonial context as the literatures of previously colonized ethnic peoples illustrate such ways of expressing themselves. According to Deep Punia, "all literature- oral or written- springs from life, but oral literature is a better projection of the innermost recesses of the socio-cultural life of a society and its traditions, customs, social values, rites and rituals" (11-12). Hence the use of oral/folkloric forms in writing would certainly demonstrate the 'innermost recesses' of a people's culture. This is witnessed in postcolonial writings, particularly in the works of indigenous women writers.

Shubha Tiwari rightly notes that "Postcolonialism challenges those parameters with which the dominant European culture judges other cultures," but it is to be remembered that "alien yardsticks applied on the history, culture and literature of erstwhile colonies have no validity" because of the very difference in basically "everything" in "any given two distinct territories of the world" (53). She further quotes Stone Mediatore who speaks of how "many third world women in particular have found theoretical discourses inadequate and have turned to experience oriented writing to communicate their struggle against an array of patriarchal and neo-colonialist institutions" (58). Similarly, Gay Wilentz, referring to the work of Black women writers, also posits that "the task of exploring works of cultures suppressed by dominant culture needs an interdisciplinary approach to criticism, an examination of the literature's historicity and social significance, attention to its oral/folkloric inheritance, and an understanding of the writer's commitment to reflect and often reform the culture that the literature represents" (xiii). She affirms that documenting alternative practices may open up other ways of seeing which have been lost both in opposition to and incorporation by the dominant culture (xxviii).

Elleke Boehmer also notes that "claiming a historical validity for the ordinary," postcolonial women writers have "situated their work alongside, and overlapping with, conventional narratives of a national, public history" (218). She emphasizes that a crucial structural function found in much of postcolonial women's writings is "the intermingling of forms derived from indigenous, nationalist, and European literary traditions" (221). This body of literature offers alternative narratives that enable a better understanding of different cultures and beliefs. It is a combination of oral tradition fused with written literature, as according to Bill Ashcroft, et al, "post-colonial cultures have all, in various ways, been influenced by the interrelationship between orality and literacy" (165). Much of the literature from North East India and particularly Nagaland, also typically reflect these characteristics. Temsula Ao terms this as "writing orality" (109). She elaborates that this is literature rich with indigenous flavour wherein "folklore does not remain merely 'folklore' as relics of a distant past but becomes the signifier of a new sensibility" (Ibid).

WEAVING FOLKORE INTO A NARRATIVE

Kire's novel A *Terrible Matriarchy* is about a society steeped in customary practices but undergoing rapid social changes. A significant aspect about the novel that has received less critical attention is the way in which the entire story is woven with threads of folkloric elements. These are incorporated meticulously in the narrative structure of the novel. During the 60s and 70s, Kohima was a new town which was in a state of flux, grappling with changing social values. Kire highlights how traditional cultural values were in conflict with modern values leading to identity crisis, violence and abuse. It is within such a setting that she endeavours to show 'living folklore' operating in the lives her characters. The narrative follows a linear progression from the protagonist Dielieno's first person point of view. The first chapter immediately sets things into context. It begins with Dielieno feeling unloved by her grandmother and ends with her dream of dreading her life at Grandmother's. The novel opens with her stating, "My grandmother didn't like me. I knew this when I was about four and a half" (Kire 1). She was made to believe this based on the preferential treatment in serving meat to her and her brother. While eating at her grandmother's house, she was denied the chicken leg because according to Grandmother, "that portion is always for boys" and "girls must eat the other portions" (Ibid). This statement introduces the theme of suppression and ill treatment of the girl child by Grandmother.

THE ANGAMI 'SCIENCE OF DREAMING'

Kire then uses dreams as a recurring motif to outline the structure of the novel. She begins with Dielieno's dream narration in the first chapter, followed by several other dreams in between, and ends with another dream in the epilogue of the novel. Besides, the presence of spirits and descriptions of food-ways are interspersed throughout the narrative. These elements form the structure of the novel, bringing the plot, setting, themes and character development full circle. The first chapter ends with Dielieno's first dream. After overhearing her parents talking of sending her to live with Grandmother, she is so horrified at the thought that she wishes she were dead. That night, she sees a strange dream:

> I saw Grandfather walking ahead of me. I ran up to him, having quite forgotten that he was dead. I tugged at his hand and we were playing together when his face changed and became Grandmother and she shook off my hand and gave me such a stern look that I woke up suddenly, in fear. (Kire 10)

Referring to past anthropological studies on dreams, Vibha Joshi comments that "the theme of moral reckoning is a significant aspect of Angami dream interpretation, which as has been documented in other studies, is often a means to predict what the future holds for a person or for the village" (76). Dielieno's dream foreshadows the successive events and foretells that her future life would be defined by the stern hand of Grandmother. The dread of her future fate is projected in her dream. For the Angamis, dreams are of great significance. They are part of the belief system and accepted as omens and divine revelations. Angamis believe in consulting their dreams and this is an integral part of their consciousness. In his monograph *The Angami Nagas*, British administrator ethnographer J. H. Hutton notes that dreams are a form of "second sight" and "the Angamis have almost a science of dreaming" (246). They read omens from dreams before undertaking any important tasks. It was generally considered foolish to ignore the dreams. American anthropologist Michael Heneise opines that Hutton himself was puzzled about "the agency of spirit entities on the dreamer, and indeed the predictive accuracy of dream mediated divination" (74).

Heneise in his recent study of Angami dream culture explores how this 'science of dreaming' relates to Naga cosmology in contemporary times. He notes that "dreams are the most common mode through which revelatory knowledge is obtained" (78). Heneise categorizes Angami dreaming into two types: *mhote* dreamers or dream experiences and *mhaphruo* dreamers and dream experiences. The first refers to ordinary dreams that are "interpreted based on community memory of symbolic meanings of dreams interpreted in the past" and the latter, "particularly cryptic, puzzling or troubling dreams" that are either "prayed upon or brought to a more experienced dreamer for interpretative consultation" (78 -9). Traditionally, the second type required shamanic healer-diviners (*themumia*) to draw truths from a spirit-mediated realm of knowledge (Ibid). The dreams narrated in the novel are mostly of the ordinary type that does not require 'interpretative consultation' but are accepted as 'revelatory knowledge.' A recent article in *Psychology Today* states that "dreaming clearly emerges out of the brain, mind, and personal life experiences of each individual. Yet also clearly reflects the individual's cultural environment – the languages, customs, concepts, and practices of his or her broader community" (Bulkeley). It further adds that studies show "how dreams reflect and actively respond to cultural, social, political, and religious influences in people's lives" (Ibid).

Kire's depiction of dreams exactly corresponds to the views stated above. Dreams function as a foreshadowing motif in the novel and the significant stages in Dielieno's character development are preceded by, or related to dreams. Dielieno is a *mhote* dreamer. Her dreams are not cryptic, but are revelatory and accurately predict what the future holds. The death of her brother Pete is foretold in her dream. She dreams that while fishing, Pete suddenly fell into the river and struggled to come out. "Leto was desperately trying to hold out his hand to him but Pete was too weak to catch it and in the end he was dragged under by the current. I woke up screaming" (Kire 70). Later, on the night when Pete dies, Lieno narrates how her father rushed into the hospital saying "I knew in my dream" as he wept unashamedly (135). Lieno shares about her father's dream with her friend Vimenuo:

> Father said that he saw Grandfather waiting outside our house and calling one of the boys out of the house. He saw that it was one of the boys, not me. Isn't it strange that dreams always come true especially if it is dreams of death in the family? (143)

Her father knew because the spirit of their dead Grandfather had come to call the boy's spirit. This alludes to the Angami belief that the spirits of the dead come to take their loved ones at the point of death. Similarly, before her father's death, Vimenuo says her grandmother too had dreamt of men digging a new grave in the courtyard and they knew someone in the family would soon die. They "prayed a lot but Father died three weeks later. So, it was like a preparation" (Ibid). Dreams are a form of intuitive and intangible wisdom that the Angamis possess, and Kire demonstrates that dreams function to control, guide and inform the people. The ways in which the characters respond to their dreams reflect that they interpret and accept them according to their past experiences of community memory of symbolic meaning and the cultural environment of their own community. In all these instances, the dreamers do not question or wonder about what they dreamt but accept the symbolic meaning of predictions of death in the family.

Lieno's dreams are omens that signify the course of future events that would have huge impacts on her life. Pete's death is a significant event in Lieno's life. This loss teaches her about empathy and the importance of friends and relatives through the presence of her friend Vimenuo. She confides: "I felt a twinge of guilt that I had not been with her when her father died" (142). More importantly, after the incident, she takes charge of the kitchen and helps the family as her mother recovers from the loss. It is a stage of progression into maturity in the process of her coming of age. This later makes her mother see and value the different strength women possessed compared to men, giving a new sense of worth to Lieno. Therefore, the death foretold in the dream is a precursor of the painful experience of having to grow up too soon, but it also moulds her character and provides her strength to become who she is meant to be.

Another significant experience that shapes her character is the pain caused by Vini to the family because of his rebellion and alcoholism which ultimately led to his death. Lieno has a sense of apprehension about Vini's fate which is again indicated in a dream. She first saw Pete standing in a garden of flowers after which he walked away, and "it was Vini in his place but instead of flowers there were thorns and burnt plants" (164) and he pulled out all the flowers leaving only black petals and thorns. After witnessing that Vini's alcohol induced violence was escalating too much, Dielieno questions her feelings for her brother. He had truly become a thorn in the family, causing discord and tension for everyone. It infuriates her so much that it drives her to speak out in anger:

> How dare you behave like this? You are the most selfish person
> I know and you have made life difficult for everyone. I wonder
> how Nisano can love you and stay with you. I'm ashamed to
> call you my brother. We should all leave you to yourself and
> get on with our own lives. (128)

This is the one instance where Lieno speaks up openly against male privilege, implying that he did not deserve the love of his wife and family members. She finds her voice and vents out her frustration at him. But Vini's response is typically male, as he counters her challenge by using his age and gender. He echoes Grandmother's views about the place of girls in society:

> What Lieno, you dare to raise your voice at me? Do you know
> that I used to carry you on my back when you were small?..
> Grandmother was right. Girls should never be educated. They
> always forget their station in life. (Ibid)

Though Lieno admits that she had spoken out of turn since she was a girl and the youngest in the family, Vini's actions cannot be justified merely on the basis of him being male and elder to her. Therefore, the fact that she speaks up and questions his irrational behaviour is significant. It gives voice to the silenced and suppressed girl child in the traditional patriarchal society. Vini however, does not change and ends up as a victim of alcoholism. The incidents surrounding the deaths of her two brothers are defining moments that shape Lieno as she grows into adulthood as a new age woman, and both these deaths are foretold in her dreams. Kire deftly interweaves Lieno's character development with the theme of alcoholism posing as a new social evil in society, the cultural environment that regulates the thoughts and behaviour of people, and the beliefs that still have a stronghold on people's attitudes. It illustrates the society's struggle to develop too, along with the social changes.

Besides these dreams about impending deaths and unfortunate events, there are two other incidences where the significance of dreams is highlighted. Sometimes dreams are consulted before deciding important matters, especially in cases of marriage proposals. When Sizo comes to meet Grandmother with the news of an offer of marriage for Bano, she was not so keen on agreeing, saying that that there would be better offers. He leaves after telling her, "Perhaps you should listen to your dreams before you say anything on the matter" (92). Grandmother of course, flouts the advice as she continually misapplies cultural norms according to her convenience, and Bano never receives another proposal for marriage.

The dream narrated in the epilogue of the novel is also significant. According to Heneise, mhaphruo dreamers may receive knowledge directly from the spirits of dead relatives and other non-human entities with whom they interact, and sustain a deeper personal linkage with their dream experiences" (79). Since Grandmother's unquiet spirit had been haunting the tenants of her house after her death, a pastor is brought to pray over the abandoned house and the unquiet spirit. That night, the pastor had a dream of Grandmother in which she tells him: "My house is not for strangers. It is for my family members. How can I be at rest when they have thrown out of my house those who cared for me and tried to make money out of it?" (Kire 286). The pastor is like a mhaphruo dreamer in this case as Grandmother directly communicates with him in the dream. After this incident, there are no more disturbances and the house is occupied by those whom Grandmother had intended it to.

The dream is a conduit for the spirit of the dead to communicate with the living and Grandmother's will is carried out, enabling her spirit to rest in peace. The Nagas believe in "a close link between the living and the dead... The living and the dead are brought together in dreams" (Jacobs, et al 85). Heneise also notes that such interventions involving "communication with the dead relatives in dreams and reverie" (76) are not uncommon. He has recorded similar anecdotes in his study. He further states that "with the advent of Christianity and particularly its numerous charismatic variants, the cultivated practice of communicating dream-mediated knowledge has entered new ritual modalities and form[s] new meaning" (79). Nowadays, a pastor is sought for intervention instead of traditional seers, as was done in the past. By incorporating this significant element into the story, the author shows how culture and dreams are intertwined. It is apparent that "the parallel existence of the spirit world and the world of the living is very firmly accepted" in Naga culture and "life is lived in such a way that it expresses this belief clearly" (Iralu 83). As noted by Kezhakielie Whiso, Kire's fiction accurately portrays "the depth to which the powers of dreams and visions are ingrained" into Naga beliefs and practices (Whiso).

THE OMNIPRESENCE OF SPIRITS

A different way of warding off the spirit of the dead is described earlier in the novel. After the death of Vimenuo's father Zekuo, he is sighted in the evenings by different people. Then he appears at the drinking house he used to frequent, seated at his usual seat at the hearth. The old woman of the house tells him directly that his path is different now and he must not return again. To ensure that he does not return, "she took a dao and struck at different places in the wooden doorway" (Kire 85). Lieno describes that she spoke with knowledge of those things because she was not a Christian but still followed the old religion. The old woman was empowered by the traditional knowledge of warding off evil spirits with iron and metal. She has a shamanistic quality and her retention of the knowledge of folk ways makes her a culture bearer. After this, Lieno says there were no more sightings reported. It is noteworthy that this is in contrast to the pastor being called to pray over Grandmother's spirit. These two incidents clearly indicate two belief systems existing concurrently. Though the society was rapidly moving towards a more urban way of life in the new town, the traditional practices and beliefs are not completely gone. This is evident in the beliefs people had about the presence of spirits.

There are many other instances of the overwhelming presence of spirits. It is a world where people live in great fear of spirits. Lieno sometimes "heard hard breathing" behind her as she went to fetch water early in the morning. She says "a real man, even if he were dead drunk, was preferable any day to a spirit" (34). She has heard the old women say that it was not a good thing to go too early to the pond because the spirit of a white man was seen by early risers. A young woman encountered him at the pond and died a few days later. The man had told her that he came to "take a bride" (32). She describes him as someone who was very fair. Her sister suspects it is a white man's spirit, as "they both knew the only white men around these parts were now spirits" (Ibid). This is an allusion to the war-torn landscape of post WWII Kohima where the locals believe that the spirits of dead British soldiers roam about in the hills. Such stories have also become part of the Naga spiritual landscape.

Grandmother and Neikuo's conversation informs us that spirits of the dead appear to those with whom they were close. Loved ones return not as unquiet spirits, but to say farewell. Three days after Grandmother's death, Lieno sees her sitting in her usual chair in the kitchen. After the spirit disappeared, she felt her presence all around the dark kitchen but incredibly, she "did not feel any fear" (266). Similarly, Pete appeared to his mother when she stood grieving at his grave and told her that he is alright and happy. She was comforted because she saw him smiling and holding out his hand at her, and he was surrounded by many flowers at his feet (Ibid 271). In "A Note from the Author" of the second edition of the novel, Kire explains that the story is set in a society that seemed to be "obsessed with spirits of the dead" (viii). She says:

> This predominantly Christian society has not come very far from non-Christian superstitions and spirit beliefs. Angami Christianity is nativised Christianity which accepts the presence and the manifestation of the supernatural in a very natural way. The dead returning to show themselves to their loved ones one last time has no logical explanation but the spirit sightings in the book are all based on reported sightings. (ix)

The dead reappear with messages for the persons who see them. Mother explains that by showing herself to Lieno, Grandmother was trying to show that she loved the girl in her own way. This is significant because Lieno had told Grandmother on her death bed that she forgave her for being harsh with her, but Grandmother was incapable of speaking at the time. However, she had cried silently and shed a tear hearing Lieno's words. Except at Vini's funeral, Grandmother had "never displayed grief openly" (257). Therefore, through this spirit sighting, Kire portrays the further development of Lieno's character. There was now an understanding between grandmother and granddaughter which could never be achieved when Grandmother was alive. This brings about the turning point in Dielieno's character as it enables her to let go of her bitterness and understand that Grandmother did not actually hate her.

Grandmother's spirit however, becomes 'unquiet' later when her sons decide to rent out her house to tenants, letting Bano go to live with Neikuo. Hers becomes the most intimidating spirit presence. It is almost as if she has come back to life to impose her will on the living. Grandmother's spirit is so strong and willful that it forces everyone to reconsider their actions and ultimately brings the conflict in the family to order. Kire affirms that "Angamis are a very superstitious people, but the spiritual world is a reality that is integral to their consciousness and worldview" (Kire). The importance she attaches to these beliefs in her writings validates the fact that unlike the western worldview, people of oral cultures have an experiential consciousness and accept mystical phenomena that cannot be explained by scientific rationalism. She portrays a world where the physical and the ethereal rub shoulders with each other on a daily basis, and all aspects of folk belief are practical guidelines that serve as survival mechanisms for the community.

The different viewpoints of the characters in the story not only create conflicts in the plot but also present multiple perspectives to the story. This is a distinct characteristic of oral storytelling in which there is never a single version of a story but various versions. The narrative is also interspersed with home-grown images and metaphors. Kire meticulously recreates these images from personal memory and the collective memories of her people. In the mornings, Bano would be heard "breaking twigs and blowing on the embers of last night's fire" to start a fire. Lieno explains to the reader, "We always buried a small burning log in the hearth (Kire 11). The dented kettle at Grandmother's house is so old it is "burnt pitch-black from the years of being used on a wood fire" (12). The bitter cold of the harsh Kohima winter is emphasized by Grandmother's cruelty of letting Lieno bathe in cold water and sending her to fetch water early in the morning while it was still dark. Lieno also describes how her "mother would dry paddy in the sunshine and would run in and do her chores and then run out again to chase birds and chickens away" and "she always got up early to fetch water" (47).

THE SYMBOLISM OF FOOD

Another important aspect of the novel is the symbolic use of food and food-ways. According to Malzeppi, one of the most important means of asserting ethnicity in the postcolonial context is through food-ways. Because "food habits are especially resistant to change – perhaps more so than other aspects of culture... Cuisine, she says, "forges an enduring link to the past" (qtd. in Clements 26). Lieno describes about dried meat that was "hung from spiked bamboos over the fire" (Kire 14). She relishes the distinct taste of having "hot rice with a broth of lentils and garlic and some dried meat" (26), or with meat that tastes better after being "left to get cold overnight" (56). Bano and Grandmother dried a lot of vegetables like "yam leaves, mustard leaves and squash sliced into thin pieces" (52) to be used during winter when they ran out of green vegetables. The retention of traditional cuisine is understandably more evident in Grandmother's kitchen in comparison to Dielieno's home where they cherish Christmas cakes. These images of food show that though Kohima was gradually progressing towards a more urban town life, the community life was still largely sustained by the agriculture produce from the land, linking them to their traditional past.

Besides these metaphors that create the cultural landscape in the novel, Kire further uses the practice of sharing food as a symbolic sign of acceptance and rejection of people. This is also in consonance with Angami cultural practice. An intrinsic part of Naga traditional life is the sharing of food which signifies the bonding and building of community relationships. In general, offering food to others is a way of expressing love and care for them. Drawing on the anthropological views of the symbolic language of food, Vitsou Yano comments that for the Angami Nagas, "the communication through food acts as a very strong bonding among the people knowingly and unknowingly. Giving food of any type to each other was a common act. Giving was highly appreciated by all without much expectation. The relationship between neighbors can be better by giving food to each other... this untold communication of food built a bridge between two people or two families" (379). Food therefore assumes a symbolic language and becomes a channel of communication. In the opening chapter, Dielieno was not served the chicken leg because Grandmother said it was meant for the boys and not for her. The rejection made her feel that Grandmother didn't like her. This significantly affects her sense of self and identity, and Lieno has to learn to continually negotiate her identity as a 'girl child,' feeling lesser than her brothers, while growing up.

On another occasion, when she and her brother Leto went to deliver a basket of vegetables given by their mother, Grandmother carried Leto on her lap though he was almost thirteen. Dielieno waited for her turn to be carried but instead she was made to fetch wood for the fire. When she returned, Grandmother didn't offer to carry her but went and gave a lump of jaggery to Leto. He gave her a bit to lick, but Grandmother shouted: "Enough, enough, it is for you," and "closed the almirah with a loud bang" (Kire 4). The lack of warmth and closeness between Dielieno and her grandmother is illustrated through such incidents that always made her feel ignored and unloved. In contrast, Dielieno remembers her grandfather with fondness. He used to give them candy and chocolates at Christmas and on Sundays. Food thus becomes a signifier of acceptance and rejection, or love and the lack thereof between the characters in the novel. As rightly noted by Sanghamitra De, Grandmother's kitchen serves as a highly symbolic space where "gender bias [is] actualized through food behavior, culinary activities, as well as the pattern of consumption and distribution" (De).

Similarly, when Vimenuo comes to play at Lieno's house, she brings a packet of "fried cookies made of pounded glutinous rice" lined in plantain leaves (59) sent by her mother. Lieno's mother accepts it gratefully but has to be discreet in associating with them because Grandmother disapproves of Vimenuo's family. Though her mother does not discriminate, Grandmother's disapproval dictates and restricts her behaviour. At Grandmother's house, when the chickens were grown, they would cook the meat and Lieno was sent to take half the cooked meat to her brothers. Since it was sent very often, it was nothing new for the brothers but she envied them because, "I knew now that I would never be sent half a chicken" (33). Lieno's devalued status in Grandmother's eyes is confirmed by this practice.

On the contrary, whenever he visited, Sizo always gave her chocolates or brought a big bar of jiggery just for her. Lieno likes him because he always acknowledges her individual presence. These treats meant a lot to her because she has always had to share things with her brothers. Besides, Sizo is the only person who could unnerve Grandmother. His unbiased attitude reaffirms Lieno's sense of worth, subverting Grandmother's devaluation, and helps her to develop her self-concept as a person who is not less important than her brothers. She also forms a closer bond with Bano through a piece of stolen meat. Grandmother's pot of meat was always guarded, but Lieno learns about Bano's subtle way of subverting her control when she sees her taking a piece of meat out of the pot and eating it while it was still cooking. At first she is surprised but Bano gives her a piece too, and this secret sharing without Grandmother's knowledge brings the two of them closer, making them allies in negotiating Grandmother's strict regime .

The mores that governed life in the past are reflected when Neikuo tells Lieno about her parents' wedding. Yano has noted that "food consumption patterns in Angami Naga society are one social aspect which is a means of cultural identity...The casteless society witnessed the difference of wealth, and depending on that, the pattern of consumption differs, where food is seen as a sign of wealth. Food categorizes and separates the people in the society into different classes" (377). Neikuo tells Dielieno that it was a big wedding and her grandfather's family killed three cows for the wedding feast. They were rich enough and could have killed four cows but they didn't because "at weddings, one has to think of those who cannot afford to kill even one cow" (Kire 108). The pattern of food consumption was definitely a mark of wealth for the rich as stated by Yano, but cultural mores also dictate that the rich do not flaunt extravagantly. Dielieno's modern perception is further contrasted with Neikuo's cultural knowledge when she asks if they served cake, and Neikuo replies, "No, it wasn't that sort of wedding. People liked to eat meat at weddings, not cake, so it was a wedding with a lot of meat" (109). All these images illustrate that food-ways embody a people's cultural beliefs. Kire writes from the matrix of her memory and recollections, approximating the sensual responses of the world she lives in and she effectively transfers her sense of the imagery and cosmology of the Angami Nagas to the reader.

Kire's writing is marked by its cultural landscape, giving it a distinct feature as she writes "Angami-centric" literature. According to her, "the landscape tends to be underestimated but in fact, every aspect of native life - the language, culture, and food originates in it and forms the cosmology of the Nagas, giving it their distinct identity" (Kire). She recaptures these thoughts, food habits, and the mindset of her people in simple prose.

There are instances in the apparently simple prose narrative that reflect the turbulent history behind scenes from everyday life. While at her parents' home, one of Lieno's happy experiences is when Mother treats her with Christmas cakes baked out of an old ammunition box. Cakes however, are not indigenous to Naga cuisine. They are a residue of the colonial heritage that has, through acculturation, become part of the local cuisine, and the ammunition box immediately speaks of the history of war.

These meticulous renderings are therefore, metaphors of a culture in transition and present the way ordinary folk become accustomed to changes through time. Grandmother's food and attitude are set in contrast with Lieno's feelings, representing two different worldviews. Two traditions simultaneously exist in Lieno's life and both components influence her new hybrid identity. Her parents belong to the in-between generation. They have seen and experienced both sides of tradition and changing modernity. They recognize the importance of getting an education for their daughter unlike Grandmother who thinks girls need no education. This awareness of the necessity of education is influenced by the changing lifestyle from farming to more urban professions such as teaching and desk jobs. Kire effectively shows the subtle manner in which major events in the form of colonialism and wars affected the traditional way of life and native worldview.

These native details form the crucial structural function of presenting a Naga cultural landscape that is steeped in living folklore. The interweaving of dreams, folk ways and beliefs into the structure of the novel illustrates what has been quoted earlier as "the intermingling of forms," (Boehmer 221) where we find the indigenous folk elements embedded in a narrative that is presented in the format of European literary fiction. Dreams and folklore are present not just for the sake of it but form the underlying structure of the narrative. They direct the plot and storytelling technique, illuminate the various themes, and facilitate character development. In consonance with postcolonial writings, this can be termed as experience oriented writing that offers alternative ways of seeing things, reinforcing a different belief system and projecting the innermost recesses of a culture as opposed to the dominant narratives of history.

Though the girl's coming of age seems to be the "subtle but principal theme," as noted by Sushmita Kashyap, A Terrible Matriarchy is also about many other things, such as "identity, culture and the inheritance of loss" (35). Kire has endeavoured to capture and retrieve the cultural beliefs and practices that continue to operate as living folklore even in the face of inevitable social changes. The novel also presents the "multifarious strata to social behaviour in the society" (Kire ix). It is a whole society's coming of age. Her writing is literature that is rich with indigenous flavour wherein folklore is definitely not a relic of the past but very much alive. Therefore, as a postcolonial indigenous writer, Kire's style of incorporating living folklore in her fiction is an assertion of her cultural moorings and reflects her commitment to her cultural identity.

WORKS CITED

Ao, Temsula. "Writing Orality." *Orality and Beyond: A North-East Indian Perspective*, edited by Soumen Sen and Desmond L. Kharmawphlang, Sahitya Akademi, 2007, pp. 99-112.

Ashcroft, Bill, et al. *Key Concepts in Post - Colonial Studies*. Routledge, 1998.

Boehmer, Elleke. *Colonial & Postcolonial Literature*. 2nd edition. Oxford UP, 2005.

Bulkeley, Kelly. "The Cultural Dimensions of Dreaming: New Perspectives on Dreams in Psychological Anthropology." *Psychology Today*, 19 April 2019, www.psychologytoday.com. Accessed 17 Aug. 2020.

Clements, William M, editor. *The Greenwood Encyclopaedia of World Folklore and Folklife*. Vol.1. Greenwood, 2006.

De, Sanghamitra. "Food, Culture, and Gendered Space: A Reading of Easterine Iralu's A Terrible Matriarchy." *Women's Writing from North East India*, issue 36, *Café Dissensus*. 14 June 2017, www.cafedissensus.com. Accessed 20 Oct. 2019.

Haase, Donald. *The Greenwood Encyclopaedia of Folktales and Fairytales*. Vol.2. Greenwood, 2008.

Heneise, Michael. "Making Dreams, Making Relations: Dreaming in Angami Naga Society." *The South Asianist*, Vol.5, No.1, 2017, pp. 66-82, www.southasianist.ed.ac.uk. Accessed 20 Aug. 2020.

Hutton, J.H. *The Angami Nagas*. Oxford UP, 1999.

Iralu, Easterine. *Folk Elements in Achebe: A Comparative Study of Ibo Culture and Tenyimia Culture*. Ura Academy, 2000.

Jacobs, Julian, et al. *The Nagas: Hillpeoples of Northeast India: Society, Culture and the Colonial Encounter*. Hansjörg Mayer, 1990.

Joshi, Vibha. *A Matter of Belief: Christian Conversion and Healing in North–East India*. Berghahn, 2012.

Kashyap, Sushmita. "The Inheritance of Loss." Book Review of *A Terrible Matriarchy*. *Biblio*, Vol. XIII. No.5 & 6 May-June 2008, p.35.

Kire, Easterine. *A Terrible Matriarchy*. 2nd edition. Zubaan, 2013.

_ _ _. Personal Interviews. 2009; 2010.

Pimomo, Paul. Review of "Easterine Kire, A Terrible Matriarchy." *Nagas: Essays for Responsible Change*. Eyingbeni Humtsoe-Nienu, et al. Heritage, 2012, pp. 186-192.

Propp, Vladimir. *Theory and History of Folklore*, edited and introduced by Anatoly Liberman. Manchester UP, 1984.

Punia, Deep. *Social Values in Folklore*. Rawat, 1993.

Tiwari, Shubha. "The Universality of the Colonial Experience of Different Parts of the World." *The Atlantic Literary Review*, Vol.10, No.1, January –March 2009, pp. 52- 60.

Whiso, Kezhakielie. "On Easterine's Novel *A Terrible Matriarchy*." *Nagaland Post*, 27 Jan. 2010, www.nagalandpost.com/ShowStory.aspx?npoststoryiden=UzEwMj E4MTM%3D-UWcDISlvvx4%3D. Accessed 15 July 2015.

Wilentz, Gay. *Binding Cultures: Black Women Writers in Africa and the Diaspora*. Indiana UP, 1992.

Yano, Vitsou. "Traditional Food Culture and Women in the Angami Naga Society." *Modern Research Studies: An International Journal of Humanities and Social Sciences*, Vol 2, Issue 2, June 2015, pp. 375-387.

05

WRITING MEMORY: THE PRESERVATION OF INTANGIBLE HERITAGE IN EASTERINE KIRE'S *SKY IS MY FATHER: A NAGA VILLAGE REMEMBERED*

Avinuo Kire

Easterine Kire's debut novel A *Naga Village Remembered* was released in 2003. It was the first novel written in English by a Naga. It has since 2018 been re-named and republished as *Sky is My Father: A Naga Village Remembered*.

As is common knowledge, the Nagas did not traditionally possess the art of script. Historically, Nagas were a highly oral society whose main pool of knowledge and information lies with the elders. In the old days, knowledge was orally passed down from generation to generation through the art of storytelling. On this, Naga historian Lanusashi Longkumer elaborates;

> (Nagas) had an effective medium of communication and records that have been preserved for many centuries through the oral tradition based on deep-rooted and time-tested foundations. Any oral narrative or traditional history, origin and migration of the people ... formation of the village, events of war, peace, festivals, and so on are transmitted by word

of mouth from one generation to another through songs, poetry, ballads, prayers, sayings, stories and tales or public oration when the situation demands. Through such means youngsters were trained not only to learn but to master them (Longkumer 11).

For centuries then, prior to being "discovered" by the outside world, Nagas carried on their daily lives, observing their many rituals, ceremonies and celebrating their varied festivals, replete with colour, song and dance. They were autonomous warrior tribes, living independently of each other. The vibrant diversity of all these activities added richness and dimension to the oral narratives (Sekhose 33). Traditional customs and teachings were generally imparted through traditional institutions which served as knowledge imparting centers. Gradually, such traditional institutions ceased to exist with the arrival of British administration in the 1800s and the American Baptist Mission in the 1830s, which ultimately resulted in the western system of education replacing traditional methods. Indian incursion into the Naga Hills followed the departure of the British in 1947 and propelled the Indo-Naga conflict which continues to this very day. For over seven decades since the end of British colonization and what was viewed as annexation of their homeland by India and Myanmar, Nagas have lived in constant conflict and unrest due to the political struggle for sovereignty and self determination. In the midst of such a volatile conflict environment, what was important for the survival of the Nagas as a people was swayed by other pressing priorities that came with a conflict situation. Hence, Nagas' encounters with non-Nagas or 'outsiders', for lack of a better term, came to occupy centre stage and was determined as detrimental towards the continuation and preservation of the oral tradition, which constitute our intangible heritage.

Being an indigenous oral society, the value of intangible heritage for the Nagas is immeasurable. Kōichirō Matsuura, eminent Japanese diplomat and former Director General of UNESCO, has defined intangible heritage as follows:

> The term 'Cultural Heritage' usually calls to mind monuments, museums, material culture, works of art and so on. However, it should not be forgotten that 'Intangible Cultural Heritage', which may be defined as the collective creations of a cultural community, rooted in its traditions, is every bit as much a fundamental part of the heritage of humankind...Intangible heritage takes such forms as languages, oral traditions, customs, music, dance, rituals, festivals, traditional medicine, handicrafts and traditional building skills. For many cultures

and for minority and indigenous populations in particular, intangible cultural heritage is an essential source of identity (Matsuura 1).

In line with UNESCO's 2003 Convention for the Safeguarding of the Intangible Cultural Heritage, the Ministry of Culture under the Government of India has classified intangible heritage into five broad domains, as manifestations of the same: Oral traditions and expressions, including language as a vehicle of the intangible cultural heritage, Performing arts, Social practices, rituals and festive events, Knowledge and practices concerning nature and the universe and Traditional craftsmanship.

Kire's A Naga Village Remembered is essentially a work of historical fiction. This literary work, set during the late 1800s, recounts the way of life of the villagers of Khonoma, a fiercely independent Angami Naga hamlet, and how this life was forever altered through their encounter with the British. The novel is embedded in historical events which irrevocably changed the Naga way of life and chartered their political future.

Fiction, particularly historical fiction, can give not only a literary experience but also serve as a powerful medium in providing glimpses of the past. While historical fiction certainly cannot be read as history, in the case of traditionally oral societies like the Nagas, it can serve as an invaluable means of preserving remnants of a heritage which may otherwise be lost. In this regard, the possibilities grow immensely when fictional narrative and intangible cultural heritage are intertwined seamlessly into a whole, which is what Kire does with Khonoma in A Naga Village Remembered

It is of tremendous significance then, that the book contains a section titled, "Oral Narratives of the Merhü clan" after the close of the story. The Merhü clan is a prominent clan of Khonoma village. In an email interview, Kire credits the clan's oral tradition with inspiring her writing of the novel.

> Without the oral tradition, I would not have been able to write this novel. Before writing the book, I worked for about two years with oral narrators translating poetry. In that period, I acquired much cultural information on the village of Khonoma, much of it literary, since I needed the information to help me with my translation project... All of this gave me the background that I needed. The next step was to collect what I term as unwritten history, the histories that our people carry in their bodies. Remember, this was nearly twenty years ago and many of my narrators were alive. One of them said that his great grandfather had participated in the battle of Khonoma where the political officer, Damant, was killed. Through his

oral memory, I could access the battle as experienced by the village, the insiders.... Leaving the battle aside, narrations of unwritten history give us so much information on the cultural life of the village. I was so fortunate to get this information as part of the process of retrieving information. This is what went into making the book.

The above lines are a testament to the author's profound commitment to historical truth in her fiction writing. Equipped with these orally transmitted lived realities, Kire weaves the memories into the lives of her fictional characters who loved and fought to protect the land and its people against foreign invasion.

This book may be read in two parts: Naga life before and after British annexation. Kire brings to life the historical trajectory of a people through an inventive device of tracing three generations of a typical Angami Naga family in Khonoma. The novel begins with Kovi, a warrior, and Vipiano, his widowed sister, the wife of a slain warrior, and her two young sons, Levi and Lato. As the story progresses, the focus shifts to the second generation- Levi, who follows his late father's footsteps by becoming a warrior himself, and his younger brother Lato, who is projected as a peace loving man. Levi, along with his fellow tribesmen, boldly resists the British, with devastating results. An embittered Levi struggles to move on and goes on to marry and have two sons of his own. Kire handles her fictional characters with fine sensitivity and as we witness how the ripple effects of colonization shape the lives of Levi's sons, Roko and Sato, we come to understand the Naga perspective better. Kire states:

So the book is about the insider perspective which is so much more important than the colonial perspective that uses definitions like "rebel village", "insurgency", "barbaric races" etc. The reasoned out reasons used by the warriors of Khonoma to engage in this battle are more significant than the colonial logic for the expedition against problematic villages (Email Interview). Subject

This chapter briefly examines a few practices highlighted in the first half of the novel, which revolves around the once pristine ancestral Naga way of life, as portrayed through the village of Khonoma. This is not to suggest that the village of Khonoma and the Angami people represent all Naga villages and Naga ways of life, but that the autonomous village government and socio-cultural traditions the Angamis practised were similar to those of most other Naga groups. Thus, Khonoma's historic encounter with the

British makes it a suitable stand-in for a history-based fictional narrative of the Naga encounter with colonialism on a broader scale.

Meanwhile, it may be noted that "Naga people, today, are spread to the Kachin state and the Sagaing Division in Myanmar, in Assam, Arunachal Pradesh, Manipur and Nagaland states of India" (Pou 52). Nagas living in Nagaland proper, so to speak, are comprised of sixteen tribes and many subtribes, each richly blessed with their own distinct language, customs and traditions. Nagas, as a collective group of people belong to the Mongoloid race, are linguistically placed under the Tibeto Burman group, and share oral traditions with similar world views, way of life and belief system.

The novel unfolds in the household of the warrior Kovi, one of the key central characters. It is poignant that the story begins with Kovi in deep reflection, expressing how it is good to remember the old ways. It is the break of a new day and as he surveys the routine domestic scene unfolding, he exclaims, "Ah, the old ways are good, he thought, our women do us proud when they show themselves so eager to keep the teaching of their fathers" (Kire 1). These sentiments appear ominously evocative of what is to come. This viewpoint recurs when Levi and his bride Peno carefully observe the rituals necessary for beginning a new life in a new house. Kovi, Levi's uncle, blesses them with the words "'...Your lives are starting now and it is good that you have heeded the old ways. May you always keep the blessings'" (65). The opening lines hauntingly sets the tone for the entire novel.

COMMUNITY CENTRIC FESTIVALS

Kire beautifully depicts how the Naga way of life is built upon a foundation of belief system, deeply rooted in spirituality, spirit appeasement and fertility of the land. Community life is centered around elaborate festivals, each involving specific rituals, lasting for days on end. Sekrenyi, which is still celebrated to this day with great flourish, although simplified without the religious rites, is arguably the most well-known Angami festival. It is essentially a festival of sanctification. We are also made familiar with Ngoyi, a festival of merry making and rest from field work, Thekranyi, a feast of the different age groups, and Kelipie, a festival in the middle of the agriculture year, especially replete with music. Other minor harvest festivals mentioned are Terhünyi andTerhase. All these festivals are interlinked and entrenched in ancestral beliefs.

Further, we are made to appreciate the sacredness of observing Genna days, i.e., no-work days. Genna days, too, are of varied nature. Thenais a semi Genna day where no other work except field work is allowed whereas

Khunuo Lievi is a strict Genna day where any form of work is taboo. The Genna days are not arbitrary but carefully linked to the cycle of agriculture seasons, field work and spirit appeasement.

> The care with which the Genna days had been adhered to filled the elders with a sense of well-being. They had successfully held the Genna to prevent the paddy dying, and another Genna to prevent sterility of the soil as well as the Genna to ensure the fertility of the soil. It should go well for this year's harvest, they said to one another (57).

During one such stringent Genna day, Vipiano receives some unexpected visitors from a neighboring village. To convey that she is observing the taboo on speaking to sojourners on that day, she fixes her eyes on a rock, pretending to be unaware of the presence of her visitors but somehow cleverly conveys her good wishes. Her visitors understand her predicament and graciously take their leave (83).

TRADITIONAL SYSTEM OF EDUCATION

With fine precision, Kire details how daily life was once centered on traditional institutions, each tailored on the basis of gender and age. "For the menfolk, there were daily meeting places. For the youth, separate male and female dormitories served as centres of learning and culture dissemination" (Sekhose 33). Thehou is the community house where the menfolk routinely gather to share their concerns and discuss important village matters. Respect and reverence towards one's elders were paramount. "But if the elders were there, the younger men listened closely without speaking much. They came to learn the stories of the village. It was good to be called a *thehou no*, a child of the thehou- it meant that such a person was well versed in the stories and customs of the village" (Kire 7).

Children and young people were sent to the Kichüki, which, translated from the Angami Tenyidie dialect to English, literally means "dormitory". These dormitories were segregated gender wise, into different age groups and accordingly, each group/ dormitory was assigned an elder to teach them. The elder is referred to as "parent". These institutions are the traditional equivalent of modern day schools, except that the "students" get to sleep over.

As Levi prepares to spend the night at his age group's Kichüki, his mother Vipiano reminds her young son not to spend all his time jesting but to listen to the parent's story. In the dormitory that night, their assigned elder not only narrates stories but also teaches them how to inculcate good values. He instills the code of ethics expected of them. The parent earnestly teaches Levi's group, "'If you are at a community feast and take more than two pieces of meat, shame on you. Others will call you glutton; worse, they will think to themselves, 'Has no one taught this boy about greed? This is the key to right living- avoiding excess in anything- be content with your share of land and fields...'" (30).

In the Kichüki is where young people learn what is important for life. The parent decide the lessons to be taught, keeping in mind their ages and mental capacity. That particular night, Levi's age group betray their tender age as they are only interested in storytelling.

> No one was ready to sleep. Evenings at the dormitory were exciting times when they exchanged stories and listened to the teachings of the man they called their parent, the elder chosen to be mentor for their age group. Each age group had a parent and the dormitory was a long bed hewn out of a single log on which ten to fourteen boys could sleep. 'Apfü, tell us again the story of Terhuotsiese', one of the boys asked, "Lonyü, that was the name of their parent, smiled and said, 'you are still young boys at heart. Your big bones deceived me into thinking I could talk to you as adults'" (31)

The Kichüki is also where young children learn the finer things in life such as music, the art of oratory, social skills, sports etc. Lato, Levi's peace loving younger brother happily informs his mother that his age group had learnt the art of ululating the *hutho* and other poem songs (40- 41). As they grow older, they learn knowledge concerning history, culture, traditional teachings and traditional art/skills. Traditional knowledge also includes ancestral wisdom pertaining to knowledge of the environment, ecosystem, medicine, philosophyand all varied aspects which constitute a people's heritage. An example of everyday traditional knowledge is Vipiano's effortless ability is read the seasons.

> 'Three weeks to Thekranyi from today' she announced to Lato
> 'Really Apfü, how do you do it? How can you tell?'
> 'Silly boy, it's only a matter of counting the lunar cycle. Today
> is the first day of the new moon, that's how I know' (39).

Naturally, therefore, the traditional system of education was immensely holistic in nature. Regrettably, too soon, western education was given precedence over the prevailing system and this adversely affected the oral tradition and traditional system of education. "There is the danger of ultra modern education and westernization, overshadowing indigenous identity" (Sekhose 37).

CUSTOMARY PRACTICES AND BELIEF SYSTEMS

To truly understand a people, it is imperative to first comprehend the belief system behind their customary practices. Many non-Naga writers have labeled Nagas as "headhunters", often in a derogatory/ condescending tone, or with a sense of morbid fascination. However, it should be noted that this is a tag given by outsiders as Nagas never considered themselves "headhunters". They were warriors. Head hunting was a way of warfare and rooted in the prevailing belief system.

> But it is an interesting fact, too, that they (Nagas) never considered or called themselves as such (headhunters), for they were "Warriors" and called themselves to be so "Terhümiavimia" in Angami/ Tenyidie; "Aghutomi"/ Sema; "Ekhyoekhung"/ Lotha; "Naomei"/ Konyak; "Nokinketer"/ Ao; "Riphienmai"/ Zeliang etc. Today, Nagas have internalized the labeling idea and call themselves "head-hunters", with a kind of savage pride even. This, perhaps, is because for their ancestors, head hunting was a matter of bravery, honour and life long reputation as an achiever, not as uncivilized bloodthirsty barbarians as others saw them (36-37).

Head hunting was bound by a code of conduct which warriors conformed to. An example of this in Kire's book occurs when the Khonoma warriors attack Gariphe village. Having supreme confidence that their own warriors could protect them, the women of the attacked village continued to engage themselves in their routine weaving. The Khonoma warriors were compelled to destroy their looms before slaying the women as "It is taboo to kill a woman while she is weaving, which is why we took out their looms" (Kire 5).

The ghastly practice of headhunting came from a worldview that believed headhunting was an act of personal heroism that enhanced community wellbeing, not an act driven by primitive bloodlust, as erroneously perceived by some observers. In *Naga Heritage Centre- People Stories*, a collection of documented oral narratives, the elderly oral narrator, Aseü Kire recounts:

> However, it is interesting to observe that in a world which
> today seems barbaric and primitive, a strict code of conduct
> and decency was always adhered to, by warriors and victims
> alike...The Konyaks (Naga tribe) believe that a person's life
> force is contained in the head. It is told that when a person is
> about to die at the hand of an enemy warrior, he/ she could
> request to be given a moment to compose a final Geizo. In a
> sense, it is like composing one's own elegy. The headhunter
> is honour bound to respect his victim's last wish...Sometimes
> the warrior would pause to ask his victim for final words even
> before the victim speaks. It was also considered taboo to slay a
> pregnant woman (A. Kire 81-82).

Thus, headhunting was bound by a firm code of conduct which
required restraint and discipline. A man did not become a warrior for
love of power, riches or violence but because of honour. In A Naga Village
Remembered, an elderly man at the Thehou explains, "'But it was a matter
of honour, you see?....That is what drives a man to battle, the need to prove
himself worthy of defending his village and his womenfolk and to earn
ornaments of war...'" (Kire 8). Other than honour, the reasons behind this
practice may vary from village to village or tribe but is generally presumed
to be grounded in beliefs pertaining to fertility of the soil, women, animals,
prosperity, better hunting and general well being of the people (Vamuzo
29).

Oral history has made it known that Nagas were a fiercely independent,
sovereign people for the most part, and, but with the exception of a few
villages/tribes, an egalitarian society with no concept of kingship. "During
the pre-British days, each village enjoyed complete independence and thus
each village was sovereign" (Venuh vii). That Nagas were a classless society
is particularly validated through the practice of the Feast of Merit wherein
a rich man would share his wealth by feasting the entire clan/village and
subsequently become an honored "title taker". In the novel, Kire, through
her character Keviselie, revives the elaborate processes required to be
fulfilled in this once celebrated practice. Keviselie is a man who has been
blessed with excellent harvest by the spirits. He dreams a dream soon
after. Keviselie accordingly consults with the elders and they agree it is
time for him to give a Feast of Merit, i.e., in simple terms, to gain honour
and esteem by throwing a feast for the entire clan or village, as the case
may be. Naturally, in preparation for the feast, he painstakingly observes
the steps and rituals for weeks prior. After it is completed, he is blessed
by the elders and gains the prestigious title of one who has hosted a Feast
of Merit.

'The village has not been feasted so well since Nikerhe's title taking feast', Vipie, an elder declared...
Two months later, Keviselie was able to feast the whole clan at his *sha*, the first Feast of Merit. His friends from the other clans received generous shares of meat. ...The village talked about Keviselie's Feast of Merit for a long time to come. (Kire 28).

Obviously, honour and gaining the respect of one's community was more important than material wealth. "As Levi had predicted, it was an excellent harvest. Some men of the village prepared to take titles again for they had been blest in grain and cattle exceedingly" (79).

GENDER ROLES

Nagas are a patrilineal and patriarchal society. In the old days, gender roles were clearly defined and demarcated. While the womenfolk looked after domestic affairs, it was the sole responsibility of the menfolk to safeguard and protect the village. Men were the governance and cultural policy makers and warriors. This demarcation is highlighted when Kovi tersely tells his wife "It's man talk. Don't ask after the business of the clan, woman" (3), when the later inquires about the soon to be held meeting. It is pertinent to note that such a reply was indicative less of the lack of affection between husband and wife than of the husband acting in accordance to the code of conduct expected of men and women. Maintaining honor through obedience to community ethics was paramount. "The women knew better than to ask after men's business. No self respecting men ever revealed talk of the Thehou to their wives...None had told their mothers, and all of them religiously came to sleep in the dormitory every night" (42). The menfolk regularly gathered to discuss important affairs at the Thehou which they referred to as "man's talk" and it was taboo for women to participate or attend these meetings (7).

SYMBOLIC WRITING AND THE ART OF ORALITY

It is interesting that although Nagas may not have possessed the art of script, our stories were conveyed through the oral tradition and also through houses and the clothes we wore. People took great care with their attire. As

Keviselie's household prepared for his title taking ceremony, he instructs his family, "'Check that you are wearing in the right order'. All of them did as he said including his four year old son. People always took care to wear their body cloths with the embroidered portion showing in front" (23). The necessity of being properly attired is emphasised again when Levi and his new wife prepare to enter their new house. "'Check your body cloth before you enter the house, my son, it must be worn in the right manner', Kovi instructed" (64).

Being a highly oral society, every Naga man and woman was traditionally a storyteller. The art of orality, of conversation and lyricism, is inherent in everyday speech. In the novel, young Lato and Levi's education includes music and poem songs (41). Poem songs are a form of Geizo, i.e., oral poetry. The late oral narrator Mrs. Aseü Kire recalls:

> Against the backdrop of a rich oral tradition, our forefathers had a deep appreciation for Geizo and spoken language was highly lyrical in nature. Almost every person appears to have a Geizo composed after him or her- against an accomplishment, a deed or simply to commemorate the person's life. Similarly, there are beautiful Geizos for every nature of relationship and also specific ones for occasions such as feasts, celebrations, funerals etc. (A. Kire 82).

Naga folk belief has it that man, tiger and spirit once lived as brothers, sharing the same mother. The death of the mother brought disunity and led to a parting of the brothers. Although separated, our Naga forefathers continued to regard the tiger as the "elder brother". *A Naga Village Remembered* unfolds during a time when this belief was actively lived out. When Vilauslays a tiger, the entire village gathers in excitement. But Vilau's uncle rebukes him and says, "'They say you have killed our elder brother who was kind and gentle. Do not come' Vilau stopped and gravely replied, 'Apfü, it was not I. It was the spear that struck him down'" (Kire 16). Following custom, they open the tiger's mouth with a stick and place the head under the waterfall in such a way that the water ran through its mouth. This was done to prevent the tiger's kin from avenging it. An elder tells the slain tiger, "When your relatives come asking for you, be smooth voiced as the straw and the leaves of the chili and may your voice be as unclear as the sound of this waterfall so that your kind will never discover who killed you" (*Ibid*).

Another instance, reminiscent of quotidian orality, rich with drama, repartee and lyricism, is when Keviselie prepares to take a title. Four priests visit his house and a nuanced exchange, seemingly insignificant but pregnant with meaning, takes place.

> In a low voice he called out, 'Keviselie'. Keviselie was ready and
> he responded 'we-e' in an equally low voice. The priest then
> called again, 'Keviselie', in a louder voice, getting the same
> response from the title taker. The third time his voice was very
> loud. When Keviselie had given the appropriate response in a
> loud 'we'e', all the priests pronounced the blessing together:
> 'May your household prosper'. Once they had pronounced
> the blessing, all four priests walked away (27).

On the morning of Peno and Levi's marriage, Peno nervously begins
her nuptial walk to her husband-to-be Levi's house (61). The marriage rituals
are carefully observed, after which the relatives go on to bless the new
householders with these traditional blessings.

> This household will fetch and drink water from the water
> source as long as others are fetching and drinking from it
> They will be able to make fire as long as other households can
> Their progeny shall be numerous
> As numerous as the progeny of spiders and crabs
> They shall be blest with long life
> They shall live to be ancestors and grandparents and prosper
> in their life (61-62).

Oral poetry was popular and speech was highly lyrical. "Sky is my
Father, Earth is my mother, I believe in Kepenuopfü", is a well known prayer
against malicious spirits and Siezo, a man who recovers from a spirit induced
sickness wonders why he could not bring himself to claim the protection of
those words during his delirious illness (71).

Speech could sometimes be playful, argumentative or rhetorical.
During the festival of Terhase, the priest exclaims;

> Spirit Vo-o, we were wondering where you were but here you
> are. We have come to solicit peace between man and spirit. Let
> there be no destruction and calamity, no death and disease
> and plague. Who is honest, you are honest. Who is honest, I
> am honest. We will compete with each other in honesty (14).

On the last day of the Sekrenyi festival, everyone congregates at the field
where an elder pronounces the moving traditional blessing, "'My paddy,
may you grow up well, though the weeds are abundant, my paddy, grow you
around the tree stumps and boulders. It will be the food of generations, the
food of wartime, grow bent over with full-husked grain'" (82).

BRITISH ANNEXATION OF THE NAGA HILLS AND IMPACT

Towards the latter half of the novel, the author focuses on the year 1879, which many Nagas recall as the year of the historic Battle of Khonoma. "This battle was marked by the spirit of nationalism, self-determination and unification already ingrained among the Angami Nagas" (Longkumer 13). Despite their valiant efforts, proud Khonoma is eventually subdued by the mighty British forces. The British burned the village four times and confiscated their lands. "This was the punishment of a proud people who had dared to control their own destinies" (Kire 108). When the wise elder Pelhu meets British General Nation to forge a peace treaty, Pelhu brushes aside any requirement for a written treaty. "'No' Pelhu shook his head and said firmly, 'If we have said there will be peace between us, there will be peace. We do not need to write it down'" (107). True to Naga tradition, the power of the spoken word was immense and a person's honour is attached to his word.

Although confined to Khonoma village, nevertheless, the Battle of Khonoma 1879 had a ripple effect and played a decisive role in shaping the history of the Nagas as a people. The "civilizing" mission, which came attached with colonization and Christianity, greatly altered the traditional way of life. In this regard, proselytization, too, played a significant role as many Nagas believed that embracing the Christian faith meant discarding tradition and culture. This way of perceiving faith came at great cost. "There is certainly the need to separate religious practices from socio cultural ones so as to enable distinct Naga identity to thrive on" (Sekhose 38). And the Indo-Naga war, which followed after the departure of the British, did not help the cause of preserving the rich intangible heritage of the Nagas.

Despite all, Nagas consider themselves a free people in heart and spirit. During the observation of the 74th Naga Independence Day on 14th August 2020, Naga elder, Visier Sanyü, a native of Khonoma village, recounts how the villagers endured a long period of displacement after the village was burnt in 1956, this time by Indian troops. "This forced the people to take refuge in the jungle for three years and live in the outskirt of the village for a decade, only returning to Khonoma proper in 1970" (Sanyü 1). The toll on intangible heritage was obviously devastating. Sanyü states, "New songs were written; new legends were created; traditions were altered; taboos were broken out of desperation; festivals, weddings and funerals began to change as result of the deep search for being" (*Ibid*).

CONCLUSION

The culture of minority and indigenous groups worldwide is particularly vulnerable and constantly in danger of being undermined by globalization and the unjust yet growing propensity towards cultural homogenization. Hence, proactive steps towards preserving, safeguarding and reviving intangible heritage are urgently needed. Specifically, the value of oral sources in indigenous societies like the Nagas cannot be overstated. In Easterine Kire's fascinating, evocative narrative, "the histories that our people carry in their bodies" constitute the very foundation of Naga heritage, which is built around the art of orality ~ what anthropologists call intangible heritage. The disruption of the age old and effective generational oral transmission of knowledge, which began during the 1800s with the Nagas' encounter with the British, as depicted in Easterine Kire's A Naga Village Remembered/Sky is My Father, continued after the departure of the British, and throughout the Indo-Naga struggle from the mid-1950s to the present. The continuous history of colonial and postcolonial disruptions have significantly muffled the indigenous voices of generations of Nagas

Amazingly, however, like opportunity hidden in a crisis, hope for the Nagas came through the gift of the art of script via the early American missionaries who rendered the various Naga vernaculars into the roman script. Learning the art of writing provided Nagas with a way to help safeguard their endangered intangible heritage. It must be emphasized, however, that this crossover does not necessarily entail a complete break from the oral or imply that writing should replace orality. This would do great injustice and disservice to the age-old oral tradition. Nor would it be possible to adequately capture the essence of the oral tradition if orality were to be discarded entirely. It is pertinent to note that the transition to script only signifies anew delicate balance wherein script could aid the cause of preserving the oral narratives. Consequently, and inevitably, then, this challenge fell upon the concerted shoulders of knowledge holders, story tellers, scholars and writers-to negotiate a way forward where the oral and written forms could complement each other, and how each necessitates the other.

> Nor is orality ever completely eradicable: reading text oralizes it. Both orality and the growth of literacy out of orality are necessary for the evolution of consciousness.
> To say that a great many changes in the psyche and in culture connect with the passage from orality to writing is not to make writing (and/ or its sequel, print) the sole cause of all

the changes. The connection is not a matter of reductionism but of relationism. The shift from orality to writing intimately interrelates with more psychic and social developments than we have yet noted (Ong 182).

Where we are now, urgent documentation of our oral narratives, be it in native or English language, is the first step towards preserving intangible heritage. This applies even to fiction writing, especially when it is told against the backdrop of the traditional Naga way of life. That in a sense, if the writer successfully tells the story, the tale could offer a link to a world in danger of being wiped from memory.

This is precisely what Easterine Kire's literary marvel A *Naga Village Remembered* does. It has the distinction not only as the first Naga novel written in English, but is celebrated as a highly successful transliteration of the collective memories of a people who, as the writer movingly describes, "dared to control their own destinies". And through this narrative act of linking the oral with script, Kire has recreated a vibrant evocation of traditional Naga intangible heritage and opened up the possibility of reviving the oral tradition.

WORKS CITED

Kire, Easterine. *Sky is My Father: A Naga Village Remembered.* 2018. Revised Ed., Speaking Tiger. First Published 2003.

~~. "Re: Some Questions please." Received by Avinuo Kire, 27-30 July 2020. Email Interview.

Kire, Avinuo. "Ancient Practices." *Naga Heritage Centre: People Stories: Volume One,* Avinuo

Kire and Meneno Vamuzo, PenThrill, 2016.

Longkumer, Joseph. "Historical Review on the 1879 Battle of Khonoma." *Journal on Frontier Studies: Collections of Academic Discourses,* edited by Visakhonü Hibo, NIDS, 2014-15, pp. 12-21.

Longkumer, Lanusashi. "Oral Tradition in Contemporary Conflict Resolution: A Naga Perspective" pdfs.semanticscholar.org/d108/19f10afdfdeffd537bda5fd2 ddc7adea9a78.pdf. Accessed 24 Jul. 2020.

Ong, Walter. J. *Orality and Literacy.* Routledge, 2002. "A Movement that came to give us our Identity." Morung Express, 15 Aug. 2020, pp.1. morungexpress. com/nagaland-a-movement-that-came-to-give-us-our-identity Accessed 15 Aug. 2020.

"National List for Intangible Cultural Heritage IHC." Ministry of Culture, Government of India. www.indiaculture.nic.in/national-list-intangible-cultural-heritage-ich. Accessed 8 Jul. 2020.

Pou, K B Veio. *Literary Cultures of India's Northeast: Naga Writings in English.* HPH Books, 2015.

Sekhose, Jano. "From Oral to Written Narrative: A Study of Naga Experience." *Journal on Frontier Studies: Collections of Academic Discourses,* edited by Visakhonü Hibo, NIDS, 2014-15, pp. 32-44.

"UNESCO/ Japan Funds-in-Trust for Intangible Cultural Heritage." UNESCO. www.unesco.emb-japan.go.jp/pdf/brochure_intangible_uk.pdf. Accessed 10 Jul. 2020.

Vamuzo, Meneno. "Contemporary Challenges of Naga Women in Nation Building." Diss., Trent University, May 2011, pp. 29.

Venuh, N. *People, Heritage and Oral History of the Nagas.* Papyrus, 2014.

06

HOMING AND THE SENSE OF BELONGING IN EASTERINE KIRE'S *SON OF THE THUNDERCLOUD*

Neikehienuo Mepfhuo

INTRODUCTION: KIRE AS AN INDIGENOUS WRITER

Indigenous/tribal societies are wholly dependent on community living and the feeling of oneness, and this is projected in indigenous/tribal literature, where a sense of place and home plays a vital role. Similarly, the search for a space called 'home' to provide a sense of belonging permeates Easterine Kire's *Son of the Thundercloud* as the traveller Pele looks for a new place to belong to after losing his whole family in a famine. Naga literature is similar to Native American literature in that imagination, place, community, people, and belonging combine to create a safe space called 'home' for their characters. These types of literature focus on fundamental leitmotifs of community, family, and, specifically, land. This chapter seeks to focus on the concept of home and the sense of belonging in Kire's novel, taking into consideration how this topic is studied in the broader spectrum of indigenous/tribal literature.

Easterine Kire's works inform and educate readers about the tribal history and the rich cultural heritage of the Nagas. She is known for narrativizing the lives of the Nagas, especially the Angami Naga tribe that she belongs to. Naga writers have always drawn inspiration from their own rich and diverse cultural history passed down through the oral tradition. They write to "recreate a resplendent past through a retracing of the traditional folklores and folksongs...and such a reverting to the past is important as identity signifier for the Nagas" (Pou 43). Kire belongs to the writing genre where women writers narrate and write their own stories and experiences. However, for indigenous writers, the additional task is to write the people's history and present indigenous voices and views simultaneously with personal stories. In the process of remembering and narrating their stories, they also have to preserve the historical and tribal heritage of their people.

Apart from a theme of hope and a narrative reminiscent of Biblical faith and beliefs, *Son of the Thundercloud* is a story about homing and searching for a place to belong to in the aftermath of misfortune or tragedy. Kire has combined the Naga creation myth with the redemption story of Jesus Christ. Kire also noted that this book is an allegory which provides the reader "a trajectory to the world of myths and legends" ('*Son of the Thundercloud* brings Sahitya...'). The protagonist Pelevotso, affectionately called Pele, ventured out of home after his village Nialhuo, in the western hills, was hit by a famine in which he lost his whole family. Pele's wife and children passed away due to starvation, and he decided to leave the village. His parents and relatives begged him to stay, and he obliged. However, after a few days, Pele's aged parents died within hours of each other. With no reason to stay, he decided to leave the village.

He left the village with just his clothes and a hunting knife, affirming the fear of village elders who seemed to have prophesied this Pele's departure before it happened, "'Our young should not think that there are lands better than this to build a home. They belong here, they must take the place of their ancestors.' They feared that if the young were not taught to love the village, it would soon be abandoned" (Kire 12).

However, for Pele, his whole existence in the village revolved around his family – the people he belonged to and the people who belonged to him. He decided to leave and "never once looked back" (Kire 15). Pele's departure is evocative of American literature in which the protagonist leaves home. Examples include *Moby Dick, Huckleberry Finn, Sister Carrie, Portrait of a Lady, and The Great Gatsby*. In *Critical Perspective on Native American Fiction*, Richard F Fleck states that in such 'leaving' plots, the individual leaves with no regard for family, society, past, or place, and the individual consciousness is the medium of knowledge. However, Pele's departure is different from the 'American Adam' in the sense that 'home' changed physically and mentally as a result of losing his whole family simultaneously, thereby losing a sense of being, identity, and the very notion of home as a result.

Fleck posits that for indigenous literature, especially Native American literature, the hero comes home in contrast to the American hero leaving home – "coming home, staying put, contracting or even what we call 'regressing' to a place, it is a primary mode of knowledge and a primary good" (Fleck 16). For Pele, his world was broken by the famine, and without any familial support and sustenance, the home must be re-conceptualized. He is forced to relocate and recreate a home away from home. As a result of his relocation and isolation from his family, his perception of the home had to evolve and grow as well.

In the introduction to the book *Painted Words: An Anthology of Tribal Literature*, G N Devy said that tribal communities "accept a worldview in which nature, man and God are intimately linked, and believe in the human ability to spell and interpret truth. They live more by intuition than by reason, they consider the space around them more sacred than secular, and their sense of time is personal rather than objective" (Devy x). Pele's intuition led him to the Village of Weavers, and he was also told that there was enough food and water and "they might let him stay and build a home" (Kire 16-17). In the beginning, he claimed that "he did not know if he wanted to build a home"; however, in due course, he did build a home for himself in the village. Not only did he construct a place for himself, but he also built and repaired the homes of Kethonuo, Siedze and Mesanuo. He repaired the home of Kethonuo and Siedze from his first meeting with them by collecting old sheets of perforated tarpaulin, jute bags, thatch, wood, and broken bricks to repair their roof. The sisters did not even seem human when he first saw them, but "the more he spent time with them, the more human they appeared to him" (30). The importance of human connection especially in tribal societies which necessarily might not be blood relations – is of paramount importance; as Peter Beidler puts it, "blood quantum is not nearly as important as love quantum" (Wilson 68).

The first meeting with the two sisters Kethonuo and Siedze, "mere skeletons covered in tattered cloth" (Kire 20) gave him a sense of home and belonging in his long and tiring journey where they warmly welcomed him to their ruined home, "you have come far, traveller. We have no food, but you may shelter in our house. That is our way. We never turn a traveller away and it will soon be night, so you may be our guest" (18).

The relationship between Pele and the two sisters is a case of how 'home' is not only formed by blood relations but also by people who have each other. People and a sense of belonging create a 'home' in tribal communities. With the coming of Pele in the lives of the two sisters, they saw rain for the first time in four hundred years, "It rained all morning, heavily, fiercely, as though the rivers of heaven were emptying onto the earth. It was seven-hundred-year-old rain. The bottomless chasm that had opened up the night before drew in all the water and saved the village from a terrible flood" (Kire 31).

These two sisters had been deprived of any human communication and connection for a long time, and their abandoned Noune village was considered cursed by other villages, the presence of Pele is symbolic of how he had revived this abandoned and cursed village, "as if the earth was newly born and creation would start all over again" (Kire 32). Apart from this, Pele noticed that the 'ancient sisters' even looked younger and more human, and their features appeared clearer after the rain for which they had waited their whole lives.

REDEFINING 'HOME'

After his displacement, Pele must locate another place, and his notion of home must be 'redefined'. In this novel, the concept of 'home' transcends the usual groupings of a nuclear family, biological relations, and fixed land relations. Pele's relationship with the sisters is unique. The sisters seemed to be in an alternate supernatural universe, nevertheless making it possible to create a home based on love, compassion, and companionship, breaking the boundaries of both time and space. Pele's journey had enabled him to forge a relationship with the sisters and, in the process, helped create a 'physical place' for him to call 'home.' After spending some time together, they left for the Village of Weavers to meet Kethonuo and Siedze's youngest sister, Mesanuo – the tiger-widow. What the readers were not aware of was that Pele would create a 'home' with Mesanuo as a result of his meeting with the two sisters. Pele realized that Mesanuo was none other than the woman whose husband and sons were killed by a tiger. He had heard of her story and even came to know that she was pregnant after "a single drop of rain" fell on her. Mesanuo told them, "nothing except for that one drop of rain. I felt the baby grow as soon as that drop landed on me" (Kire 37).

The next morning, to Pele's astonishment, Mesanuo has already given birth. The birth of her son has also given birth to new trees and saplings, which seemed to have sprouted overnight. Also, stones, stones, and grains appeared out of nowhere. The birth of the Mesanuo's son has made the "very air felt holy, and the headman sensed that his authority had no jurisdiction over the little house of the tiger-widow" (Kire 44). As Jill Jepson argues, "... home engages the individuals associated with a network involving family relations, larger communities, geographic space, and 'cosmic networks.'

Home refers both to a physical place and a network of belonging and history" (Wilson 69). It can be assumed that the presence of Pele had accelerated all the good things in their lives or the fact that he had brought the rain with him, which gave rise to all the good things they had been waiting for. In his subconscious search for a home, he created a home for the people he met along his journey.

Tribal communities believe in the importance of harmony, reflected in their strong sense of communality and cooperativeness. They give utmost importance to cooperation and good relations within the group, which is demonstrated in communal rituals, work and prayer, and decision-making. The river was a place of gathering or coming together for the village as it fed the village with fish, frogs, herbs, and water. The river had been a connecting source for the people in the village, but with the drought, that connection had been lost. After the rain, they declared with gratitude, "Our mother has come back to feed us" (Kire 55). However, with the rain, the communal feeling and connection had been restored in the village where "the people laughed and sang, and the oldest among them wept tears of joy" (56) and "people went to their fields and came back singing" (59). Before the rain, they restricted newcomers from coming and settling in the village, but after the rain, "they changed the laws on newcomers and welcomed the ones who came to share their prosperity" (59).

Thus, after the rain brought enough food for the village, the ethical community values were reinstated. The people considered generosity, helpfulness to others, and respect for age and experience as highly valued virtues defining them as one tribal community. Mesanuo, before going off to meet her sisters, left a sack of grain over her doorway so that "any stranger who needs food may help himself to the grain...it will be a sign of hospitality to guests even if I'm not around to host them. Now that we have food, we should not hoard it all for ourselves, lest we lose it all again" (Kire 77). Pele also thought about his grandmother in her remote hut where injured animals came for healing. So, in tribal community settings, there is sensitivity and kindliness that creates a safe space not just for people but for animals too.

This novel shows that it is far more important for characters to come together instead of focusing on the superficial differences relating to where they came from. People, regardless of their origins, could create a space called 'home' despite their differences. The birth of Mesanuo's son Rhalietuo – the redeemer, had also reunited her with the rest of the village. Called the 'tiger-widow' and dismissed as a ghost inhabitant of the village, the village finally accepted her into the village after the birth of Rhalietuo. She even appeared "young and beautiful, like a skywoman" (Kire 57). More than that, it was only after the birth of her son that her name was uttered by the tongues of the villagers. Before this, she was only called the 'tiger-widow.' Mesanuo corrected the village headman, "I'm no longer the tiger-widow, headman, so you can stop calling me by that name. My son has given me the right to be called by my own name, Mesanuo" (45-46). The presence of Pele helped create a new life for Mesanuo. After Pele reached the Village of Weavers, a drop of rain fell on Mesanuo, which made her pregnant and brought about the birth of her son. She tells Pele towards the end of the novel, "you brought the rain and see what it has brought me" (105).

Rhalietuo's birth had salvaged a home for Mesanuo and also reclaimed her space in the village, which had been lost for years. Her former unacknowledged state of being "isolated from the village, even while living within it" (Kire 104) was changed when the village headman begged her to stay in the village – "Live here with us, Widow. I request you not to leave the village. Stay here as you have done and share your blessings with us as you did with our ancestors" (45). Before Rhalietuo was born, parents did not allow their children to go to Mesanuo's house. However, Rhalietuo became friends with the village headman's son Viphrü, who came to their house for the first time, even though he refused to come inside. Also, Rhalietuo was even allowed to visit the home of the village headman, which was something unexpected.

Larry Evers and Paul Pavich have said that a sense of place is made possible by the "cultural landscape" created "whenever communities of people join words to place" (Patton 187). Pele decided to settle a little longer in the Village of Weavers than he had planned. "He wondered if he should start travelling again, but he felt no real need to" (Kire 59-60). After the ruin of his first family unit, he had not searched for any particular space in which to create an alternate home. However, in this village, he felt his first sense of belonging after leaving home. This feeling is interpreted in his decision to build a home in the Village of Weavers, and it is also an indirect indication of his desire to belong there.

"In any case, he had no destination to reach, and he did not have much to return to. He did not feel the call of his ancestral village. He had let his past die a long time ago. He asked the headman for some land to build a house and was given a good plot of land" (60).

THE QUEST FOR HOME

VS Naipaul's A House for Mr. Biswas also explored the theme of the quest for home, which stands for both "spiritual and physical shelter" (Baviskar 2). However, Pele's pursuit of a home proceeded considerably faster than that of Mr Biswas. In this novel and Kire's Son of the Thundercloud, a house stands for "stability, self-respect and identity" (2). Mr Biswas and Pele were aware of their rootlessness, and each strived to build their own house. For Pele, after he built his home, it was made in such a way that there was the provision to add more rooms if he wanted to. Thus, he had long-term plans as he settled into this village. He even bought a field from the village headman to till. The village headman gave it to him for free, but he insisted on paying for it. In the course of time, Mesanuo and Rhalietuo became his family, and he visited them every evening after work. He always kept a portion of fruits and vegetables for them from the fields. He ate with them often, and, in tribal societies, this symbolizes welcoming and accepting somebody into the family. After spending time with Mesanuo and her son, Pele saw the possibility of creating a home with them and even "felt his heart stir." (Kire 65). A tiny part of him acknowledged the fact that he stayed for them even after Mesanuo's sisters left. He was initially alarmed, "He could not possibly be falling in love with her! The thought was blasphemous to him. Yet, why had he stayed on in the village? Unsettled by these revelations, he hurriedly took leave of her and went home" (65).

The construction of a 'home' for Pele was a response to losing his family, his migration towards the Village of Weavers, and his ensuing attachment with Kethonuo, Siedze, Mesanuo, and Rhalietuo. In addition to his house in the Village of Weavers, Pele also built a home in the abandoned village where he had met the two sisters Siedze and Kethonuo for the first time. He built a home, making sure "it was close enough to their house" (Kire 105) on his second visit with Mesanuo and Rhalietuo. At first, he repaired the house of the two sisters, and "he had managed to build an extra room for Mesanuo and Rhalie, and low beds for them all" (101). He then asked the sisters for a small portion of their land to build a shed, to which they readily agreed, and he built a two-room shed for himself. After building his home, he built one for Rhalietuo too. In his first home, he left some provision to add extra rooms if he needed them in the future. In the abandoned village as well, he built an extra room for Mesanuo and Rhalietuo. Subconsciously, he had been creating and saving spaces to accommodate Mesanuo and Rhalietuo all along. Creating a space for oneself or others is a symbol of attachment to a place and the people of that place.

Pele fixes homes or builds homes throughout the novel. Mesanuo told Pele after he fixed her sisters' home that "for the first time, they have a real home to live in" (Kire 102). By creating homes for others, Pele compensates for the loss of his own family so that other people can "have a real family to share it with" (103). He even established the value of building homes in the mind of young Rhalietuo, as he also wanted to be a carpenter – "because houses are important. If we didn't have houses, we would have to sleep outdoors in the rain and cold. Anie Pele said he will teach me to make houses," (108).

Transferring knowledge and skills dominates tribal societies. It is passed on from one generation to the other. For young boys, skills are usually acquired from male members of the family, mostly from the fathers. In this book, Pele is the undeclared father figure for Rhalietuo – he looks out for him, he offers to accompany them to meet Mesanuo's sisters, and even the act of him making a slingshot for Rhalietuo is something a father would do for his son.

Pele was reunited with Mesanuo's sisters after seven years. He went with Mesanuo and Rhalietuo to visit them, and everything was transformed since his first visit. There were plentiful grains, various berries, and wild mushrooms that grew everywhere. The village had not seen such life and exuberance for a long time. The sisters inhabited the Noune as if the village had never been abandoned. To an outsider, this displaced group of people could not be considered a typical family unit with a father, mother, and children. Undoubtedly, the group presented an unorthodox family, but the elements that brought them together were location, love, and a search for belonging. They were so complete in themselves that it did not matter whether their unit was perfect in the eyes of other people or not – it only mattered that they had each other. Of their imperfectly whole unit, Pele declared that "I actually feel...reborn – if I may use such a term. Things that I learned as I was growing up no longer fit or belong, and this is the only reality I want to hold on to" (Kire 94-95).

Towards the end of the novel, when Rhalietuo is killed in the community hunt, Pele removes all the spears from Rhalietuo's body and "refused to accept help from the boys. Carefully wrapping Rhalie in a cloth, Pele lifted him on his shoulders and carried him home to the village" (Kire 136). Pele is the male figure Rhalietuo never knew he needed. When Rhalietuo got hurt as a result of Viphrü hitting him on the nose and making him bleed, Pele was "confused, and unaccountably sad, he turned and walked out of the house" (74). He was slowly getting attached to Mesanuo and her son and the idea of building a home with them as he recovered from losing his own family. It was not like he was replacing his original family with a new one, but there was a sense of belonging he had not felt since he tragically lost his whole first family.

The death of Rhalietuo symbolized how tribal community life could be destroyed by hatred and jealousy, as Mesanuo lamented, "They were consumed by hate. They hated others..." (Kire 141). It was as though she had known Rhalietuo would be killed from the beginning. She told Pele, "When people are overtaken by greed, they are going to bring a lot of trouble into their own lives and into the lives of others" (64-65). After Rhalietuo was killed, Mesanuo insisted on taking his body back to the abandoned village. She was only staying in the Village of Weavers for Rhalietuo, and without him, there was no reason for her to stay. He was her "home", the reason for her existence. So, when he was buried in the abandoned village, she decided to leave the Village of Weavers, never to return – "This part of my life is over. I cannot return to live here. I don't know what I will do but I will make my home where my son is buried," (140). Perhaps she wanted him to be buried in the abandoned village because this was a place where Rhalietuo knew he was loved and a place he also treasured dearly. Mesanuo believed that it was "instinct that brings us back to a place where we've been happy. I want to stay here. I want to make this my home for the rest of my life on earth" (144). The abandoned village was even renamed Nouzie, the village of compassion – the lack of which had killed her son.

When Mesanuo died, the traveller Pele left Nouzie village. These people were the reason he was staying. It may have been another relocation for him; however, this time, he left feeling content that he brought people together and united them both in life and death – "they belonged together, and his destiny was to be part of their life, briefly" (Kire 149). He felt like "he was the last man on earth", but he left with the satisfaction that "they would always be together now" (149). The novel does not end with Pele finding a home; instead, we find him in search of another place to belong to.

According to Paudel, in post-colonial literature, "the notion of home is unhomeliness, the feeling that one has no cultural home or sense of cultural belonging" (Paudel 71). However, he further explains that unhomely is not homelessness but feeling not at home even if one is in one's own home. This is evocative of the condition of Pele as he relocates from one home to another. 'Home' is not fixed or static, nor is it a place that can be considered if one remains on indigenous lands. Home evolves with the person; it can be created and recreated. This was his third relocation or displacement, but it was different this time. In the film *Contrary Warriors: A Story of the Crow Tribe*, Janine Windy Boy-Pease said, "Wealth is measured by one's relatedness, one's family, one's clan. To be alone, that would be abject poverty..." (Fleck 15). Here, Kire's characters are scattered people looking for a home in each other, starving for a sense of belonging in a world that had consciously and unconsciously isolated them. Thus, the concept of 'home' is ever-evolving, and it is created and recreated as it is the "singular yet webbed intricacies of people, land, memory, identity, space, language, and community" (Wilson 1).

WORKS CITED

Baviskar, M B. "Concept of House in V.S. Naipaul's A House for Mr. Biswas". *Pune Research, An International Journal in English*, vol. 4, Issue 1, Jan-Feb 2018, pp 1-7.

Devy, G N. *Painted Words: An Anthology of Tribal Literature*. Penguin Books India, 2002.

Fleck, Richard. *Critical Perspective on Native American Fiction*. Three Continents Press, 1993.

Kire, Easterine. *Son of the Thundercloud*. Speaking Tiger, 2016.

Patton, Venetria K. *Background Readings for Teachers of American Literature*. Bedford/ St. Martin's, 2006.

Paudel, Rudra Prasad. "Unhomely Home: Cultural Encounter of Diaspora in Jhumpa Lahiri's

The Namesake". *NUTA Journal*, 6 (1& 2), 2075, pp 70-76.

Pou, K B Veio. *Literary Cultures of India's Northeast: Naga Writings in English*. Heritage Publishing House, 2015. "*Son of the Thundercloud* brings Sahitya Akademi's Honor for Easterine Kire." Morung Express, 24th June, 2018

Wilson, Jonathan Max. *Native Spaces of Continuation, Preservation, and Belonging: Louise Erdrich's Concepts of Home*. 2008. PhD Dissertation. University of Texas of Arlington

Section 2

SITES OF RESISTANCE: EXPLORING COLLECTIVE MEMORY

07

NARRATIVIZING HISTORY THROUGH THE EVERYDAY IN *BITTER WORMWOOD*

Bendangrenla S Longkumer

INTRODUCTION

Easterine Kire's *Bitter Wormwood* (2011) is a historical fiction that revolves around the life of Mose, who lives through the history of the Naga freedom movement. Mose, the protagonist, is the metaphor for the history of a people thrown into a bloody conflict engineered by external forces outside their control, much like his own destiny. Mose is also a lively young man in a very real world defined by intricate relationships between the individual and society. Mose's experience in the novel has the dual characteristic of being personal and collective simultaneously.

In recent years, the study of the everyday and the 'quotidian' has emerged as one of the most fertile grounds in literary studies. Kire's *Bitter Wormwood* (henceforth *BW*) offers the possibility of not only speaking and coming to terms with the history of the bloody relationship the Nagas share with the Indian state but also provides us ample space to narrativize the history of the Nagas through the writing of lived experiences of the everyday, of life as experienced by the common people. Spanning over 70 years that encompasses the history of a family over four generations, *BW*, which is incontestably a historical novel, narrates the history of a people and their lives swept over by events of historical magnitude. Kire's genius lies in these events being embedded within the lived experience of the ordinary people. In her novel, it is as if history is the rude intruder that disrupts the continuum of the otherwise peaceful, idyllic existence of the characters.

Kire in her introduction to *BW* cautions her readers, "This book is not meant to be read as a history textbook... This book is not about the leaders and heroes of the Naga struggle. It is about the ordinary people whose lives were completely overturned by the freedom struggle. Because the conflict is not more important than the people who are its victims" (121). She has been able to consistently portray the mundane and the everyday lives of ordinary people in her works which, coupled with the simple and poignant language, replicates life as it is in the Naga society. The unnamed, the unacknowledged, and the erased experiences are always of the common people, as official historical records often evade these narratives. On the other hand, it is the everyday lives of the common people that are disrupted and their identities dislocated by such histories. *BW* reconciles this loss by weaving historical events into the lives of the characters she has created.

BW responds to the fundamental questions of how literature illuminates the everyday and how the writing of the everyday and personal experiences in literature fills in the gaps that are not documented by formal history. Pasco, in his discussion of whether literature can serve as legitimate historical sources in the context of the revolutionary era of France in the 18th century, suggests that official records of history are exclusionary as they fail to record the details of how a certain era is experienced by the commoners who are often the 'silent majority'. He writes:

> In fact, we are very poorly acquainted with the lower and middle classes that made up the vast majority of the population. As a consequence, it is important both to develop new resources for uncovering the past and to find new perspectives on older resources...when handled judiciously, and in answer to appropriate questions, literature can provide a reliable window on the past. Used carefully—and remembering that reality is never pure, simple, or linear—literature and the arts can bring fresh light to our perception of history. (374)

Pasco is astute in his observation of how official historical sources are inadequate to understand the human and the lived experience dimensions of history, thereby asserting the importance of everyday lived realities of the ordinary population as essential to understanding human history.

NAGA HISTORY WRITING AND ITS TUMULTUOUS SAGA

History writing for the Nagas is still in its nascent stages. According to Chasie, history writing for the Nagas became possible only in the 1970s, with a few Nagas who could afford to write because of their education as well as a sense of security over their livelihoods (3). He argues in the same article that prolonged years of intense fighting made survival take precedence for the Nagas, leaving no room for any kind of writing to develop. The post-independence era for the Nagas was also an era of extensive censorship and surveillance. T. Senka Ao, who was the editor of the Ao regional newspaper *Ao Milen* for over two decades in his memoir, recounts how even newspapers were often censored by the Indian government during the occupation era—an era defined by curtailing of freedom of speech, expression, and movement. The Emergency era would again ban all suspect materials in print between 1974-5 (Ao 55-76). Iralu, in his preface to the second edition *The Naga Saga*, writes about his inability to find willing publishers for what would become one of the most important historical accounts of the Naga Freedom struggle. He writes, "In Nagaland, prior to the 1997 NSCN-IM and Government of India Cease-fire, many Naga activists who had tried to tell the truth had suffered because of their attempts. Many publishing houses had also been subjected to severe harassment because of publishing factual accounts of the conflict" (Iralu v). It is between the erasures of the truth by dominant discourses and the stunted growth of the written form of the lived history because of the violence that Kire's body of literary work stands as both custodian and mediator.

In the essay "The Value of Narrativity in the Representation of Reality", Hayden White writes, "So natural is the impulse to narrate, so inevitable is the form of narrative for any report of the way things really happened, that narrativity could appear problematic only on a culture in which it was absent—absent or, in some domains of contemporary western intellectual, and artistic culture, programmatically refused" (5). Following Hayden's line of argument, Naga culture is based on narrativization to the very core. Being oral in nature, the art of narration in the form of folksongs, poems, and tales is a quintessential part of Naga society. Hence, even history writing by Naga writers tends to be narrativized. For centuries, history for the Nagas has been passed down from one generation to the other through narratives in the form of storytelling, songs, and folklore. The narration of the personal lived experience is interspersed with historical events, much like Kire's *BW*. The problem arises when these texts are put under the lens of academic research because of the academic parameters that are defined by rationalistic and empirical definitions of modes of knowledge following the Age of Enlightenment.

As White observes, Western academia has 'programmatically' rejected narrativization over discourse because of the hierarchization of objective as being rational and scientific and subjective as being unreliable. "This distinction between discourse and narrative is, of course, based solely on an analysis of the grammatical features of two modes of discourse in which the 'objectivity' of the one and 'subjectivity' of the other are definable primarily by a 'linguistic order of criteria'. The subjectivity of the discourse is given by the presence, explicit or implicit, of an 'ego' who can be defined only as a person who maintains the discourse. By contrast, 'the objectivity of narrative is defined by the absence of all reference to the narrator'" (7). The advent of positivist thought in academia has led to the denigration of subjective forms of expression.

It is undeniable that the formal annals of history reduce the multi-dimensional facets of the human experience into mere numbers and statistics. The Western and Eurocentric modes of writing history as a record of the facts and enumeration of events in the official annals have defined *history* as a discipline in academic discourses. This is an offshoot of the Enlightenment, as White claims. The subjective experiences of ordinary people do not feature in the conventional defining modes of official history writing, which according to Partha Chatterjee, is "characterized by institutions such as the professional historical journal and the academic monograph, writing conventions such as the footnote and the bibliography. It is the space where rational causation and scientific methodology are the dominant sentiments" (9). This also leads to the inevitable marginalization of the mythic and supernatural narratives that form the important lived experience of oral-based cultures like the Naga tribal communities. For Naga society, the mythic and the supernatural are part and parcel of the community. In the novel, Khrienuo warns her son Luo-o to be careful while going into the deep forest because they were considered to be "unclean regions in the old days" (242). True to the seer's warning and Khrienuo's fears, Luo-o is crushed by the tree the men had cut down. To the Nagas within this mythopoetic cosmos, such supernatural events would not seem strange or improbable and would be evaluated with much caution and wisdom. However, such interpretations of events would be dismissed as 'malarkey' by formal history writing modes.

As Chatterjee suggests, "Vernacular histories exist in their difference from the authorized forms of modern academic history...vernacular history frequently use other literary genres such as the novel, drama, autobiography, and even poetry" (19). By applying the parameters set by Chatterjee, Kire's *BW* plays an important function by narrativizing history through the everyday as she states in her introduction. In the author's own words on historical fiction that she has written, she states, "They contain a lot of unwritten history that I want today's generation to know. And the good thing is, they learn it better when history is presented in a novel. Family history helps to give structure and authenticity to the writing" (Pou).

No doubt the characters are fictional, but Mose's musings about how "the almost daily killings, the young men on the streets calloused by hate and shouting at everyone in sight and the complete collapse of cultural life" is an instance of how the collective feeling of the Nagas are captured in the novel (157). Kire mentions in an interview that some of the experiences in *BW* are based on real-life incidents of the 60s that she herself has lived through (Pou). Such instances, along with beliefs, customs, and sayings that form an important part of the Naga lived experience, infuse the narration of *BW* with authenticity. For instance, the naming of our protagonist as 'Moselie' is a practice that is still an intrinsic part of Naga tribal communities. Naming a child is sacred and done with much thought, with the belief that a child's name charts his/her destiny. Mose's name means 'one who will meet life without guile' according to Khrienuo, the grandmother, and, true to the name, Mose lives an honest, upright life, much loved by everyone in the community (Kire 217). Her text becomes the site where the collective lived experiences of the people are documented. Akin to the oral culture that she is located in, it is pertinent to note how some of the historical events that unfold in the novel belong to a time the writer would not have lived through, but the collective memories of people and the acts of 're-membering' are what weave her narrative together. Kire speaks of the importance of collective memory and remembering in her historical fiction in these terms:

> Mari and my own mother helped me a lot by giving me their memories of a Kohima I had never seen – pre-war Kohima under British rule.
>
> I used my older cousins and my mother as sources to write sections of *A Respectable Woman*. The last part of the novel, "Mapping Kohima", is the input I received from them. They could describe what kind of shops were there in the fifties and the very interesting trading communities – the big Manipuri traders and the Nepali women selling herbs and chickens. (Pou)

THE KITCHEN HEARTH: THE SITE WHERE RESISTANCE IS FORGED

The kitchen hearth, in the cosmos of the Nagas occupies a very important place. As Easterine Kire comments on the loss of oral literature among the

Nagas, "The peace that is essential to the continuation of oral narrative when the grandmother's hearth in the village world was destroyed and the villages burnt and its inhabitants tortured and killed or forced into evacuation" (Stricklan). Between the destruction of the kitchen hearth where the soul of the community resides and the adverse conditions that made writing impossible, much of what constitutes the Naga identity and history would be lost. It is in this gap that writers such as Kire stand and fill in the erasures through literary works. A particular instance in *BW* drew my attention to Kire's craft as a writer who effortlessly weaves in historical narrative into the everyday:

> One Sunday morning, the pastor announced at the end of the service: "We need to pray for our land. The Indian government has taken Zapuphizo prisoner for saying that the Naga people want independence. Hard times are ahead of us. Please continue to pray in your homes for peace in our land." After church, everyone was discussing what the pastor had said. Some people had more information about it. They said that Phizo was in jail in central India for writing letters to the British Parliament.
> Later that day when they were at home, Khrienuo asked, "Can it be such a bad thing to write to the white man's government? What did Phizo write about?"
> "They say he wrote asking that Nagas should not be made a part of India," Mose tried to explain. "Well, that is quite right. We have never been a part of India before. Why should we join them now?" Khrienuo asked. (Kire 550)

This is a reference to the series of events after India got her independence from British rule that would eventually lead to the Plebiscite of 1951, drafted by the Naga National Council with A.Z. Phizo as the President and signed by 99.9% Nagas according to Iralu (27). The Plebiscite continues to remain a very important historical landmark for the Nagas in their assertion that "they were not Indians and would not join the Indian Union" (Iralu 27). The innocent conversations between grandmother and grandson reflect the collective sentiment of the Nagas and their inability to comprehend how the sovereignty of an entire people can be taken away against their will. Khrienuo's naïve hope that the Prime Minister "surely cannot ignore it (the Plebiscite) when so many villagers have expressed their wishes" (584) becomes the collective, yet unattainable dream of the Nagas for their wishes have surely been ignored and instead have been rewarded with decades of violence.

Kire's act of writing a novel based on the individual and collective experiences of her people mired in their contentious history is also a political act of reclaiming the kitchen hearth that would ensure the survival of the collective memory of the Nagas, an intrinsic part of the Naga identity. Kire's politics of reclaiming the space that was forcefully taken away from the Nagas by writing about collective experiences is also reminiscent of the Native American poet Joy Harjo's politics in her poem "Perhaps the World Ends Here" where the domestic "kitchen-table" is central to the existence of the values and history of oral tradition-based communities. Much like Harjo's kitchen table, it is by the kitchen hearth that men and women are made, where values are instilled, and where the community lives on. The experience of the everyday, therefore, not only makes history but also ensures the survival of the community.

Mose's upbringing by his grandmother and mother in the absence of a male role model does not impair his abilities or worth as a young man. The values of an honourable man who would take on the role of protector and provider of the family are the lessons he learnt at the kitchen hearth from the women in the house, which would also define the direction he would take later in life. At nineteen, he has already taken on the reins of the household and has already made up his mind to join the freedom movement with his friend Neituo. The narrative of resistance against the claims of the dominant discourse is built in the domestic space even as violence intrudes into the domestic space:

> "I don't feel right to be studying when we are living in such troubled times. Let me take over the field-work so you can stay at home safely."
> "What makes you think I'd be safer at home, son? They are everywhere, and they attack everyone. Only Jisu keeps us safe." (Kire 819)

BITTER WORMWOOD AS A COUNTERNARRATIVE TO DOMINANT DISCOURSES

Narrativized history writing is criticized for its inability to provide 'objective' facts and truths. Subjective experiences and narratives drawn from the everyday are judged on the basis of the inherent biases and prejudices they might harbour. However, even formal history writing, although seemingly objective, is also mediated by "ideological presuppositions" which decide the documentation and writing. History is also written by those in power, thereby leading to the erasure of events that may indict them. For instance, the first General Election of India in Nagaland was a massive failure as the Nagas did not cast their votes. However, this point never made it to the mainstream narrative:

> Later, there was nothing on the radio about the empty ballot boxes that were returned from Nagaland. People got to know about it from the few Nagas working in the Government sector. It was retold in whispers. (Kire 649)

Contrary to the claims made by dominant narratives, the failure of the General Elections in Nagaland has survived in people's collective memory, filling in the deliberate erasure of the history-making projects of those who hold power. Hence, one can conclude that all forms of history writing are mediated; therefore, even the objective and positivist claim of academic history writing becomes suspect.

All forms of history writing are inadequate. What claims to be official history is often distorted by the subjective taste and sensibilities of historians. More often than not, history writing is also an authoritarian exercise of power where the history of the people on the margins is erased without any opposition simply because there is no space for these voices to be heard. Just as elements of narratives such as experience and memory are subjective, formal history writing is also not absolutely objective; neither is it innocent in its claims.

Secondly, *BW* also functions as the site where the history of the ordinary Naga people is written. As people on the margins, their voices are erased from official history recorded by the dominant discourses. Even when the dominant discourses talk about them, these communities/people/groups are always misrepresented or misappropriated. Writing, therefore, becomes a conscious political act of allowing their voices to be heard. For instance, it has always been the claim of the Government of India that the Nagas were a part of the Indian Territory. Udayon Misra writes, "Nehru was clearly stating that the Naga territory was too small to exist as an independent nation and for strategic reasons it must join the Indian Union" (620). Contrary to such claims, we see the protagonist and other characters in the novel finding it impossible to relate to the new national identity that has been thrust upon them forcefully by the Indian state. Unsurprisingly, such sentiments of alienation from the national identity are harboured by many even today. Kaka Iralu's passionate claim in *The Naga Saga* that the Nagas have "no affinity with India whether racially, historically, politically, culturally, religiously or any otherwise" is a sentiment that runs through the novel (5).

Even as the novel ends on a hopeful note, the characters never retract from their identity of being a sovereign people. If there is reconciliation, it is in terms of forgiving and moving beyond a shared violent past between the oppressor and the oppressed.

Gopal Guru, in his ground-breaking book *Cracked Mirror*, suggests the possibility of the construction of counternarratives to the modes of knowledge that are accepted in formal institutions through lived experiences. This, in many ways, finds resonance in Kire's *BW*, where her intention is to talk about the everyday experiences of ordinary people in an era and a space torn by strife. The grief, the anger, the fear, and the helplessness, interspersed by moments of domestic bliss and comfort, are part of the author's own lived experiences and of the many Nagas who have lived through this tumultuous history.

The dehumanization and villainization of the freedom fighters as mere terrorists and insurgents in the dominant discourse perpetuated by official records of history become overwritten by the sense of humanness, love for their people and the very clear purpose they have in the narrative. They are portrayed as a people who have been unjustly deprived of their rights and are measured in terms of the immense sacrifices they have made to free the Nagas from the authoritarian rule of the Indian Government, which offers a very different picture than that of "terrorists" and "insurgents". By locating these characters within the domestic and social spaces they inhabit, Kire is able to reclaim the humane in her portrayal of freedom fighters like that Mose and Neitou. As Gopal Guru states in *The Cracked Mirror* on the importance of narratives based on experience:

> It becomes the moral responsibility of those who are recipients of torment, crushing experiences to vocalize the experience of past silence. The tormentor avoids writing the history of social evils for which he or she is responsible. It becomes the added responsibility of the tormented to resurrect the history of experience, reflect on it and use it radically for the political and intellectual organization of masses who then would be ready for the annihilation of the structures of domination that underlie this experience. Thus, reference to experience becomes important in order to detect the absence of the ethical principal of co-responsibility within the tormentor. (117)

Hence, these narratives based on the subjective experiences of individuals are sites of resistance that subvert the dominant discourses. These narratives are a source that speaks out for the silenced and oppressed on the margins and therefore fill the gaps and silences in the histories documented by the elite and the privileged.

Thirdly, these narratives are drawn from the everyday of the common people that inhabit marginal spaces. Chatterjee, like Pasco, asserts that the site of the everyday is where "real history of the people is" as opposed to formal histories that are documented based on evidence from archives and monographs. He writes:

> The real history of the people lay beyond the reach of archival documentation; the methods of academic history were unsuited to recovering that history. Indeed, the true history of the people resided, untouched by the vagaries of political history as a sort of timeless essence suffusing the ordinary lives of people. (16)

The narrative of *BW* similarly revolves around the everyday lives of ordinary people. If it does talk about war or times of conflict, such stories are narrated in terms of how these catastrophic events affected the normal, ordinary lives of the Nagas, who mostly inhabited the rural areas. The site of the everyday is also the site where culture in terms of religion, language and tradition exists. Hence, it is also the site where a shared identity of the people emerges. This is very true of the emergence of a Naga identity where the collective sense of belonging ties the people together in the demand for a separate nation.

Chasie, in his article on Naga literature, writes, "People usually write about what concerns them the most...The obsession of Nagas for politics and history...has given rise to a category of writers who might be described as Naga politico-historians who would try to prove that historically the Nagas have nothing to do with India" (3). This group of "politico-historians" has already undertaken the project of scripting a history for the Nagas as a counter-narrative against all discourses that threaten to silence them. The Naga freedom movement is one of the longest unresolved conflicts in the world. In an attempt to cover up the atrocities, huge resources have been spent by the government. In spite of all the efforts to suppress the voice of the oppressed, these personal and subjective narratives based on everyday lived experiences remain to tell stories of resistance. An alternate history is being scripted by the Nagas for themselves, asserting their right to independence. As Chatterjee writes, "Effective histories are being made in the vernacular" (23). In Kire's case, effective histories are being written in her body of literary works.

As Pasco rightly argues:

"Raw facts of history can be revitalized with a human touch when historians have a better understanding of the fantasies, beliefs, fears, and loves of the people. Such attitudes are crucial to the ways people see their world and go far in explaining their actions. Novels, plays, poems, and essays, many of which include extensive social commentary, can bring considerable depth to history and the study of culture." (388)

The mundane joys, personal sorrow, and grief of Mose and the wailing and mourning of the community around him in the novel give *BW* an authenticity and a depth missing in official historical records. Kire, no doubt, informs, but her redeeming quality is in the humanizing aspect of her works that acknowledge the ravages of history and its consequences on the ordinary men and women she has set out to write about.

WORKS CITED

Ao, T. Senka. "Milen Ka Asoshi." *Kishi Tezülen* (*Off the Doorway*). Author, 2016, pp. 55-76.

Chasie, Charles. "The History of Nagaland Reflected in Its Literature." *Eastern Mirror*, 4 January 2015, https://easternmirrornagaland.com/the-history-of-nagaland-reflected-in-its-literature/ Accessed on 13 Sept. 2016.

Chatterjee, Partha. "Introduction: History in the Vernacular." *History in the Vernacular*, edited by Razuiddin Aquil and Partha Chatterjee. Permanent Black, 2008, pp. 1-24.

Guru, Gopal. "Experience and the Ethics of Theorising." *The Cracked Mirror: An Indian Debate on Experience and Theory*. Ed. Gopal Guru and Sundar Sarukkar. OUP, 2012, pp.107-127.

Harjo, Joy. "Perhaps the World Ends Here." *The Poetry Foundation*. https://www.poetryfoundation.org/poems/49622/perhaps-the-world-ends-here Accessed on 15 Sept. 2020.

Iralu, Kaka D. *The Naga Saga*. Kaka D. Iralu, 2000.

Kire, Easterine. *Bitter Wormwood*. Kindle ed., Zubaan, 2011.

Misra, Udayon. "The Margins Strike Back: Echoes of Sovereignty and the Indian State." *India International Centre Quarterly*. 32.2/3. (Monsoon-Winter 2005): 265-274. Jstor, www.jstor.org/stable/4366506. Accessed on 16 Nov. 2016.

Pasco. Allan H. "Literature as Historical Archive." *New Literary History*, Summer, 2004, Vol. 35, No. 3, Critical Inquiries, Explorations, and Explanations

(Summer, 2004), pp. 373-394. *Jstor*, www.jstor.com/stable/20057844. Accessed on 10 July 2020.

Pou, Veio. "Years of Listening to Stories Grows a Wealth of Knowledge Within Your Spirit." *Scroll.in*. 23 August 2020, www.scroll.in/article/971141/years-of-listening-to-stories-grows-a-wealth-of-knowledge-within-your-spirit-easterine-kire. Accessed on 27 Aug. 2020.

Stricklan, Kate. "Bitter Wormwood: Interview with Author Easterine Kire." *Sampsonian Way*. Jan 2012. www.sampsonianway.org/literary-voices/2012/01/16/bitter-wormwood-interview-with-author-easterine-kire. Accessed on 18 Dec. 2016.

White, Hayden. "The Value of Narrativity in the Representation of Reality". *Critical Inquiry* 7.1. (1980): 5-27. *Jstor*, www.jstor.org/stable/1343174. Accessed on 11 Nov 2016.

08

TRACING NAGA HISTORY: A STUDY OF EASTERINE KIRE'S HISTORICAL NOVELS

Limayangla Pongener

INTRODUCTION

Easterine Kire writes extensively across genres and subjects. A prolific and versatile writer, a glance at her work could suggest that it is predominantly based on Nagaland and its people, wherein the cultural and traditional life of a Naga individual is represented. However, upon closer reading, it can be observed that much of her work is also preoccupied with Nagaland's history. Colonial contact which brought major changes to the social, political and religious practices of the people; the Battle of Kohima during the Second World War, which brought Nagaland into focus on the map of the modern world; and finally, the Naga fight for independence – these continue to affect every aspect of a Naga's life. These are important events in the history of Nagaland on which a number of her novels, fiction and historical fiction, are based. By writing about these occurrences, Kire makes the world or the reading public aware of the historical significance of these events in shaping Nagaland and its people. Therefore, this chapter traces and highlights elements of Naga history in the selected texts. To do so, it devises a framework in which Kire's interviews, along with the selected texts, are closely read.

APPROACHING KIRE THROUGH HER INTERVIEWS

Through the medium of the interview, a writer offers a reader an opportunity to understand his or her work at a more intimate level. It provides an almost direct insight into the worldview of the writer from whom the stories originate. Examination of Kire's interview responses indicates an individual who is deeply moved by the social, political, and historical scenarios of Nagaland. Her writing is a contribution to the larger discourse directed at a collective attempt towards a reasonable and peaceful understanding of the various factors that have led Nagaland to its present situation. To illustrate the point, perhaps we can consider her responses over the years in detail. In a 2006 featured article titled "In Her Own Words", Kire candidly writes about her life, from the meaning of her name to how the Naga fight for independence affected her personal and professional life; from her relocation to Tromso under ICORN to the kinds of issues that she takes up in her writing, which enables her to articulate her hopes and dreams for the future of Nagaland:

> I continue to pray and dream of peace for my people and reflect it in my poetry. At the same time, I am now able to admit and talk about the long-term damage to my people the years of protracted conflict have inflicted and I have slowly begun to address this in my new writings . . . I am now thinking of new ways to help my people, especially the young.

As one studies Kire's interview responses, one begins to understand that for her, the documentation of Naga history, especially by Naga writers, is of utmost priority and therefore needs to be treated as a matter of urgency. In a 2019 interview with Namrata Kolachalam, she explains why she writes historical novels. She says:

> We have an ancient oral, unwritten literature and a young written literature dating back to the 1970s when academic works by Nagas appeared in print. Before that, the writings that existed on Nagas were by western anthropologists and British political officers and American missionaries. I started writing historical novels on my people's history because the insider's voice was silent in all the historical narratives on us. Writing historical novels gave me the opportunity to give a socio-cultural presentation of my community. I always include the spiritual element as that is a big part of our reality as a

people. I see the role of Naga writers as one of chronicling our history and our socio-cultural reality in the format of written literature.

Kire reiterates the point in another interview in the same year while discussing the non-fiction *Walking the Roadless Road: Exploring the Tribes of Nagaland* (subsequently *WRR*), with Sudipta Dutta:

> Written Naga literature is still very young. For many years we have relied on our rich oral literature. But Naga society began to change from the 1980s. The age-old tradition of the age-group houses where stories were passed down orally has fewer members now as many have migrated to the towns to get Western education, and jobs. The old keepers of the stories are dying out. The present time is such a crucial moment when we can document the collective wisdom, village narratives, and history of the tribes. This was one reason why I wrote this work of non-fiction. I have been doing it constantly in my fictional work, but universities and such need this kind of boxed-in, authenticated information which attends to formalities like indexing, referencing etc. (2019)

In these statements, it can be seen that Kire is extremely conscious of the loss of a rich oral tradition through which Naga history, tradition, culture, and belief, in short, the whole Naga way of life, were handed down orally from one generation to another through the institution of what the Angamis call *thehou*, the Aos call *ariju*, the Konyaks call *pan*, and the Changs call *sochum*. This setup is commonly known as a *morung* and translates as "community house" (166) or "male dormitories" (25) as described by Kire in *A Naga Village Remembered* (subsequently *ANVR*). Another important domestic setup was the kitchen hearth, where elders, especially the women folk consisting of grandmothers, mothers, and granddaughters, spent time imparting similar traditional knowledge. It is a trope that Kire uses in most of her novels with nostalgia. However, the modern lifestyle and emulation of Western culture have led to the discontinuity of this rich Naga custom, and, with time, most of the elders who were storehouses of Naga history have passed on. Kire also advocates the need for the Nagas themselves to tell the stories about Nagas, calling this the 'insider voice' and pointing out that the stories have been written about or represented by outsiders for a very long time. Keeping all these factors in mind, before the onslaught of time completely ravages everything that remains of the past, Kire believes that "The present time is such a crucial moment when we can document the collective wisdom, village narratives and history of the tribes." This, she says, was one of the reasons for writing the non-fiction WRR, even though she has already been "doing it constantly" in her "fictional work". She makes a defining statement about Naga writers: "I see the role of Naga writers as one of chronicling our history and our socio-cultural reality in the format of written literature." Kire further elaborated on her writing process in an interview with Sangeeta Barooah Pisharoty in 2016 where she said:

> I have been writing my novels chronologically in order to give the historical background of my people and their lives. Therefore, the first novels I wrote were historical fiction, centring on historical events. I felt this was important to chronicle our history in the form of a novel.

Thus, in keeping with Kire's paradigm, this paper traces the historical events in chronological order in its examination of the historical novels *ANVR* (2016), *Mari* (2010) *Bitter Wormwood* (2011) and *A Respectable Woman* (2019).

OVERVIEW OF THE EARLIEST NAGA-BRITISH RELATIONSHIP THROUGH A RECONSTRUCTION OF THE HISTORY OF KHONOMA VILLAGE

A Naga Village Remembered (2003)[1] is the first novel by Kire and also the first one to be written in English by a Naga. It is based on the warrior village of Khonoma, inhabited by the Angami Naga tribe. The village earned a formidable reputation because it managed to protect its sovereignty and maintain its supremacy among neighbouring villages. The small but brave village resisted colonial advances from the very first contact until it was brought under colonial control in 1880. Prior to the final suppression of Khonoma, the village warriors besieged the Kohima garrison in October 1879. After the siege failed, the British attacked and eventually conquered Khonoma; the village was destroyed, and the inhabitants were banished from their homes.

---

[1] The second edition of the novel was published in 2016 and in 2018, it was reissued under the title *Sky is My Father: A Naga Village Remembered* (Speaking Tiger Books).

In the introduction, Kire chalks out important events in the history of Khonoma on which the novel is built. She highlights the four expeditions carried out against Khonoma: the first expedition led by Captain E.L.D Wood was in 1844 in order to suppress the "anti-colonial feelings of the village" (12) and resulted in the village being burnt down. The second punitive expedition in 1849 was against what the colonizers termed as "Khonoma defiance" after they helped a "group of men of Mezoma who were opposed to the Government". During this expedition, "Houses of the Thevo clan and Merhü clan were burnt" (12-13). The third expedition, on the 10th of December 1850, was led by Captain J. Butler, Major Foquett, Lieutenant Reid, and Lieutenant Bivar. During the burning of their houses, the villagers took shelter in "the mountain fort called Phegei, or Tsiekha, also referred to in British records as Chakka fort" (13). The fourth and the last expedition in November 1879, known as the Battle of Khonoma, was carried out as punishment for the killing of Deputy Commissioner Damant in October 1879 and also to punish Khonoma for the siege of Kohima. Details of these encounters have been extensively recorded in several colonial writings[2]. The novel also provides a detailed account of the Angami way of life governed by strict traditional and cultural beliefs, which were followed for generations until the arrival of Christianity. Kire adds explanatory or introductory notes, which are an integral part of historical novels termed by Jerome de Groot as "external scholarly apparatus" or "extratextual information" (7). Thus, Kire draws from colonial records as well as oral narration as she meticulously reconstructs the historical events by incorporating both *insider* and *outsider* sources.

In the first few chapters of the book, Kire highlights the reasons that drove the warriors of Khonoma to attack the British. Kire presents a series of scenes at the *thehou* to highlight the kind of talk that the menfolk dwelled upon. "Reminiscing about hunts and battles in the past" (25) was one recurring topic among them. Such deliberations reveal that the men are proud of their ancestors' exploits, which in turn encourage them to carry on with their warfare and even challenge enemies mightier than them. One example is the proud recollection of the revenge exacted at Piphe by killing twenty-two soldiers, including Bogchand, for burning houses of the Merhü clan under Bogchand's order during the second punitive expedition. The

---

[2] In the introduction, Kire gave her source of information for these historical details, "Accounts of the siege of Kohima and the Battle of Khonoma have been taken from Mrs Cawley's report in *Nagas in the 19th Century*, Johnstone's *Manipur and the Naga Hills*, Mackenzie's, *The North East Frontier of India*, and Visier Sanyü's, *A History of Nagas and Nagaland*" (15).

speaker explains the philosophy behind such action. He says that "it was a matter of honour" because a man will be looked down on as "Thenumia" (which means woman) if he does not seek revenge when his kin is killed, and his house is burnt. He explains that it is "the need to prove himself worthy of defending his village and his womenfolk, and to earn ornaments of war" that "drives a man to battle" (26).

The killing of the Political Agent Mr. Damant on 14th October 1879 led to the eruption of the tension brewing on both sides for a very long time. In the encounter, "thirty-eight men were killed and nineteen wounded" (107). This success fueled Khonoma with the confidence to attack the Kohima garrison. However, they wasted time in their traditional feast of victory called *rüpi*, during which the British garrison fortified itself and sent out messages to other headquarters calling for reinforcements. Thus, the Angamis faced fierce resistance and their estimate of an "easy victory... stretched into a twelve-day siege" (109) until they retreated after learning about Colonel Johnstone's march towards Kohima with his huge party. In order to punish the villagers for their rebellion, on 22nd November 1879, the British launched an attack on Khonoma under the command of Brigadier General Nation. Khonoma was surrounded on all sides, and the villagers retreated to the mountain fort called *Tsiekha*. Before surrendering, however, "55 warriors marched through the Zeliang territories into Assam, raided the Baladhan tea garden, killed Mr. Blyth, the manager and 16 of his labourers" (122). After plundering and burning the place, they returned to their village. This further pushed the British government to inflict severe punishment on the small warrior village. As a result, it was "razed to the ground". This was interpreted by the British as their victory. However, Kire points out an interesting fact. She highlights the totally different code of honour practised by the villagers when "the elders explained that this raid on a British territory and its subjects was necessary because the men of Khonoma were culturally bound to avenge their fallen men" and that since they killed last, it was "all right to talk of peace now" (122).

Another important aspect of the Battle of Khonoma was the manner in which the peace treaty was agreed upon. When elders approached General Nation "at Mezoma for a peace settlement", (123) he asked them to bring the warrior Pelhu because he had "heard of Pelhu's legendary fame" (122). When they met Pelhu at Kenoria, he refused to go with them because "the British had killed Sakhrie, Zapusau, and Levolhu" of his clan. The elders managed to persuade him by explaining that it was necessary to make peace with the white men, at least for the sake of their women and children. Therefore, along with representatives from different clans, he met General Nation and gave him a tragopan as a "token of peace" (123). Kire explains:

He wore a *Padi* cloth and he would not don his ornaments
for it would dishonour his dead kin. In front of him walked
Zhütsülie of the Semo clan, and Zhüwhelie of the Thevo
clan. Zhüwhelie looked splendid in his breast ornament and
Zhütsülie wore his black men's kilt. Rhitso of the Vihutsu clan
of Mezoma accompanied them carrying a *duda* spear. (123)

This passage has great significance at many levels. For one, it is an
excellent demonstration of oral narration. It will not be lost on a reader
familiar with oral tradition as it immediately transports one to a typical
traditional setting where oral narrators proudly list every detail of a particular
event as the listeners listen in awe taking mental notes. It also holds
immense cultural and historical significance as it records the participation
of representatives from each clan by naming the individuals and describing
their bearing and attire for the solemn occasion. Finally, through a verbal
contract which is a Naga tradition, as opposed to a Western written contract,
"The treaty was concluded between village representatives of Khonoma and
representatives of the British Government at Mezoma on the 27th March
1880" (124) with a shake of hands between General Nation and the great
warrior Pelhu. Thus, Kire further elaborates on the nature and worldview
of the people of Khonoma while highlighting and documenting the kind of
interactions and negotiations the two parties were forced to work with.

It can be deduced that the manner in which Kire reconstructs
Khonoma's contact and exchange with the British, by drawing from both
oral and written narration, is a display of the method that Nagas in general
and Naga scholars in particular use in the search for their past story. At the
same time, it also demonstrates how the Nagas uphold oral tradition and,
thus, is a powerful assertion of the importance of Naga customary practices
to date. In fact, it is an example of the politics behind the writing of a
historical novel, which Jerome de Groot describes in his book, *The Historical
Novel*:

> Often writing back is deployed as a means of cultural
> reparation and leveling. Within the context of the historical
> novel it does signify this, but it also demonstrates a desire to
> bring figures from the margins to the centre and to dissent
> from the authoritative narrative of the past. At the same time
> using language, history and cultural references in a different
> setting makes them something new, uses them to create
> something owned by the writer, and therefore challenges
> hegemonic models of cultural capital. (165)

WORLD WAR TWO: EXPERIENCES RECOLLECTED AND RECOUNTED

After a detailed account of Naga life before colonization, Naga resistance to British rule, and the coming of Christianity through a reconstruction of the history of Khonoma village, Kire writes about another important event in Naga history, which is the coming of World War II to Nagaland in the novel *Mari*. She then goes on to describe the rehabilitation process carried out by the British India Government in *A Respectable Woman* (subsequently *ARW*). *Mari* is the story of Easterine Kire's aunt, Khrielieviü Mari O'Leary. It is based on her diary during the war and the narration of her own life story to the author. *Mari* and *ARW* together reconstruct a detailed description of Kohima, the common people, and the soldiers before, during, and after the war through the memories of people who lived through it. Kire demonstrates how she uses, verifies, and corroborates oral accounts of different individuals to write the stories. In the author's note to *Mari*, Kire explains:

> The pre-war town of Kohima has been recreated mostly through Mama's and Mari's eyes. They told me about landmarks in the town such as the shops and the school and the hospital. They remembered the gallows used during British times to hang murderers, the pillory set up to deter wrongdoers from repeating their offence, the names of their teachers and the number of cars in town. (viii)

Similarly, in *ARW* she explains:

> My mother, Khrienguü Kire, could attest that the pillory set up by the British government was located at the former site of the yarn stores owned by Yachutuo and Zasitso at the end of the Mission Road.
> Corroborating my mother's information, T. Solo added that petty criminals "were shackled in wooden frames and pilloried. This was publicly done in what is now the junction of Mission Compound and High School road on the eastern side of Vikrulie Belho's shop". (164-65)

In *Mari*, Kire is able to present first-hand experiences of the people when the Battle of Kohima was fought from 4th April to 22nd June 1944. She writes, "In 1943, the war that had seemed such a distant thing for so long finally reached us" when refugees from Burma reached Naga soil "in wretched bands; starving, diseased dregs of humanity, droves of them dropping down dead by the roadside or in the refugee camps" (17). Another sign that made the war a reality was when young Naga men "left home to join the army, the RAF and the navy" (18). In *ARW* too, she writes, "Many young Naga men were running off to join the British army in those days because the pay was good and no young man could resist getting a rifle to call his own" (52). Mari also talks about employment opportunities that the war provided everyone. For instance, while Mari and her friends could find employment as civilian contractors to build roads, the army recruited "Uneducated men ... as coolies in Moreh and Tamu," as "paid labourers in Tiddim in Burma", and "Even grown girls left home to join the military nursing service" (18). While *Mari* closely follows the battle in Kohima and recounts in detail the ordeal people had to undergo, *ARW* gives a detailed account of the rehabilitation period after the war. Mari writes about her experiences of being separated from her family, fleeing from home and hiding in jungles to escape Japanese atrocities, walking from camp to camp seeking food and shelter and also about the roles played by Nagas in the war, performing duties of coolies, stretcher-bearers, and spies. For example, Sam, Mari's brother, was a King's Scout (64) who worked with "the British troops as a guide for the Wingate Chindits" (91).

The first part of *ARW* is based on Kohima immediately after the war. It presents the tenacity of the people in the face of destruction as they start rebuilding their lives along with aid provided by the government. The character Khonou recalls how "DC Pawsey and his men drove up with truckloads of tin and timber" (11). One of the developments introduced after the war was the replacement of thatch roofs with tin, which was hailed for being less flammable. Another innovation was the distribution of a new and "fast growing variety of paddy seed", which the people called "*rosho lha* as they could not pronounce *ration lha*" (13). She recalls that the DC's Angami assistants "set up a table" and "wrote down the names of all the people who had lost their homes. . . the exact losses suffered by the household, such as loss of grain, houses, and so on" and distributed monetary compensation as well (11-12). Yet another significant change was that of the landscape after the British heavily bombed "Kohima, Viswema, Khuzama, Phesama, and Jakhama" (Mari 91) to drive out the Japanese who were in hiding after their defeat. In *ARW*, Khonou notes that before the war, the only proper road they had was a narrow, one-way road between Imphal and Dimapur, but after the war, many interconnected roads were built that brought about further changes to the topography. It can be seen that Kire constantly uses Government records to corroborate oral narration in her stories, and the mere numbers and figures in official records are amplified by the experiences and opinions of the people who lived through the changes. Kire also evokes pathos, which academic history writing fails to do by imagining the life of common people in the midst of these historical events and not focusing on the military exploits of brave generals who led the war or the diplomatic competency of politicians and statesmen of the countries engaged in war. In this way, the particular historical events covered by Kire are no longer seen as simply part of an academic exercise dealing with a distant, intangible past. It is proof of Allan H. Pasco's statement in the essay, "Literature as Historical Archive" that it is the literary medium in the form of "Novels, plays, poems, and essays, many of which include extensive social commentary," that "bring considerable depth to history and the study of culture" (388).

INDO-NAGA CONFLICT THROUGH THE STORIES OF THE COMMON PEOPLE

The departure of the British from India and Naga soil, leaving behind unresolved political issues, led to the beginning of a new chapter in the history of Nagaland. Kire explores this ongoing political problem in the novels *Bitter Wormwood* (subsequently *BWW*) and *ARW* by tracing the Naga independence movement through the lives and perspectives of ordinary people. *BWW* is a historical fiction that traces the story of a family from 1937 to 2007. It starts with the birth of the protagonist Mose in 1937 and ends with his tragic death trying to save a migrant worker from Bihar in 2007. Mose and his friend Neituo, who were still teenagers, voluntarily joined the Naga freedom movement after witnessing the atrocities committed by the Indian Army. It was the time when the Naga fight for independence was gaining momentum after the British left India in 1947. Throughout the book, Kire brings up the many incidences of human rights violations committed by the Indian Army, which still live on in people's memories and mentions the various Government Acts that allowed them to happen. For example, when Mose was just seventeen years old, his grandmother was shot while working in the field. It was 1954. Kire uses this incident to explain the workings of the "Assam Maintenance of Public Order Act 1953". She writes that the soldier who killed Mose's grandmother would not be prosecuted because "The Act empowered a soldier to 'shoot and kill, in case it is felt necessary to do so for maintaining of public order'" (73). Another incident still fresh in peoples' memories occurred on 5th March 1995, when the Army killed seven civilians and injured twenty (167). This incident took place in one of the busiest parts of Kohima town, where the only famous hotel at the time, Hotel Japfü, was located. A convoy of 16 Rashtriya Rifles, travelling to

Dimapur from Imphal and parked below the hotel, started indiscriminate shooting and bombing (166) because "The soldiers claimed they had been shot at". In reality, "one of the tyres of the army in the lead had punctured loudly", which made them think that "they were being ambushed" (167). Kire records:

> For more than two hours they terrorized the civilians who were making their way home and held people at gunpoint. Reports came in that civilians were being stripped and beaten by the soldiers. The Chief of Police rushed to the spot. He started a long negotiation before the soldiers relented to his authority. (167)

Later, "The Justice Sen Commission's report, which came out in April, stated that the Rashtriya Rifles had fired 1700 small arms and 9 rocket-propelled grenades and 52 mm mortars into a civilian area" (167-68). Again, in the next chapter, "The AFSPA", Kire talks about this draconian act that sanctions unlimited power to the armed forces. The Armed Forces Special Powers Act (AFSPA) was passed in 1958, "sanctioning search and seize and arrest without warrant and shooting even to the causing of death, with complete protection of the military and paramilitary forces from legal charges" (246). To show the kind of immunity the AFSPA grants the Army, she cites an incident when an innocent "young father returning home late at night was shot by an Indian soldier" (169) who did not face prosecution because the soldier was provided immunity by the AFSPA, despite protests by the people.

It should be noted that Kire traces historical facts and phases with an objective perspective - neither demonizing the Indian Army nor presenting the Naga freedom workers as above reproach. Kire is openly critical of the factionalism among the freedom fighters that led to the degeneration of the ideals with which the movement was started by its leaders and carried on by members like Mose and Neituo. In one of her latest interviews, she says:

> Very sadly, a cause that started so nobly was destroyed from within by factionalism, and it suffered the erosion of unity that factionalism always brings. We started well, no doubt about that. But we are not finishing well, that is what makes our story so sad. Disunity and the struggle for power has diminished the aspects that made the struggle noble and worthy. (2020)

During one of the many contemplations and discussions between Mose and Neituo long after they had left their life as freedom fighters, Mose says, "Sometimes, I wonder if those young new soldiers in the factional groups even know what they are fighting for" because along with "the bogus members, there were many jobless young men joining the factions and extorting money". To this, Neituo replies, "Cannon fodder. That's all they are. Somewhere along the way the cause was kidnapped and now it has metamorphosed into a mind game" (162). Through this passage, Kire draws attention to the attitude of many Naga people who are disillusioned with the turn that the Naga freedom movement has taken. Kire makes an honest commentary on the deterioration and degradation of the movement by presenting the lived experience of hardworking civilians who have had to live in constant fear and endure threats to their lives, properties, and freedom. Again, in the previously mentioned ICORN article of 2006, Kire writes:

> I am now able to admit and talk about the long-term damage to my people the years of protracted conflict have inflicted and I have slowly begun to address this in my new writings. While many of the writers in cities of refuge have experienced prison physically, my people and I have been living within an invisible prison for many years, denied freedom of expression, freedom to nationhood and most painfully, freedom to life itself.

A few years later, in a 2012 interview about BWW with the online magazine Sampsonia Way Kire again opens up about the motivation behind the stories she writes; "I'd like people to know the truth, unadulterated and ugly though it may be at times. Not my version of the truth, but an objective truth that people in their heart of hearts will have to agree with as true, even if it paints an unattractive picture of the conflict and of the people who became its prisoners." The often-neglected history of the Naga people, who were plunged into another war even before they had managed to recuperate from the Second World War, is highlighted in ARW. People were scrambling to build their lives back after the destruction caused by the Second World War when armed resistance for Naga independence began right after India's independence, and another war started. Kire writes about the prolonged darkness that engulfed Nagaland as Khonuo and Kevinuo talk about the infamous strategy of grouping that resulted in the death of young and old because of starvation and torture and of the numerous accounts of human rights violations and of rapes by the Indian Army soldiers. As a result, "So many men joined the Naga army to fight against the Indian government. So many of those men died; it was like a whole generation of men disappeared because they were all killed, one after the other" (58). Thus, when young men left their families and homes to join a war, history repeated itself. Once again, women were left behind, but this time they did not compose songs to dissuade their male friends and lovers from joining the war as was done during the Second World War. This time, "Even women joined the Underground and fought alongside the men for many years", seeking to avenge the killing of "their brothers or fathers" by "the Indian army" (61-62). Those who were left behind, wives, sisters, and mothers, quietly bore the burden of managing the household, children, and aged parents even as their day-to-day life was heavily restricted by curfews, military surveillance, and subjugation. Khonuo explains that "Life was so much worse than it was during the Japanese war" because, during the Second World War, the British and the Indian soldiers "were there to protect" their "lands" and now, because of the atrocities committed by the Indian Army even "the sight of the Indian soldiers" (59) created fear in the people. However, despite the unrest, Kevinuo says that "in the townships people tried to live their lives as close to normal as was allowed." She explains that there were exchanges of "gunfire in encounters between the army and the Underground" which would disrupt "any semblance of normal life in an instant. But the next morning, the townspeople would pick up their lives and go back into the routine of daily life" because "That was the only way to survive" (63). The bombing of Ruby Cinema Hall on 4th February 1973, which killed many civilians, is one such example. In both novels, Kire writes that people tried to live a normal life, but they were suddenly made aware of the abnormality of the times in which they lived when the Ruby Cinema Hall was bombed. In an interview with Veio Pou in *Scroll* (2020), Kire recounts her own memory of the period. She says:

> I grew up in the sixties and seventies in a Kohima that witnessed many changes. In the sixties, the army would clamp curfew on town areas. In spite of all the dark experiences of army occupation, the late sixties and early seventies were a bit more peaceful and there would be concerts, variety shows and school shows in the town hall. There even was a cinema hall which showed both English and Hindi movies.
> The hall was blown up in 1973.

Kevinuo, in *ARW*, states that "it was one of the worst local tragedies" (97) they witnessed. Ruby Cinema Hall was not just a movie hall, but as Neituo says, it was "the lifeline of the town" (125) where "Kohima schools organized all their annual functions and variety entertainment evenings. In winter, the up-and-coming rock bands liked to hold noisy concerts in the hall. A few weeks before the bomb blast, sedate ladies of the town had organized a flower show at the same hall" (*BWW* 125). However, "The bomb blast destroyed the illusion of peace and progress in the new state of Nagaland" and reminded the people "that the conflict between the Naga Underground and the government of India was still highly volatile and begging a solution" (*ARW* 98).

CONCLUSION: NAGA HISTORY DOCUMENTED IN KIRE'S HISTORICAL NOVELS

Kire writes with a clearly defined purpose, which is to give a voice to the marginalized and suppressed by documenting and passing on various facets of Naga history in the form of her historical novels. Another important motive driving Kire to explore and document the history of the Naga people as extensively as possible and as soon as possible is the loss of its richest tradition, namely, the oral tradition. The themes and techniques she works with are heavily inspired by Naga oral tradition through which she ensures its conservation. In this regard, Kire stresses the importance of insider narratives because they reinforce authenticity in the representation of a particular group of people and their worldviews. In re-examining historical events using memory and oral narration as an important means to delve into the past, Kire not only foregrounds oral tradition as a vital source of history but, through the stories, provides a much-needed voice and representation of the ordinary person. Hence, in *ANVR*, it is the perspective of the villagers of Khonoma that she brings to the forefront. She achieves this by writing about the traditional practices, the customary laws and by simply presenting the day-to-day life of the villagers, from the private kitchen hearth to the communal activities such as festivals, hunting, and war. This practice of writing from the perspective of the Naga people, who were the subject of many anthropological works during the peak of British colonization but never given a platform from which to speak for themselves, is seen throughout her works. In *Mari* and *ARW*, she uses sources such as the diary of Mari, the oral narration of Mari herself, of Kire's own mother, of relatives and people who had experienced the war years to document the ordeals of the common Naga people who lived through the world's greatest war, namely, the Second World War. Their side of the story has not yet reached the rest of the world and could, therefore, fade into oblivion if not recorded urgently. Finally, one of the longest political conflicts, the Indo-Naga conflict, which again remains the least talked about conflict in world politics, is highlighted in *BWW*. By tracing its genesis and impact on the people of Nagaland in novels like *ARW* and *BWW*, Kire again successfully documents historical facts, giving them the much-needed coverage that the international media and academics have failed to provide. In this process, Kire's historical novels adopt a powerful stance by identifying and recording issues and concerns that have not found a space in traditional historiography.

WORKS CITED

Groot, Jerome de. *The Historical Novel*. Routledge, 2010.

Kire, Easterine. *Bitter Wormwood*. Zubaan, 2011.

—. "Bitter Wormwood: Interview with Author Easterine Kire." Interview by ICORN. *Sampsonia Way*, 16 Jan. 2012, www.sampsoniaway.org/literary-voices/2012/01/16/bitter-wormwood-interview-with-author-easterine-kir/

—. *A Naga Village Remembered*. Barkweaver Publications and Ura Academy, 2016.

—. *A Respectable Woman*. Zubaan, 2019.

—. "In her own words." *ICORN*, 16 Feb. 2006, www.icorn.org/article/autumn-06-featured-writer-easterine-kire-iralu

—. "Years of listening to stories grows a wealth of knowledge within your spirit: An Interview with the Writer from Nagaland" Interview by Veio Pou. *Scroll.in*, 23 Aug. 2020, scroll.in/article/971141/years-of-listening-to-stories-grows-a-wealth-of-knowledge-within-your-spirit-easterine-kire

—. "Of the Lesser Known." Interview by Sangeeta Barooah Pisharoty. *Nezine*, 11 Feb. 2016, www.nezine.com/info/Of%20the%20lesser%20known

—. "Stories of Nagaland" Interview by Namrata Kolachalam. *Helter-Skelter Magazine*,11 March 2019, helterskelter.in/2019/03/interview-easterine-kire-a-respectable-woman-nagaland/about:blank

—. *Walking the Roadless Road: Exploring the Tribes of Nagaland*. Aleph Book Company, 2019.

—. "War and the Silencing of the Naga Narratives." *Seven Sisters Post*, 13 Nov. 2011, nelitreview.blogspot.com/2011/11/war-and-silencing-of-naga-narratives.html

Pasco, Allan H. "Literature as Historical Archive." *New Literary History*, vol. 35, no. 3, 2004, pp. 373–394. JSTOR, www.jstor.org/stable/20057844.

09

SOVEREIGNTY AND BARE LIFE IN EASTERINE KIRE'S *BITTER WORMWOOD*

Boniface Gaiguilung Kamei

The idea that sovereignty and literature can interface might appear incongruous. After all, they are two separate domains: the former concerned with state laws and governance, and the latter the domain of arts and aesthetics. Despite this chasm, an interface occurs when literature explores ideas of sovereignty. This can happen when literature plays a statist role by romanticising or validating state ideologies. In his study on the poetics of American sovereignty, Andrew Hebard writes that literature offers imaginary situations to readers to help them understand how the state exercises sovereignty through its laws. Hebard cites Owen Wister's novel *The Virginian* (1902), which supports the state's practices and highlights the use of lynching as a necessary and permissible form of governance for the Native Americans in reservation centres (105). Wister's novel can be argued to play a statist role in the production of American sovereignty as it normalises lynching as a part of governing the Native Americans. However, literature of the resistance convention performs an antagonistic role contrary to the statist one. Moving beyond the statist or antagonistic role of literature, Jonathan Arac, in "What is the History of Literature?" argues that certain literary texts are 'national' because they constitute the collective memory of specific national spaces and populations. For instance, Mark Twain's *Adventures of Huckleberry Finn*, which engages with the practice of slavery in America and the highly hierarchal racial relationships, has this national characteristic (30). Texts like *Adventures of Huckleberry Finn* possess a historical agency that makes them a legitimate source for studying a nation's history.

It is in these two frames suggested by Hebard and Arac that the essay will approach Easterine Kire's novel *Bitter Wormwood* to understand the history of sovereignty and how it is exercised in post-colonial India. Here the engagement with sovereignty and the novel's central narrative is not the discourse about a sovereign Naga nation countering the claims of India's sovereignty. Instead, sovereignty is understood in the sense of the declaration of a state of exception and the creation of bare life. Here an engagement with the concept of sovereignty, state of exception, and bare life can provide insights into Kire's novel. The following section will engage with the works of Partha Chatterjee and Giorgio Agamben to get a sense of the history of sovereignty and how the state has exercised it.

SOVEREIGNTY, STATE OF EXCEPTION AND BARE LIFE

In *The Black Hole of Empire*, Partha Chatterjee argues that the concept of sovereignty underwent a radical change in the nineteenth century. This was primarily due to the rise of legal positivism and the normative framework of comparative government. The period witnessed the shift to legal positivism from the universal natural law in the legal domain. The primary distinction between the two is that natural law was based on moral principles and legal positivism on legal acts passed by sovereign state authorities. The change in legal regimes from natural law to positivism was primarily due to the changing political relations between the European powers and Eastern rulers. The increase in the production capacity of the new industrial Western states forced them to expand and acquire territories in Asia and Africa for raw materials and markets. However, this also created the need to develop a legal system based on sovereign agreements to prevent the emergence of a single dominant power or coalition in Europe. The change to legal positivism was also due to the rise of democratic and nationalistic movements in Central and Eastern Europe. The rise in legal positivism also meant the undervaluing of the universal natural law and the Westphalia Treaty that underpinned sovereignty between European powers and non-European rulers (187-89). This change immediately affected the sovereign status of the nations in Asia and Africa because the rulers of these continents governed with laws shaped by religion and culture. Therefore, since these nations did not value the underlying precepts that underpinned the law of Western nations, they could not be regarded as subjects of international positivist law, making sovereignty solely a European concept according to the imperial jurists and theorists. However, this became problematic because the denial of sovereignty to the non-Europeans would mean that treaties the Europeans had engaged in had no legitimacy (192). It is here that the normative framework of comparative government came into play.

Based on a normative comparative government scheme, Europeans would distinguish between civilised and uncivilised. The former consisted of the European nations and settler nations in the Americas, and they constituted the family of nations and the proper subjects of international law. The latter consisted of the rest of the world that did not have proper state formations or legal regimes, and where the rulers ruled with laws shaped by religion and culture. Moreover, since the uncivilised nations had no understanding of the concept of legal positivism, they could not be regarded as subjects of international law (191). The political strategies deployed to normalise vis-à-vis discipline the non-Europeans to the desired standard of governance were through the pedagogies of violence and culture. The former refers to the use of imperial force, and the latter to institutions of education, ideological, legal, social and economic (187). Through this scheme, the non-European entities possessed some degree of sovereignty, but they possessed it only "precisely in order to give it up through a valid legal agreement with a civilised European power" (192). In India, the protectorate system illustrated the contingent and undefined nature of the sovereignty of the non-European states, which was conditional on imperial interest. The protectorate system enabled one state to control another state without taking over the administration of internal affairs. However, the protecting power could take over the internal administration by citing a provision or clause in the treaty or the failure of the native rulers to provide proper governance. Thus, the grounds for the imperial state to intervene were not defined, giving the paramount power the strategic flexibility to frame its policies for the protected states (193). In most instances, the colonial state declared exceptions to intervene in poorly administered or misgoverned territories by using the pedagogical techniques of violence to take over the administration and bring it to the desired normal standard. Alternatively, as Chatterjee puts it, "the imperial prerogative lies in the claim to declare the colonial exception" (194).

In the twentieth and the twenty-first centuries, the declaration of exception has become the paradigm of governance even in modern democratic constitutions. This practice of exception has also been developed as a theory of sovereignty. Carl Schmitt, in his work *Political Theology*, developed his theory of exception in the form of the theory of sovereignty. According to

Schmitt, the "sovereign is he who decides on the state of exception" (as quoted by Agamben in *Homo Sacer*, 11). In other words, sovereignty lies in deciding what constitutes normal order and when and where the norms can be suspended for the state of exception to be proclaimed or declared. The sovereign temporarily suspends the norms or laws to create the conditions required for the law to operate. Therefore, in this sense, the sovereign exception decides what is normal and what is exceptional, and this deciding function makes it the fundamental distinction between what is inside the law and what is outside the law (16-19).

Giorgio Agamben, in his works *Homo Sacer: Sovereign Power and Bare Life* (1995) and *States of Exception* (2003),[1] developed the theory of the 'state of exception', which first appeared in Carl Schmitt's works *Dictatorship* (1921) and *Political Theology* (1922). Agamben posits that the state of exception that suspends the law is not merely a foundational localisation of the normal and exceptional; rather, it has a very ambiguous centre. The state of exception that suspends the law introduces an anomic (normless) zone where what is public and private, law and lawlessness, and order and chaos become indistinguishable (HS 19). The suspension of law entails two things: the expansion of military authority to the civilian space; and the suspension of constitutional safeguards, especially the ones that protect individual liberties (SE 5). Agamben further argues that when the law is suspended, it continues to be in force but without significance. By this, he means that the law neither has any meaning nor positive content, nor does it perform its primary function, which is to protect life (HS 51). Constitutive to this law 'in force without significance' is a force of law, which Agamben writes it as force-of-law, that operates as the rule when the law is suspended.[2] Agamben says that this force-of-law is not the law in the formal sense but rather 'acts' that have the binding force of law. In other words, the decrees and measures taken by the military are not formally laws, but they have the binding power of the law (SE 38). The actions carried out during the exception do not have any juridical determination because the state of exception that is proclaimed by suspending the laws cannot be a juridical fact or right. As Agamben puts it, the actions carried out during the sovereign exception can be described only as 'executing the suspension of the law' (*Ibid* 50).

Agamben also makes the case that the state of exception is a kind of exclusion, and what "is excluded in it is not, on account of being excluded,

---

[1] The two texts by Agamben will be abbreviated as HS for *Homo Sacer*, and SE for *States of Exception* for citation clarity.

[2] Agamben writes the phrase 'force of law' with an erasure as force-of-law. This is to distinguish the force of law in normal condition and in exceptional condition.

absolutely without relation to the rule. On the contrary, what is excluded in the exception maintains itself in relation to the rule in the form of the rule's suspension" (HS 17-18). He further posits that the sovereign ban best exemplifies the structure of the state of exception. What is captured or excluded in the sovereign ban is life. Agamben writes, "He who has been banned is not, in fact, simply set outside the law and made indifferent to it but rather abandoned by it, that is, exposed and threatened on the threshold in which life and law, outside and inside become indistinguishable" (Ibid.28). In the sovereign ban, the subject of the ban is abandoned and exposed to the violence of the force of law. Agamben draws on the figure of the Homo Sacer from ancient Roman law to illustrate the life of the subject of the sovereign ban. The Homo Sacer is a condemned man who can be killed without the act committed against him being considered homicide, but he cannot be used for sacrificial purposes. The Homo Sacer is subjected to double exclusion from profane and theological law. The Homo Sacer is abandoned by the law, or he is outside the purview of the law. He is banned as a sacrificial object, but he continues to be under the rule through the sovereign ban that excluded him. His life is the figure of bare life without any legal status or protection, and this is the figure which Agamben says any individual could be reduced to in a state of exception (HS 71-3). The bare life represents the indistinguishable form of life between *bios* (political life) and *zoe* (simply the natural life of all living beings). The bare life is a form of life that can be described as merely surviving, in contrast to the aesthetics that political and natural life entail.

According to Agamben's concept of the state of exception, the frontier territories of India have been in a permanent state of exception as the state persuasively used the technique of exceptional violence as an emergency or necessary measure to suppress any political unrest that threatened the territorial integrity of the nation. In India, the state of exception manifests in the forms of the Assam Maintenance of Public Order Act (1953), Disturbed Areas Act (1955), Armed Forces Special Power Act (1958), and Defence of India Act (1962). These acts originated during British colonial rule in India as necessary measures to suppress anti-colonial nationalism. Stephen Morton traces the increasing use of emergency law in colonial India to the partition of Bengal in 1905 and the subsequent increase in political assassinations and bombings in Bengal, Maharashtra, and Punjab. These incidents provided grounds for implementing martial law, and, in 1915, the police were given special powers to search and arrest under the Defence of India Act. In 1919, the Rowlatt Act was passed, enabling the use of extra-legal measures not only during war but in any state of emergency (63). The reason why it has remained embedded in post-colonial India is because of the nationalist project of the modern Indian state. Partha Chatterjee in

The Nation and Its Fragment posits that nationalism in India operated in two domains: the material and the spiritual. The material domain refers to modern statecraft, economics, arts, science, and technology. The spiritual refers to cultural areas such as language, national education, family, nation's history and outcaste. The nationalist project in the discourse of nationalism was "to cultivate the material techniques of modern western civilisation while retaining and strengthening the distinctive spiritual essence of the national culture" (120). The project of modern national culture was achieved through the development of native languages, national education (including women's education), the creation of a classical history, and the creation of a synthetic theory of caste based on an ideological ideality of caste. With regard to the material domain of statecraft, the nationalists who represented the new state "chose to retain in a virtually unaltered form the basic structure of the civil service, the police administration, the judiciary, including the codes of civil and criminal law, and the armed forces that existed in the colonial period" (204). This ensured that the Indian state also retained the exceptional colonial acts; and these acts, albeit with some changes, provided the framework for the military to operate in the civilian space and also authorised the military to arrest and detain without a warrant and even kill any individual suspected of engaging in activities threatening the state. The permanent inclusion of exceptional rules with no juridical forms into the rule made it impossible to know the norms and distinguish between lawfulness and lawlessness.

THE INDIAN STATE AND ITS FRONTIERS IN *BITTER WORMWOOD*

The Indian state's relationships with the frontier territories in the formative years of its independence can be best described in the words of Sardar Vallabhbhai Patel to Jawaharlal Nehru. Patel writes, "Our northern or north-eastern approaches consist of Nepal, Bhutan, Sikkim, the Darjeeling and the Tribal Areas in Assam. From the point of view of communications, they are weak spots. Continuous defensive lines do not exist. There is almost an unlimited scope for infiltration. Police protection is limited to a very small number of passes. There too, our outposts do not seem to be fully manned. The contact of these areas with us is, by no means, close and intimate. The people inhabiting these portions have no established loyalty or devotion to India... During the last three years, we have not been able to make any appreciable approaches to the Nagas and other hill-tribes in Assam." He further writes, "in my judgment, therefore, the situation is one in which we cannot afford either complacent or to be vacillating. We must have a clear idea of what we wish to achieve and also of the methods by which we should achieve it. Any faltering or lack of decisiveness in formulating our objectives or pursuing our policy to attain these objectives is bound to weaken us and increase the threats which are so evident" (Chopra and Chopra, 275-79). The problems that the frontier territories posed in independent India were identical to those during colonial rule. The frontiers were not natural territories and were inhabited by communities with little or no social and political affinity with mainland India, yet they were essential for the consolidation and defence of the state.

In the colonial period, the imperial state categorised the frontier as the zone of the different, the primitive, and the backward and unruly, and colonial violence was the only system the savage people on the frontiers were thought to understand. In the second half of the nineteenth century, Punjab was a Non-Regulation Province in the empire's northwest frontier. In the Non-Regulation Province, ordinary law and regulation did not apply unless it was extended by the British India government. Here the colonial official possessed the discretional authority to govern the province and suppress any violent unrest, especially if it threatened the officials. One such law that empowered them was the Murderous Outrageous Act (MOA, 1867). Under this legislation, the legal category 'fanatic' was created based on the frontier people's religion and ethnicity. A person was termed a fanatic if he posed a threat to colonial officials. He could be detained in jail for any period of time, and the rights and procedures provided in the British-Indian Codes, such as the right to legal counsel, the right to appeal a conviction, and rules of evidence, were withdrawn in this case. The logic and rhetoric for deploying such exceptional disciplinary methods were that the frontier was occupied by the primitive and unruly, and any exceptional circumstances legitimised or required exceptional disciplinary methods of sovereign violence as the tactical tool of control (Kolsky 1219- 23). The Indian state's approach to frontier control did not rest on racial differentiation; instead, the methods used to control and secure the frontiers created their own exceptional conditions, laws, and bare life.

Easterine Kire's novel *Bitter Wormwood* characterizes the national in terms of history telling because it considers the history of state institutionalised military rule. Through the experiences of the Nagas, Kire provides a discourse on how the Indian state exercised its sovereignty. These two frames are key to understanding *Bitter Wormwood* as having a historical agency and comprehending the expression of postcolonial sovereignty in India. Through the central protagonist, Moselie, the novel presents the Naga world in its ideal rustic form, with humans living in peaceful coexistence with nature and society. This idyllic world is soon caught up in the whirlwind of two nationalisms: one, the Nagas' aspiration to regain their sovereignty following the end of colonial rule, and two, the territorialization of the Indian nation-state. The former claimed that the Nagas were neither part of India nor subjugated by Indian kings and further justified its claim to be sovereign through the assertion of social and cultural differences. The latter claimed that the Naga Hills were an extension of India that must be secured for defensive purposes and to provide proper governance to people incapable of modern governance. The political deadlock and the descent into the state of exception following the boycott of the 1952 general election and the attempts to submit a memorandum of independence to the Indian political diplomats are captured in the novel. This act of defiance to India's sovereignty by drafting a memorandum of independence justified the Naga nationalists being viewed as threats to the stability of the nation-state. The discretion on the part of the state to order the arrest of Naga nationalists and impose a curfew for the maintenance of law and order marked the beginning of 'exception as the rule'. In the chapter 'The Darkness Descends', Kire consciously attempts to depict the suspension of the law through the imposition of a curfew that marked the inclusion of the exceptional rule into the normal rule. The beginning of the state of exception is described in the following words:

> The headmaster announced at assembly that curfew had been imposed in town...The new law said that if people were seen moving in a group of more than three, they would be arrested immediately. The students understood now that the situation had become very serious. No longer was this just exciting skirmishes with the law that the boys discussed in secretive whispers. It had become something much bigger, and it was rapidly spiraling out of control (59-60).

This event also foreshadows the impending declaration of the Naga Hills as a disturbed area through the Assam Maintenance of Public Order Act, 1953 and Assam Disturbed Area Act, 1955. These acts turned the state apparatus into a surveillance machine monitoring the activities and movements of the people minutely and also suspending the restrictions determining the licit and illicit conduct imposed by law on the police and the army in executing their duties. The repeated manner in which exceptional rules were used for governance manifested in the form of a military occupation that introduced a zone of indistinction in which what was normal and lawful could not be easily distinguished from lawlessness and chaos. This zone of indistinction or the state of exception is an anomic zone or normlessness where the law is suspended but continues to be in force without significance. Here, the law does not perform its primary function, protecting life. By supporting or sympathizing with the Naga nationalists, the people became the subjects of a sovereign ban. In the sovereign ban, life is imprisoned in the zone where the law applies in no longer being applied and is exposed to the violent force of law. Life in the sovereign ban is vividly captured in the novel.

> Mose and Neituo were on their way home when they saw four men being beaten by the army. The men covered their bleeding heads with their hands but the soldiers continued to rain down blows at them. One man lay unconscious on the ground, but the soldiers did not stop kicking him in the head. The two boys ran off as one of the two soldiers shouted out in Hindi, "Hey you two! Stop!" (79).

Two things are evident here: one, the action taken by the army has the force-of-law even though it is not the law in the formal sense; two, living in the sovereign ban is a form of bare life with no legal rights or status. The relationship between the two: the army to whom the sovereign power is delegated and bare life to whom the law applies through suspension as the subject of a sovereign ban is a catastrophic one. To put it in Agamben's words, "the sovereign is the one with respect to whom all men are potentially *Homines Sacri*, and *Homo Sacer* is the one with respect to whom all men act as sovereigns" (HS 84). This relationship is catastrophic because the Homo Sacer who lives a bare life could be killed, and his death, although a murder, would not be considered one because the law defining a certain act as murder or homicide is suspended. The creation of this bare life that is neither *bios* (political life with rights) nor *zoe* (simple natural life of animals and humans) is illustrated by the way in which Moselie's grandmother, Khrienou, was killed and buried. This Kafkaesque atmosphere in which the distinction between human and animal life becomes blurred is described by a fellow villager:

> We have seen them (army) for the past five days in our woods. We thought that if they saw us peacefully cultivating our field, they would not harm us. But when we finished working, there was a shout and they began to shoot towards the fields. We don't know if they were trying to scare us or if they were aiming at us and missing. It happened so fast. One of the shots hit your grandmother. I'm sorry lad; this is such a terrible thing (71).

Through the description of the events leading to Khrienuo's death, Kire conjures up a Kafkaesque atmosphere in which individuals are powerless and unable to comprehend their situation. This lack of certainty and security transforms life into bare life in which an individual cannot resist but only lament their condition. The transformation into bare life is further exemplified when absolute power strips the individual of the politicity[3] tied to language that distinguishes man from other living beings. Language has a supplement of politicity founded on the sense of good and evil, and just and unjust, which is different from the sound or voice of pain and pleasure of other living beings (HS 2-3). The inability of the people to articulate Khrienuo's death in terms of just and unjust is indicative of their being removed as political entities and forced into a bare-naked life that is mere survival. The transformation is pronounced when the "clansmen came and arranged Khrienuo's funeral. There was loud weeping all night" (71). Men who can only weep loudly and not use the language of law exist in the form of a bare life between *bios* and *zoe*. Here Khrienuo represents the Homo Sacer whose death through violence does not constitute a crime because the norm that defines an act of killing as murder or homicide is suspended. Her death and the action of the army that killed her fit Agamben's description, "if we wanted at all costs to give a name to a human action performed under conditions of anomie, we might say that he who acts during the *iustitium*[4] neither executes nor transgress the law, but *inexecutes* (*ineseque*) it" (SE 50). In other words, the action of the army is just an act of executing the suspension of the law and what is in force is the force-of-law that has the binding force of law but is not the law in form and content. The Assam Maintenance of Public Order Act, 1953 and Assam Disturbed Area Act, 1955 appear to empower the police and the armed forces, but the unrestrained powers of the executive come from removing the restrictions of the law by proclaiming the exception that suspends the law.

The state of exception declared during unrest, which temporarily suspends the law to make suitable conditions for the law to be applicable, does not perform this function. Instead, it has become the rule because of the state's obstinate manner of using exceptional rules. In this situation, the norm and the exception become indistinguishable (SE 58). This becomes apparent in Kire's novel from the manner in which India has repeatedly extended the deployment of the Armed Forces (Special Powers) Act, 1958 (AFSPA). The AFSPA in the disturbed areas through which a state of

---

[3] Rights and sense of right and wrong that a political life entails (bios).

[4] Agamben draws on the institution of *Iustitium* in Roman law to distinguish the state of exception from dictatorship, the institutional form through which Carl Schmitt theorized the state of exception. The term *iustitium* means suspension of the law and administration of justice, which is different from dictatorship that requires the appointment of a special magistrate to whom all power is bestowed.

exception is exercised has "the juridico-political system transform itself into a killing machine" (SE 86). In the novel, Neitou's exasperation reveals the condition of living in a state of exception. To quote Neitou, "It is an excuse for the army to kill us; that is all that AFSPA does" (169). With regard to the withdrawal of AFSPA for the normal rule to be reinstated, Neitou puts it, "Feels like we have been asking for that forever. The damnable thing is, these laws are almost impossible to remove once they are in place" (171).Until 2016, The Armed Forces (Special Powers) Act gave legal immunity to the army's actions and left the citizens at the mercy of the army in situations in which what is lawful and unlawful cannot be easily known. This is because the army has the discretionary power to arrest, detain, and even kill any person on mere suspicion or refusal to cooperate. Through her character Neitou, who witnessed the imposition of AFSPA and lived through its rule to see the horizontal spatial expansion of the draconian law to other states of India, Kire makes the case that the frontier territories of the North-east have always been in a state of exception.

Through her novel, *Bitter Wormwood*, Kire creates a discourse against the state military occupation in Nagaland. The discourse that she offers counters the state's narrative. The state covered up its orchestrated violence through censorship and surveillance and came up with the narrative that the military was protecting the people from the rebels. Moreover, it explained that the military was thereon the frontiers as "friends of the hill-people" to prevent the people from being misled by misguided Nagas. The novel as a historical agency provides a counter-narrative to the nation-state building narrative and reveals a history of violence and forced occupation that constitute a part of the history of the political and territorial integration of India. Kire's novel, which can be categorised as resistance literature, can be argued to be playing an antagonistic role in India's nation-building process. The novel narrates a history of India's use of the force-of-law that constructs sovereignty based on absolute and exceptional powers. In other words, the creation of bare life is the originary function of sovereign/ty or the state creates bare life for the assertion of sovereignty, at least in the frontier territories.

WORK CITED

Agamben, Giorgio. *Homo Sacer: Sovereign Power and Bare life*. Translated by Daniel Heller-Roazen. Stanford University Press, 1998.

Agamben, Giorgio. *State of Exception*. Translated by Kevin Attell. University of Chicago Press, 2005.

Arac, Jonathan. "What Is the History of Literature?" *The Uses of Literary History*. Durham, NC: Duke University Press, 1996, pp. 23-34.

Chatterjee, Partha. *The Nation and Its Fragments: Colonial and Postcolonial Histories*. Princeton University Press, 1993.

Chatterjee, Partha. *The Black Hole of Empire: History of a Global Practice of Power*. Princeton University Press, 2012.

Chopra P.N and Chopra Prabha, editors. *The Collected Works of Sardar Vallabhbhai Patel, Vol. XIV (1 January 1949- 31 December 1949)*.Konark Publishers, 1998.

Hebard, Andrew. The Poetics of Sovereignty in American Literature, 1885-1910. Cambridge University Press, 2012.

Kire, Easterine. Bitter Wormwood. Zubaan Books. 2013.

Kolsky, Elizabeth. "The Colonial Rule of Law and the Legal Regime of Exception: Frontier "Fanaticism" and State Violence in British India". *American Historical Review*, vol. 120, no. 4,2015, pp. 1218-1246.

Morton, Stephen. *States of Emergency: Colonialism, Literature and Law*. Liverpool University Press, 2013.

Twain, Mark. *Adventures of Huckleberry Finn*. Harper Press, 2010.

Wister, Owen. *The Virginian: A Horseman of the Plains*. Chelsea House, 2018.

10

BEYOND THE FRONTLINE: LOCATING CONFLICT AND REFIGURATIVE READING OF *A TERRIBLE MATRIARCHY*

Rengleen Kongsong

INTRODUCTION

Literature from the Northeast has often been typecast as belonging to the margin, or simply relegated to a geographical, psychological, and epistemological borderland, thereby marginalizing these voices by simply relegating them to existing stereotypes—as exotic "other" or dismissively labelling them as synonymous voices of conflict literature. These communities, in turn, whose history and civilization has, for many years been devalued because it did not conform to Eurocentric standards of modernity, have taken up the task of re-creating their past and re-inventing tradition so as to represent the present as a stage in the continuous process of marching from the past to the future. Many of these older voices have grown up with shared experiences of the all-consuming multiple political conflicts and have had close proximity to people who experienced and remembered the violence associated with the insurgency and counter-insurgency movements. Meanwhile, the younger groups of writers are continuously embroiled in the contemporary experiential reality of daily incidents of violence that continue to traumatize individuals and society.

The reconstitution of the Angami Literature Committee in 1970 and the subsequent publication of *Kelhoukevira*, seem to have inspired multiple Naga voices to assume the roles of cultural, political, and historical observers, in turn articulating collective consciousness, shared history, and experiential reality in an attempt to negotiate the overwhelming defining marker of Naga identity— the prolonged Indo-Naga political impasse, inflicted upon itself both within and without, with varying "other" ranging from geographical and political "centre", to that of internal "otherization". These emerging voices have articulated pluralistic viewpoints ranging from passive and distant observations to active identification and portrayal. However, contemporary representations by writers such as Temsula Ao, Nini Lungalang, and Easterine Kire have more often than not endeavoured to find a balanced treading ground, where the conflict-ridden immediate past is prefigured, relooked, re-imagined, and recreated or refigured in an attempt to understand and make sense of an otherwise fragmented present and transcend this parochial and limiting valuation and identification thereby redefining and re-configuring the relationship that such all-encompassing Conflict ('Conflict' with capital 'C' from hereon is used to specifically refer to the Indo-Naga conflict and differentiate it from any other conflict/s that may or may not be related) and conflict-effects that have influenced and potentially continue to influence the individual and collective self. Kire's *A Terrible Matriarchy* (subsequently *ATM*) attempts to move beyond the literary representation of the Conflict per se and critique its working dynamics and its interactions with other forms of social and political structures. As a vehement critic of violence on either side of the spectrum, she transcends generic representation and chooses to explicate *systemic* and hegemonic propagation of *objective* violence by ushering the reader into the inner domestic spaces (*home*) of three female characters belonging to three generations inhabiting the same social and historiographical spaces, in turn providing insights into the relationship between the *home* and the outer political space thereby providing a new paradigm of locating conflict and violence.

"I now have [Indian] army friends who called me *didi*" states Kire in a 2006 interview with *Sampsonia Way*. This seemingly common utterance belies the weight of the qualifying "now" in the context of the lexical meaning construction, which is indicative of the impossibility of such a mundane situation before, and hence is a testament to the very "real" perception of the Indian soldier as the "other" and the concrete psychological and social compartmentalization of the *us* and *them* binary. Recalling the circumstances leading to her and her family's exile, she reiterates: "...the conflict took on a much uglier face with the emergence of infighting in the 80s" (*Woman's Panorama*).

> From 2000– early 2005, I personally experienced the stress
> of living at home stalked by armed men at night...tapped
> telephones, every movement of my family closely monitored...
> the horror of sitting up in the night with a double barrel gun
> to protect my children against stalkers...My older daughter
> was traumatized...by a group holding them at gunpoint. Her
> sister came within five meters of being shot...My grown son
> was kidnapped for three days. (*The Storyteller*)

These are only a few of the many instances of the social and political realities that threaten to overshadow one's very existence and humanity. Therefore, having heard, witnessed, and experienced the ugly nature of what she calls uninhibited "gun culture", her initial days of empathy with a justifiable cause seem to have undergone a significant change and an effort to address that through her writing serves as an attempt to mediate the Conflict. The paper intends to explore the author's position as an *insider* in exile, thereby presenting a critical outsider's perspective of the Conflict navigating a seemingly "treacherous", but measured reconciliation of lived experiential reality and collective memory in the process of personal and collective mediation and consequently articulating a new framework of locating conflict. It will do so by exploring how geographical *distanciation* allows her to employ *emplotment* as a configurative and *refigurative* narrative tool to articulate the narrative "self" and the narrative discourse. The aporetic and polysemantic possibility of meaning construction in her post-exilic novel *ATM*, a literature of diaspora, becomes an important site through which one can examine this.

CONTEXTUALIZING CONFLICT: LOCATING CONFLICT IN ATM

Conflict theory generally posits loss or deprivation at the root. In the Indo-Naga context, the persistent deprivations of one's culture, tradition, history, a way of life, loss of basic rights, and the right to rights, which are constantly threatened by armed tussles and repressive state apparatuses like the Armed Forces Special Powers Act (1958) are some of the more prominent examples. The constant presence of military power made the region a zone of conflict resembling what Agamben, Primo Levi and Michael Taussig variously refer to as a *state of exception*, *grey zone*, or *space of death*, respectively. Rhetoric such as "war against terror", or "a war to end all wars" only serve the larger interest of the people in power and markets the cause, in a very capitalistic sense, as one that transcends the body, the individuals, and the everyday ordinary issues of its subjects. Just as the "great" wars were fought in order to "defeat" oppression, protect human rights, and defend freedom and liberty, similarly, the conflict in the Northeast has assumed dramatic proportions in its magnitude due to claims of national integrity and nationalism on the one hand and counter-claims of ethno-nationalism, illegal annexation, and marginalization by a bullish neo-colonial enterprise of modern state-making project, on the other. Hence, the shadow lines demarcating states have become seemingly unsurmountable emotional and psychological barriers, whereby processes of continuous inclusion and exclusion are initiated, compartmentalizing the "us" and "them" binary more rigidly. Thus, the very idea of this conflict, irrespective of the writer's political ideology, is also embedded within the language of the narrative itself and is inseparable from the "self". This inherent *internality* of this external conflict produces further marginalization of the subjects reeling under its effects where the personal and collective "self" itself becomes the story and vice versa, albeit in a tenebrous figuration of the narrative identity.

A bildungsroman traversing the journey of its protagonist Dielieno in a large Angami family, *A Terrible Matriarchy* takes the audience along a series of events forcing Lieno, as she is affectionately referred to, to grow up before her time. The novel shows how her childhood is divided between unending household chores at her grandmother's, and later, at the tender age of eleven and a half, she has to assume the responsibilities of an incapacitated mother at home. These circumstantial realities consequently force young Lieno to try and make sense of a complicated and insensible adult world, taking the readers on a journey of *bildung* not only of the protagonist but of the entire community.

The narrative offers a glimpse of the inner worlds of three generations of women, each trying to steadfastly hold onto their beliefs and value system. The grandmother symbolising the "terrible matriarch" in the novel, believes that empowering a girl child should mean teaching her how to take care of household chores which would put her in good stead later in life as a dutiful wife and a good mother. She believes that boys are overburdened with the tasks of looking after the village, continuing the lineage, and protecting the women in the house. Lieno, on the other hand, is portrayed as this fierce, free-spirited young Angami girl who is passionate about school and envies every privilege enjoyed by her four brothers and actively resists the "taming" of her woman self. Lieno's mother, Nino, on the other hand, is juxtaposed between these two competing value systems— her beliefs reflective of the progress the Angami society had witnessed in the aftermath of India's Independence. As such, while she understands the views of Vibano, her mother-in-law, she is also aware of the needs and aspirations of new emancipated female members of society.

At the outset, the narrative is deeply occupied with the internal world of these women characters, which is seemingly shielded from the world outside.

Occasional surreptitious glimpses of the external reality are presented in the form of quiet whispers and quick conversations in hushed tones, making the conflict simultaneously palpable yet paradoxically invisible, or at least meant to be, to the characters and the prying eyes of the readers. The first instance of the *presence* in the novel is conveyed through a voyeuristic moment where the inquisitive sixteen-year-old protagonist overhears a "shielded" conversation between her father and brother discussing the fate of sixteen captured recruits around 1970 (the grandmother, born in 1890, just turned 80 that May) when the atmosphere was filled with the fervour of nationalism, especially amongst the Naga youth. This reminded her of the similar atrocities meted out by the army that continue to shape her lived experience and those of others around her. Violence lurks all around the child protagonist in the sense that it informs every action and decision around her while the adults in her life attempt to conceal and demarcate those seemingly separate worlds. This attempt to shield and conceal the Conflict and its effects on the "vulnerable" population in the narrative is also symbolically mirrored in the sporadic mentions of the political actions of the outside world at the level of the text, where admittedly only three chapters actively allude to such events or their effects in the lives of the protagonists.

Presenting the reality from the perspective of a girl child, the seemingly rare *presence* to which the narrator, and the reader, are witnesses functions as narrative aporia where this un/intentional *symbolic* slip offers the reader a relational interpretation. Ricoeur refers to this as *prefigured experience*, where received experiences and memory of the past configure the temporal present action providing a possibility of *figurative* reading of the all-invasive and pervasive nature of the conflict no matter how demarcated the world seems to be. The relative absence of its representation elevates the visibility of the all-pervasive aspect of the Conflict, which is at once fully present in its representational absence. Moreover, the truth of the reality is all the more revealing in its absented *presence*, whereby the absence itself functions as a simulacrum of the Conflict. Thus, it will be pertinent to look at the physical, psychological, geographical, and temporal spaces where conflict and its effects reside vis-a-vis the narrative.

CONFLICT AND OBJECTIVE VIOLENCE:

Žižek identifies two broad structures of violence: *objective* and *subjective*. He further categorizes *objective* violence into *symbolic* and *systemic* forms. These forms of violence are not only ubiquitous; they are also structured, naturally powerful, and deeply entrenched in almost every society as they are embodied in languages and their forms and also embedded in the functioning of economic and political systems. However, Žižek argues that the seeming "brutality" of *subjective* violence, such as is evident at times of conflict, offers a disguise under which *objective* violence is protected, upheld and hegemonically proliferated. In the context of the narrative in *ATM*, *subjective* violence emanating from the Conflict has relegated the perception and quotidian prevalence of *objective* violence, such as patriarchy, gender differentiation, and its sub-forms, as a normative that requires participative social and cultural preservation, even escaping the powerful and insightful gaze of the matriarch or the prying eyes of the gossiping aunts. In a way, the all-encompassing nature of the subjective violence that conflict produces becomes the basis for justifying patriarchal values and beliefs upheld by even the best-intentioned. Those values, in turn, justify the further marginalization and subjugation of the already oppressed. Very often, frustrations and bloodshed associated with the "external" conflict are deposited onto the women in the family—the marginalized and sacrificial scapegoats of society. The call to extremism and militarization in the aftermath of the arrival of factions in the Indo-Naga saga, surreptitiously but prepensely inserted into the narrative in Chapter Seventeen of the book, led to further marginalization of Naga women, in particular, inhibiting their participation in a conflict that was clearly divided along gender lines. Nādirah in *Militarization and Violence against Women in Conflict Zones in the Middle East: A Palestinian Case Study* theorizes that every act in a conflict zone is "affected by, dependent on, and mobilized by militaristic values" (3) further masculinizing patriarchal powers, which actively draw hegemonic dispensation from such conflict.

Another important aspect vis-à-vis patriarchy that the novel addresses is how patriarchy as a power structure interacts with other forms of political power structures. In the Preface to the second edition of the book, Kire posits the breakdown and displacement resulting from the political conflict as the main causes of alcoholism, unemployment, and other societal vices. "Alcoholism has other causes in the Naga situation, yet all are interrelated to the political climate of the state." She goes on to say:

> "The fallout of the occupation is visible in many of the social
> evils rampant today in Naga society: corruption and nepotism,
> factional killings, sexual crimes and economic instability...for
> the deep violence seen in the streets—brawling that spill over
> into domestic violence." (X)

This relation between ostensibly disparate power structures in the text is explored in Chapters Twenty-three and Twenty-four. Vini aptly symbolizes the abusive nature of internal violence within conflict zones and becomes a caricature of how *systemic* violence becomes complicit with *subjective* violence to further oppress the already-oppressed sections of society. His violent brawling habits on the streets often spill into his domestic life, where his wife, Nisano becomes a frequent victim of his violent temper. The violence outside is literally and symbolically brought to the domestic milieu, shattering the comfortable compartmentalization of an erstwhile imagined reality. This physical invasion of the sacrosanct and sacred interior of the *home* symbolically tears down the wall and exposes the fragility of the *imagined* reality of the division while denoting a metaphorical *symbolic* order in the *bildung* of the protagonist and the reader. Lying on a hospital bed, Vini asks Leto: "Do you want to know why I drink, why all of us drink and brawl? Because life here in Kohima is so meaningless." (225). This existential meaninglessness, stemming from a sense of helplessness of not being able to contribute towards the Naga cause, is redirected in the forms of alcoholism, street brawls, and ultimately towards his wife—the sense of "impotence" in the external front being satisfied within the domestic sphere becoming, in the process, an ironic caricature of what motivated him to take up arms against the Indian army in the first place. He turned his marriage into a site of abuse, making Nisano's body a hapless weapon for him to defend his masculinity. Violence against Naga women, in the form of rape and murder, enrages Vini. Yet, he ironically becomes another tormentor to his wife, forcing her to move out of the literal and metaphorical *home*. Wing argues that "during conditions of occupation and political oppression, men within an oppressed group feel emasculated...and so resort to expressing their maleness by exerting their frustration through women in their private sphere." (Nādirah 69) Similarly, Loraine Dowler, writing in the context of West Belfast, claims that politically conflicted zones sometimes provide ground for "hypermasculinity". Men assume a socially irresponsible identity devoid of human emotions, while women are often expected to play a passive part in the stereotypical role of a subservient and subordinated woman. (127) Hence, under the influence of overtly numbing physical and psychological experiences that are increasingly overpowering, subsuming its subjects and redefining normativity, various power structures, such as patriarchy, find ways to assume more violent textures and spread their influence. Thus, modern conflict theory characterizes conflict as not a disruption of an existing system but rather a structure under which various existing social structures, such as patriarchy, emulate, reconfigure, restructure themselves, and interact with other oppressive elements of the conflict. These further marginalize and subjugate women in multiple ways and silence their existential voices of victimization, resistance, and survival.

The violence co-opts everyone into its downward spiralling slippery slope—there are no in-between spaces for any of its subjects. External political violence is inevitably reflected in social and personal space. Consequently, the micro-politics of resistance in the domestic front influences and is as potent as the macro-politics of military rebellion in the public space. The inclination to dismiss women's participation in the struggle as one of incomprehension and the subsequent relegation of their experiences of victimhood and narratives of resistance and survival as literal and symbolic "gossip" is subverted in the narrative in the forms of the transgressive acts of characters like Lieno, Nino, and Nisano. They continue to take charge of their lives and persevere on their path to education and empowerment and walk out of abusive domestic environments if and when needed. The narrative chooses to critique this "domestic militancy" by illustrating that patriarchy exercises its stranglehold upon many societies and has continued to survive in different forms over the ages, irrespective of any progress or modernity, precisely because of the complex interconnected and hegemonic dispensation of its power. Therefore, Lieno's protests against her grandmother are indirect protests against this hegemony. Her objectives interrogate the normative standards and the new status quo that has somehow managed to internalize and uphold patriarchy, even in the wake of modernity and women's empowerment in a Naga society that is on the verge of a new realization.

CONFLICT AND WOMEN'S BODIES

The social, cultural and economic location of a zone of conflict is, more often than not, actualized through military state apparatuses thereby creating a narrative discourse where militarism becomes a salient expression of its existence as well as paradigms for its societal imaginary wherein the history of the occupation is concealed under the mythography of security. As such, conflict in confluence with other power structures manufactures rhetoric based on nationalism, security, and cultural preservation equating its subjects (often its "most" vulnerable subjects, the women population by way of structural dispensation as discussed above) such as women and their bodies with veritable zones of conflict. Notions of a pre-*culpa* assignation of the motherland as chaste and sacrosanct delineate women's lives and bodies into boundary markers and sites of violence, transforming them into *exceptions* and *bare lives* vulnerable to brutal racialized and gendered measures based on *bio-politics*. In fact, there is no better illustration of the deployment of *bio-politics* in conflict zones than a systemic annihilation of women's lives and bodies, used as targets to expedite and "teach a lesson" to the whole community, particularly in the realm of the public space symbolically translates to an invasion of the sanctity and sacredness of the "pure" woman's body – the imagined *home* designated by patriarchy, which it vows to protect. Breaking down that protection by the enemy hence becomes a potent military weapon, and a number of direct and indirect references to this are narrated throughout the novel. The "truthful" narration of such incidents through passing remarks or hushed conversations conveys an illusion of *absence* only to be elevated by the occasional narratorial *presence* to emphasize the idea associated with this constructed *need* to uphold patriarchal notions of equating the female body to interior domestic space, bequeathed with notions of *home* with "honour", necessitating male protection and *shielding* of that world by the male characters in the novel. Hence, as articulated through the matriarch's voice, boys are needed for the "important" things in life, which include protecting the weak and vulnerable in society, which is equated with protecting the home. Consequently, Vini's rhetoric and justification for his and his friends' actions are all premised on that same supposed male and community pride. This becomes a lot more prominent when the male-only inheritance system in the narratorial context is juxtaposed with the leitmotif of constant *going* and *coming* for female characters symbolizing literal and metaphorical attempts at transcending these constructed identifications: Lieno leaving home to stay with her grandmother only to come back home later in the narrative; Nisano moving out and finding a home later in life; the heirless and hence homeless Bano eventually finding a home when Vibano leaves for her heavenly abode, and so on. Thus, the female characters can only find a "home" when they seem to leave these imposed identity markers.

SUBJECTS IN CONFLICT OR CONFLICTING SUBJECTS?

As illustrated in the novel, the male ego looks for a scapegoat in the form of the most vulnerable in society and finds one in the wife/daughter/ or "ill-reputed" woman. In contrast, women have no option but to try and cope with every obstacle, along with the added burden of looking after the men in the family. Girard characterizes this scapegoat concept as an attempt at collective *meconnaisance* or a misrecognition to divert the violence from the original target. Both Agamben and Girard are cognizant of the lack of sacredness associated with the idea of *scapegoating* in modern conflict as a theoretical or philosophical concept (as might have been the case in the Biblical story); yet, a similar notion of this scapegoat continues to exist in the form of the subaltern and the marginalized in society. This especially affects women, who are the modern repositories of this misrecognition. Thus the status quo is prolonged as a weapon of war to heighten the notion of victimhood, which *objective* violence chooses to appropriate, consequently reducing women's bodies to sites of contestation through which highly gendered power structures assert themselves.

The gendered structure of Naga society (rendered more so by the conflict) means, in an ironically hegemonic way, that the womenfolk become responsible for the smooth functioning of the society. Daily existential activities such as starting the kitchen fire in the morning, cooking, cleaning, fetching water, nurturing the children, and looking after older parents become more or less the sole responsibility of the female/s in the house, as is amply illustrated in *ATM*. Paul Pimomo states that the women characters in the novel, *like all Naga girls* [emphasis added], "are the keepers as well as the reformers of the traditional practices that marginalize them, the preservers of social etiquette and the upholder of the community's virtues."(Kire 292) The "terrible" matriarch Vibano, a victim of that same patrilineal structure herself, becomes the repository of traditional patriarchal values. Further, she internalizes these values to the extent that she, in turn, becomes an unconscious advocate and preserver of the power structure that she so resents. The fact that she has been mentally scarred enough to adopt a differential attitude towards a girl and a boy child, where the boys in a family are believed to be protectors of not only the family but the village/community, is a testament to the internalization of such value system in society. According to Coser, conflict makes any arbitrary division more robust: "conflict sets boundaries between groups within a social system by strengthening group consciousness and awareness of separateness, thus establishing the identity of groups within the system" (Corwin 34). Hence, at a time of conflict where arbitrary gender values and boundaries are heightened, women in society are further expected to assume this untenable position of standing up for themselves and their rights while also ironically assigned the responsibility of upholding existing value systems and *normalizing* and maintaining normalcy in an otherwise fragmented and disrupted environment. Lieno is constantly reminded by her mother about how her desire to break free is as legitimate as her grandmother's attempt to "tame" her and how it becomes her responsibility to sieve and weave through that apparent contradiction. This inherent aporia is illustrated through the journeys of the other female characters—the "gossip aunts" at the village well, the fate of the heirless Vibano, the marriage-less Bano, the widowed Nisano, and so on, exemplifying this *unliveable* existential reality.

Nancy Scheper-Hughes qualifies conflict as a "slippery concept—nonlinear, productive, destructive, and reproductive" spreading like spirals linked in chains, often mimetic of a "desired model" and producing a continuum of violence. Violence only begets further violence, and, in a way, Vini and his friends' violence on the street is reminiscent of the violence meted out on either side of the spectrum. Interestingly both the insurgency and counter-insurgency movements became the very things they each sought to suppress in an ironically mimetic way. This is further replicated by people like Vini and Rocky and exacerbated by a sense of heightened patriarchy and hypermasculinity. These elements become cogs in the wheel of the endless cycle of violence to the extent that, after a certain point, the approximation of it becomes extremely close, leading to a position of indistinctness where one could very well be substituted for the other, producing more antagonism and conflicts as more individuals and groups get mimetically drawn into the circle of desire. Girard claims that in due course, the object of desire is eventually forgotten, and the groups only imitate each other's antagonism, and a continuous cycle of violence ensues. This is a particularly painful existential reality for Kire who experienced and continues to witness violence associated with the conflict. In her own words, Kire talks about how the grand design and the initial fervour of nationalism that swept the region in the early phase of the struggle were eventually reduced to an indistinguishable enemy where the "us" and "them" eventually culminated into a self-otherization, and the grand design was reduced to disillusionment. She believes that the beginning of the conflict evoked profound feelings and the poetry of the time "bled, touching chords in non-Naga hearts." (*Through a Poet's Eyes*). However, the great right cause is now "wandering in the wilderness of political betrayal and suppression by India and the curse of ideological divisions among Nagas themselves".

LOCATING CONFLICT IN THE INTERSTICES:

It is important to realize that it is not just the physicality and materiality of the violence that qualifies as violence from the conflict, it is also the disruption of everyday lives, routines, works, fear, and tension that creeps into the minds of ordinary citizens, that is as destructive and complicit with other forms of conflict. Violence resides in the interruptions and reversals of the expected and predictable proceedings of daily lives, inflicting terror on the ontological security of the subjects' lives. Disruption of existing economic, social, and cultural activities, disrupted gender equation, interrupted flow of social and familial events, uprooting of the sanctity of the grandmother's hearth, to name a few, all lead to a sense of unrecognizability. The fact that existing schedules and ways of life have to be altered amidst the looming presence of an altogether superior alien force creates the need to imagine a new norm. This further necessitates a revision of the role and position that subjects occupy in society and a re-imagination of the self.

All the characters in the novel are forced to deal with this new normative in their own different ways, and inevitably, more often than not, a few individuals come out of it less embittered and broken. Despite being forced to skip her childhood altogether and ushered into a world of adult responsibilities, Lieno dug deep within herself to make the best of the situation. Likewise, Leto and others did to a certain extent. However, there are equally, if not more, many Vinis and Rockys, who, left to cope on their own, just fall by the wayside and seek out destructive outlets to vent their anger and helplessness.

Vini's voice as the narrator of the conflict within the narrative also presents interesting problematics. His coming-of-age moments before his eventual demise as a repentant individual serve as an aporia within the text. His voice is, at one level, the voice of a concerned and involved Naga, particularly during the initial years of the struggle, but at the same time, it cannot be construed as singularly representative. His rhetorical questions, hitherto addressed to his family and Leto, in particular, reverberate with shared sentiments of hurt and wounded pride, instilling a desire to act, while at the same time, his ways are not necessarily a representation of the collective sentiment. Rather, he is presented within the narrative as someone misguided, misappropriating his lived and shared realities as the totalizing truth of the struggle and casting doubts on the truthfulness of his position as a witness and collective conscience. He is subtly portrayed as resembling one of Yeats' "worst [who] are full of passionate intensity", while others like Leto could be construed as representing disassociation and disillusion while trying to find fulfilment elsewhere. This presence of discordant and contradictory voices, which are paradoxically cohesive, is symbolic of the gaps that lurk between contrasting sentiments, geographical and temporal spaces, and competing loyalties. Vini becomes an embodiment of a subject that conceptualizes his identity and self within the narrow construction of singularity and binary opposites—the almighty *us* against the myriad *them*, a narrow perception of a hitherto fragmented, pluralistic, and hybrid existential reality that post-modern and post-colonial individuals are subjected to apart from the further identity-scattering effect of conflict. Thus, his voice becomes submerged in the rhetoric of hate and vengeance, echoing a parochial version of victimhood. As such, he becomes a paradigmatic figure in which the author critiques the need to transcend the all-totalizing and unitary identity marker that has shaped, continues to shape, and subsumed the story of the Naga people. Rather, the author locates the narrative identity in the psychological and sociological reality beyond the realm of the ugly politics of the conflict-ridden outer space and resists being defined by its totalizing nature. She would prefer to bring out the narratives of gaps that lurk behind and beside the political drama, a deliberate act of *distanciation* and political disassociation. In other words, it is an attempt to voice the interstices, the underbelly of the narratives that get submerged within a larger monopolizing voice of the Conflict.

VICTIM AS WITNESS

Many of the characters in the novel, like the author, are simultaneously unwilling or reluctant victims, as well as witnesses to the conflict. As such, the different ways in which the conflict and its myriad effects interact with a character inform the subjects' subjective perception and articulation of the same. The subjective nature of these responses lends plurality and multiplicity of voices either as victims or as subjects or both and consequently culminates in the subjects' ultimate fate. Sometimes, as in characters such as Vini, multiple voices can haunt the same subject at the same time or at different phases in the character's life. This multiplicity of differing voices is a testament to the impossibility of being a victim as well as a witness and the enormity of the task involved in being an unwilling stakeholder in both.

Agamben argues that comprehending *Muselmann*-like witnesses such as Vini requires the realization that the value of testimony lies essentially in what it lacks; at its centre, it contains something that cannot be borne witness to. Kire asserts that the horror had taken the people beyond words and into the silence of inexpressible pain. The fundamental task then of a witness becomes that of the impossibility of witnessing oneself, of a notion of non-responsibility, not in the sense of nihilistic amorality, but rather non-responsibility as a confrontation with a responsibility that is greater than one could ever assume; hence *unassumable* in nature. However, this is an intrinsic form of *unassumability*, which lends validity to it, and *asserts* its very *unassumability*. Alexander Hirsch summarizes this responsibility of witnessing as one borne out of a condition of unattainability, though unavoidable, unachievable, and yet interminable. The polysemic possibilities of interpretations induced by the presence of fissures and disjunction in the authorial voice provide a truthfulness in that it may be a fictionalization of historical truth, but in its very factual unreliability and inconsistency, the truth is implicated. Žižek claims that "if the victims were able to report on their painful and humiliating experiences in a clear manner, with all the data arranged in a consistent order, this very quality would make us suspicious of its truth." (4) Kire navigates the conundrum emerging from this duality through simultaneous association and disassociation. Her association is reflected in her rootedness to her consanguinity in the story she tells, and her dissociation emanates from her altered and hitherto newly acquired frame of reference—distant and inward-looking rather than outward-projecting.

ASSOCIATED *DISTANTIATION* AS CONFLICT MEDIATION AND *REFIGURATION*

Although multiple conflicts have uprooted the literal as well as the metaphorical "grandmother's hearth" and, with it, the conditions for its survival, as a first-generation diaspora, Kire fondly harps on the ties that bind her to her native land. Her stories are drawn from disparate fragments, sieved through, distilled, and contemplated upon to form a whole and, as such, her voice eternally echoes sentiments of the past and present, where the present is also rooted in the richness of the past, whereby cultural association remains immanent enriching the narrative associatively. As such, the subjects within and without the narrative are at once the same, albeit separated by time, layers of memory and generations of experiential reality. Parag M. Sarma reiterates similar sentiments when analysing literature from the Northeast: "rooted as they [narratives] are in the community, [they] can never be of pure self-expression, but to bring isolated private self into harmony with the larger ethnic world." (43) Hence, narrative dissonance and gaps, where immanent, are filled by a *refigurative* reading by subjects with shared experiences, collective consciousness, and memory, constantly navigating between form and content, between individual and society, and between politics and aesthetics.

Kire mentions the idea of the "self" becoming a "treasure trove of knowledge sitting within one's spirit, waiting to be pulled out." (*Scroll*) This storied self, which is a repository of memory, nostalgia, lived experience, inherited values, and experiential reality, is then *reconfigured* with a stamp of ownership wherein the fragmented otherness of the received and storied past is taken up through what Ricoeur calls *emplotment*. This is simultaneously a receptive and creative process of imaginative transference and assimilation of the past into linguistic form. *Emplotment* entails a receptive prefiguration of lived diversity of temporal experiences and creatively configures such historical elements into narrative unity or unifying plots in order to refigure our experience in the process of locating ourselves as subjects and readers in the narrative discourse. Kire attempts to capture the dynamic character of the relationship between a pre-understanding of the received world, its meaning construction, its symbolic resources, and its temporal character, to that of its refiguration of the world of the text to that of the reader. Her narratives offer an intimate and necessary connection and mediation between the stories her subject knows, tells, and receives and the structure of human experience from which they arise and to which they return. This results in reorganizing and refiguring the assimilation of the interconnected experience of the present into more meaningful patterns, where the past assumes a lived dimension of contemporariness and reconfiguring expectations of the future. It is with this responsibility that Kire gave voice to these, at once real (with real inspirations) and fictive, visibly identifiable marginalized subjects and narratives in her works, locating them in the midst of the overwhelmingly dehumanizing conflict that has forcefully entered every Naga life, without replicating or perpetuating it—carried out with proper distance from the subjects—not so close so as to convey only a sense of pity, contempt or public spectacle; yet not so distant so as to objectify it. This is accomplished without overtly aestheticizing or entering into the rhetoric of politics and polemics. This is the delicate balance that she seeks—putting herself on the side of humanity by being sympathetic and by being one of them, and yet engaged in truthful witnessing—of being there with them: a cathartic position of what can be termed as *associated disassociation*.

The characters tell us their stories and truths as they must and do it as best as they can. The validity and veracity of those truths are best left to the readers and stakeholders to adjudicate. Perhaps the process of telling itself trivialises the obsession with the former. Likewise, Kire continues to tell us these stories, not because its power lies in its truthfulness but rather in its telling. Achebe talks about the need for writers from newly independent countries to transcend the role of being a traditional literary writer as defined by western literature and reading audience and rather embrace the added responsibility of being a political, social and cultural historian, among others. Likewise, Kynpham Sing Nongkynrih, in *Dancing Earth: An Anthology of Poetry from North-East India*, states: "the writer from the Northeast... living with the menace of gun he cannot merely indulge in verbal wizardry and woolly aesthetics but must perforce master the art of witness". This act of witnessing is often a recollection of what Temsula Ao calls a "memory of pain", of one's own self and of others. Kire is able to effectively navigate this through a position of disassociation—unintentional as well as intentional *distanciation* in the form of her political and ideological exile. Edward Said in *Reflections on Exile and Other Essays* states:

> "Exile can produce rancour and regret, as well as a sharpened vision. What has been left behind may either be mourned, or it can be used to provide a different set of lenses. Since... exile and memory go together, it is what one remembers of the past and how one remembers it that determines how one sees the future". (XXV)

ATM narrates Kire's subjectivity in a literal and metaphorical new home, reflecting her position as a critical insider looking inwardly from a geographical and ideological distance in an attempt to maintain objectivity by resisting the all-consuming stereotype of falling prey to the "'mega-narrative' that silences all other narratives" and she states:

> "The one year in a city of refuge... I am now able to admit and talk about the long-term damage to my people the years of protracted conflict have inflicted... has given me the distance I needed to become an objective writer and thinker." (ICORN)

The palpably disillusioned voice brought about by this *distanciation*, both deliberate and otherwise (her political exile being a forced one), treads a path between a conscious rerouting from the brutality of the Conflict and one that advocates a "solution"—a mediation through a refusal to cater to its all-consuming nature; a studied refusal to adhere to a stereotypical representation of the self as inhabiting a strife-torn region, and only spewing off revolutionary rhetoric and propagandist literature. Kire asserts this through symbolic and metaphorical exile as a form of retreating to a world of an *inner émigré* where the personal *daimon* is politically *deterritorialized*, "free from all procession" in order to find a *home* in *homelessness*. Choosing this form of exile, perhaps aided by her political exile, is to function within a mechanics of distancing, removal from the familiar, an imaginative journey to another stratum of being away from one's usual frame of reference in order to find a "home", a poetic home, a "place of writing" that remains disaffected by the system. This act of *distanciation*, as a way of writing distances, and writing from a distance, displaces, and de-familiarizes the author, insulating and transporting her within an elsewhere that produces a more objective perspective. This is the inherent quality of exile that both Joyce and Heaney talk about as a "'homecoming', a freeing and empowering element that appeals to universalism while being rooted in tradition, space and time." (Niekrasz)

Žižek states that when dealing with the representation of violence, there is a thin line between participating in its horror, on the one hand, and oversimplifying or portraying an inaccurate description of it, on the other: "The overpowering horror of violent acts and empathy with the victims inexorably function as a lure which prevents us from thinking." (4) Yet, on the other hand, "there is a sense in which a cold analysis of violence somehow reproduces and participates in its horror." (4) Just as her characters have no escape from their histories, so is her act of *authoring*, not one of political exorcism but an act of mediating and reconfiguration. In the absence of formal written history, writers across the world with similar relations with colonialism and neo-colonialism assume the role of articulating past traditions and history, giving voice to silences and absences, with as little adornment, exaggeration or pretension, but honest, empowered voices that are otherwise suppressed or unheard in the annals of formal history-making, in order to emancipate the collective "self" from various strands of political interpolation, ideology, and parochialism. Such an act of subversion redefines the *story* in *history*, transcending the existing defined domain. This disruption and escape from existing structures and value systems, in turn, give rise to recognizing alternate spaces as active sites of contests and resistance through the creation of counter spaces and identities outside the measuring yardstick of patriarchy and other defined power structures, thereby producing new forms of heroism, bravery, and courage, often relocating existing tales of victimhood as one of survival and marginalized subject as resisters and *frontliners*. This disruption, as Nidirah argues, also becomes the agency for marginalized subjects in society, such as women allowing them to open new paths, speak up, interact, and network, challenging existing structures of oppression, thereby creating alternate spaces and countermeasures. She designates such spaces as the battle's "frontline" and posits such subjects as *frontliners*. Therefore, just as conflict and its effects have the ability to seep into the interstices and reside in unusual places, so would our ability for a balanced mediation of the same depend upon our ability to locate these spaces as shown in *ATM* as a way to reconfigure the subject figure within and without the novel thereby equipping one with the possibility of *refigurative* reading and understanding of the legacy of the past, however, devalued and fragmented, as a way of negotiating the present and revisioning new possibilities.

WORKS CITED

Agamben, Giorgio. *Homo Sacer: Sovereign Power and Bare Life*. Translated by Daniel Heller-Roazen. Stanford University Press, 1998.

~~. *Remnants of Auschwitz: The Witness and the Archive.* Translated by Daniel Heller-Roazen. Zone Books, New York, 1999.

~~. *State of Exception.* Translated by Kevin Attel. University of Chicago Press, 2005.

Corwin, Alan. "Conflict and Critical Theories Part I: Conflict Theory: Lewis Coser (1913-2003) Ralf Dahrendorf (1929–) Randall Collins (1941–)" www.corwin.com/upmdata/13636_Chapter7.pdf. Accessed 05th June 2015.

Critchley, Simon. Review: "A dream of divine violence". *The Independent*, Friday, 11thJan, 2008. www.independent.co.uk/arts-entertainment/books/reviews/violence-by-slavoj-Žižek-769535.html. Accessed 05th June 2015.

Depoortee, Friederiek. "Reading Giorgio Agamben's *Homo Sacer* with Rene Girard. *Philosophy Today* 56.2 (2012): 154-163. Accessed 13th June 2015.

Gray, John. Review: "The Violent Visions of Slavoj Žižek", *The New York Review of Books.* www.nybooks.com/articles/archives/2012/jul/12/violent-visions-slavoj-Žižek/. Accessed 6th June 2015.

Hirsch, Alexander. *Theorising Post Conflict Reconciliation: Agonism, Restitution and Repair.* Routledge, New York, 2012.

Kire, Easterine. *A Terrible Matriarchy.* Zubaan, New Delhi, 2007.

~~. "Bitter Wormwood: Interview with Author Easterine Kire", Interview, *Sampsonia Way.* ICORN, January 16, 2012. www.sampsoniaway.org/literary-voices/2012/01/16/bitter-wormwood-interview-with-author-easterine-kire/. Accessed 05th March 2015.

~~. **Interview with** Stricklan, Kate. **International Cities of Refuge Network (ICORN), January, 2012;** http://icorn.org/ . Accessed 03rd Jan 2015.

~~. "The Conflict in Nagaland: Through a Poet's Eye". *Skarven Magazine.* Tromso, Norway, 2004. nagas.sytes.net/~kaka/articles/art006.html. Accessed 3rd Jan 2015.

~~. "Years of Listening to Stories Grows a Wealth of Knowledge Within your Spirit" Easterine Kire". Interview with Veio Pou. Scroll.in, August 23, 2020. scroll.in/article/971141/years-of-listening-to-stories-grows-a-wealth-of-knowledge-within-your-spirit-easterine-kire. Accessed 30th Aug 2015.

~~. The Women with the Golden Pen, *Woman's Panorama. womanspanorama.com/index.phpoption=com_content&view=article&id=504:easterine-kire-iralu-the-woman-with-the-golden-pen&catid=11:otherarticles&Itemid=17.* Accessed 03rd June 2021.

Lawrence, Bruce B and Aisha Karim. *On Violence: A Reader.* Duke University Press, Durham and London, 2007.

Ngangom, Robin and Kynpham Sing Nongkynrih, editors. *Dancing Earth: An Anthology of Poetry from North-East India.* Penguin, New Delhi, 2009.

Niekrasz, Andrzej. "'I Will Live Content Elsewhere': The Importance of Exile in the Poetry of Seamus Heaney", W.W. Norton and Company. books.wwnorton.com/books/aboutcontent.aspx?id=16919. Accessed 03rd Jan 2015.

Nordstrom, Carolyn. *A Different Kind of War Story (The Ethnography of Political Violence),* University of Pennsylvania Press, USA, 1997.

Ricoeur, Paul. *Time and Narrative*, Vol. 2. Translated by Kathleen McLaughlin and David

Pellauer. The University of Chicago Press, Chicago, 1984.

Said, Edward. Introduction to *Reflections on Exile and Other Essays*. Harvard University Press, Cambridge, MA, 2002.

Sarma, Parag M. "Towards an Appreciative Paradigm for Literatures of the Northeast." *Emerging Literatures from Northeast India: The Dynamics of Culture, Society and Identity*, edited by Margaret Ch Zama, Sage Publications, New Delhi, 2013, pp 37-46.

Shalhūb-Kīfūrkiyān, Nādirah. *Militarization and Violence against Women in Conflict Zones in the Middle East: A Palestinian Case Study*. Cambridge University Press, 2009.

Skjelsboek, Inger, and Dan Simth. *Gender, Peace, and Conflict*. Sage, U.K. 2001.

Yepes, Ruben. "Contrasting the Thought of Rene Girard and Giorgio Agamben, *Academia.edu*. www.academia.edu/5480305/Sacred_Violence_Sovereign_ Violence_Contrasting_the_Thoughtof_Ren%C3%A9_Girard_and_ Giorgio_Agamben. Accessed 6th Jan 2015.

Žižek, Slavoj. *Violence: Six Sideways Reflection*. Big Ideas/ Small Books, Picador, New York, 2008.

11

GENDER, INDIGENEITY AND THE SECOND WORLD WAR: THE BATTLE OF KOHIMA IN EASTERINE KIRE'S *MARI*

Maisnam Arnapal

Out of the huts of history's shame
Up from a past that's rooted in pain
Leaving behind nights of terror and fear
Into a daybreak that's wondrously clear
I Rise.

Maya Angelou, "Still I Rise" (1978).

Easterine Kire's *Mari* (2010) is an auto/biographical narrative of her aunt, Mari, (natal name, Khrielieviu Mari O'Leary), a survivor of the Second World War. The turning point of the life narrative is the Battle of Kohima (4 April–22 June 1944), one of the decisive battles of the Second World War. Arguably, the Battle of Kohima heralded the end of Japanese imperial expansionism in the twentieth century. Using gender as the optics, this essay argues that when 'The War', as referred to by the Nagas, is written from the perspective of a woman survivor, the text problematizes the rubric of war writing, which has predominantly been a masculinist genre. It can be argued that *Mari*, among many other contemporary writings by women from the region, presents a way of reimagining feminist politics in the Northeast India by its very (re)definition of 'woman' in the context of war and conflict. Drawn primarily from oral history, the text foregrounds the experiences of the Nagas during the Second World War from the perspective of a cultural insider; at the same time, it maintains a critical distance on the legitimacy of the war. By doing so, the text centers the history and culture of the Angami Nagas by subverting the hegemonic colonial writings on the Naga Indigenous [1] people. It is through this imbrication of the Indigenous and the feminist discourses that the essay attempts a critical reading of *Mari*.

(UN)DOING THE CONVENTIONS OF WAR WRITING

A significant number of works have covered the Battle of Kohima as part of the Burma Campaign in/and the Second World War. Notably, most of these writings are written from a military historian's point of view, both British and non-British. Martin Evans, in his article "Opening up the battlefield: War studies and the cultural turn", talks about decentring war studies and the many possibilities of writing about war from an interdisciplinary approach beyond the traditional war historians' focus on 'technology', 'battlefield tactics' and 'military leaders/genius' (47). Referring to the shift in war studies from the 1960s onwards, he writes about the new war specialists who wanted to study war not just as a military phenomenon but also as a social and cultural phenomenon by drawing upon different disciplines such as sociology and cultural theory (49).

In *Gendering the War Story*, Alison Fell maps two important developments in the field of gender and war studies: (i) rewriting history books and deconstructing the literary canon by including women's experiences and writings that can alter our perceptions of conflict; and (ii) using gender as an optics to study the cultural representations of war and the political debates about conflict (53-4). Drawing upon the critical interventions of Evans and Fell, reading Easterine Kire's *Mari* opens up radical possibilities, especially in

---

[1] The word 'indigenous' has been used throughout as a substitute for 'tribal', especially due to the conceptual and political significance of the former vis-à-vis the colonial anthropological invention, 'tribal'. Emerging in the 1970s primarily out of the struggles of the American Indian Movement and the Canadian Indian Brotherhood, the term 'internationalizes the experiences, the issues and the struggles of some of the world's colonized peoples' (Smith 7).

the context of the Indigenous gender discourse of the Nagas in post-colonial times.

Located at the interface of literature and history, *Mari* remains an important text from Northeast India that can illuminate the complex relationship between war, conflict, and gender. The protracted low-intensity conflict in the Northeast and the Naga insurgency movement have been matters of serious academic and political concern for a long time. A close examination of the gendered perspectives of the Second World War in Kohima, as shown in Easterine's work, can help us reorient the discourse in post-Independence Nagaland's chequered history by incorporating the complexities and specificities of the issues at hand.

Mari marks a radical departure from the conventional histories of the Battle of Kohima. There are two parallel narratives in the text: the story of Kohima and of Mari's life, with the Battle of Kohima as the turning point. In other words, it is a survivor's account of the war in which the experience, the consciousness, and the desire of a woman survivor take centre stage. Given that community relationships are a hallmark of the Indigenous Naga community, and war is a collective experience for the survivors, this particular gendered perspective of the war also qualifies as a collective Naga experience.

Building on György Lukács' thesis on the ideological and political implications of formal and compositional choices in historical novels, Diana Wallace argues that "they need to be seen in relation to women's engagement with history and not dismissed as 'unhistorical', 'factually inaccurate' or merely 'irrelevant' according to a male-defined model" (15). It is here that Mari's engagement with the Second World War makes it a distinct historical novel through the lens of an Angami Indigenous woman.

WRITING 'THE WAR' STORY

In *The Majority Finds its Past: Placing Women in History* (1979), feminist historian Gerda Lerner argues,

> Traditional history is periodised according to wars, conquests, revolutions, and/or vast cultural and religious shifts. All of these categories are appropriate to the major activities of men [...] What historians of women's history have learned is periodisation distorts our understanding of the history of women (qtd. in Wallace 13).

A close reading of Easterine Kire's *Mari* reveals a different narrative of the war in terms of its formal and structural aspects as well as the historical and cultural overtones disrupting the colonial masculinist accounts. The text de-emphasises the facets of war – the battlefield tactics, the technology, and the military might – and brings to the fore the affective, personal and community relationships and the cultural worldview of the Angami Nagas.

In the "Author's Note" to the text, it is mentioned that the Nagas of Easterine's generation grew up listening to the tales of 'The War' from the survivors' mouths. The text is the culmination of decades of stories the author had heard from her aunt since childhood, the latter's diaries, and several long interviews. It can be broadly divided into three periods: the pre-war, the war, and the post-war. It starts with life in Kohima, a few years before the war, which is recreated through the eyes of Mari. "In these pre-war years, there was a steady rhythm to our lives in our little town [...] But certain changes became quite visible at the beginning of 1942" (Kire 14). These changes were the sight of the increasing presence of the British Army and the preparations for war: "We were told what we should do if we were caught in the middle of a war and heard sirens" (Kire 16). Within a year, normal life came to a halt with the departure of the shopkeepers, the shutting of the Mission School, and many others fleeing to far-flung places for their safety, turning the once-idyllic Kohima into a ghost town.

It was in 1943, a year before the Battle of Kohima, that the Nagas saw for the first time what modern warfare could do to humanity. Hordes of refugees from Burma entered Kohima and adjoining areas after crossing treacherous forested mountains as the Japanese invasion in the Burma Campaign became more aggressive: "They came in wretched bands; starving, diseased dregs of humanity, droves of them dropping dead by the roadside or in the refugee camps" (Kire 17). This narrative runs parallel with Mari's love affair with Sergeant Victor Hewitt, alias Vic of the Corps of Royal Engineers. In 1943, when the road construction began in full swing as part of the war preparations, Mari was a supervisor at a construction site on the Bokajan road, fourteen miles away from Kohima. Their love blossomed into a full affair, and they were accepted as a couple without a wedding due to the wartime uncertainty. When the Battle of Kohima began in April 1944, Vic joined the war, and Mari fled to Chieswema with her siblings and other family members.

The portrayal of Mari and Victor in the text is of critical significance in examining the construction of gender in war writing. In the essay, "Portraying the Contemporary Spirit of War and Violence in Easterine Kire's *Mari*", Aghatoli Sema and Dayananda Pathak argue that Mari's courage and determination amidst the adversity of war and the aftermath have given her a new identity. According to them, this 'identity' is also predicated on the relationships she had with the men in her life: Mari's journey of self-strengthening starts with Victor, who gave her a new name "Marigold", with whom she starts a new life with a 'new identity'. Then, towards the end, she chooses to live her own life happily by getting married to Pat (273). However, such a reading that war and marital alliances shape Mari's identity and progression upholds patriarchal assumptions. The text rather reveals the centrality of a woman's experiences and desires, allowing radical ways of thinking about gender, war, and colonial resistance. In expressing her love and desire for Vic as well as for her other two future partners, the gaze is shifted from the colonial-masculinist one to that of an Indigenous woman. When gender is used as an analytical category in reading the text, the ideas of desire and identity cease to remain patrilocal concepts.

In her work, *Writing War: Fiction, Gender, and Memory*, Lynne Hanley argues that war literature often misrepresents war, giving a false sense of security:

> Our war literature of this century, or at least of that selection of if that we have come to know as our literature on the subject, is permeated, I think with this "secret unacknowledged elation" at the thought of war, with the conviction that war is exciting and that soldiers experience in combat uniquely profound and intense emotions and relationships [...] (4-5).

Mari is a survivor's tale of the Second World War. Although the war was fought on their soil, the Nagas had absolutely nothing to do with the aetiology of the war. The text shows that the question of victory and defeat in war is a mere absurdity, and more so for the Nagas in this case. The resultant humanitarian crises and the moral flaws of war can be inferred from the reading of *Mari*. The narrative detailing of the survivors' escape from the war – first to Cheiswema, then hiding in the thick jungles and the camps – evokes extreme pathos. This involves the splitting up of families, starvation, disease, wild animals, and the constant fear of being killed. When Kohima was turned into a battlefield from April to June 1944, Kire writes:

> We realised that we were much closer to the sources of firing, and closer to the battle zones, and therefore in great danger for our lives. Bullets flew over our heads and all around us. *But we had reached a point where we didn't really care whether we died of a Japanese bullet or a British bullet.*
> Immensely tired, sick, and starving, all we wanted was for everything to come to an end. From the fields, we could see Garrison Hill in the distance. The thick forest cover has now

burned away and there are a few leafless trees dotting the hill.
Colourful parachutes hung from the branches of some of
the trees. The slopes of Garrison Hills looked as though they
had been burnt for rice cultivation, so bombed were they. I
thought of Vic and his friends and prayed for their safety (79-
80, emphasis added).

Here the 'I'/Mari became the 'we'/Nagas talking about the collective
suffering of the survivors when their hometown was burned to ashes amid
the din of constant shelling and firing. The absurdity of this human-made
disaster is poignantly expressed in the line, "[...] we didn't really care whether
we died of a Japanese bullet or a British bullet."

Another critical dimension of *Mari*'s gendering of war writing is its
engagement with military masculinity in the representation of Sergeant
Victor. In Kire's writing, Vic is portrayed not just as a soldier fighting in the
war but also in the role of Mari's lover and a family member. The emphasis is
more on the conjugal-familial side, that is, the affective masculinity of Victor
rather than the military masculinity, which is a leitmotif of conventional
war writing as seen in Robert Lyman's retelling of the same story, *War
Comes to the Nagas* (2011), where Victor is portrayed in a different light:
"Sergeant Victor Hewitt lies there still, but not forgotten, on Garrison Hill."
Lyman's work not only makes Victor the martyr, but the latter's story is also
juxtaposed with a vilification of the Japanese forces in the war with a clear
ideological position.

While *Mari* relates the torture and sufferings the Japanese forces
inflicted upon the Nagas as part of the overall horror of war; Lyman depicts
a Manichean view, the good British army versus the evil Japanese army.
According to Khrienuo's essay, "Naga Role in World War II", the Nagas
played an important role in the British victory over the Japanese; and of
the many reasons, it was the benevolent attitude of the British rule towards
the Nagas. However, her argument reinforces the colonial stereotypes – the
colonial master as the saviour vis-à-vis the infantile natives who are incapable
of decision-making and self-rule. Referring to historian Arthur Swinson's
statement on the Naga-British relationship in the Battle of Kohima, she
writes:

Swinson was of the opinion that the part played by Charles
Pawsey [the Deputy Commissioner of Kohima], both directly
through his courage and indirectly through his influences,
was important and should never be forgotten. *He also adds that
Charles Pawsey considered Nagas as his children and, in return, the
Nagas also considered him as their father.* The Nagas trusted him

completely; they knew that in no circumstances whatsoever his word would be broken...Nagas remained loyal to the British cause, despite the loss of their homes and territory, despite danger and death"[....] (65, emphasis added).

The depiction of the white officer, Charles Pawsey, as the 'father' and the Nagas, the 'children', is the same orientalist binary used by the colonizers to legitimize their rule over the natives (in this case, the Nagas). The crucial role played by the Nagas could not be simply attributed to the favouritism of the British towards the former. As Easterine Kire's work shows, many Nagas helped the British and some others, the Japanese, yet it is not clear from her writing whether it was forced or voluntary. Indeed, it is presented as part of a larger moral complexity and ambiguity during a humanitarian crisis. This was a war fought between the powerful nations of the twentieth century with equally apocalyptic imperial expansionist ambitions. It should also be noted that Zapu Phizo, the founder of the Naga National Council, fully supported the Japanese forces who promised the Nagas an independent sovereign nation-state (Bendanganshi quoted in Khrienuo 64). In the history of the Naga nationalist movement, the Japanese influence was of extreme significance right from the beginning, and any depiction of the Japanese in accounts of the Battle of Kohima demands a critical eye.

It is worth mentioning that, while Charles Pawsey's role was hailed by historian Arthur Swinson (Khrienuo 65), he was the man who was responsible for the split between Mari and her husband, Richard Harris, alias Dickie thereby presenting a complex character sketch:

> Just around that time, Mr Pawsey sent the word that he would not allow Dickie to stay behind in Kohima nor take his small family with him to England, and Dickie felt pressured to do as he was told[...]When he finally left, I thought I would die from the heartbreak. Vic was dead and gone so I knew he would never return to me. But to have Dickie wrenched from me while we were still living seemed harder to accept than while parting Vic (Kire 130).

Severing Dickie's ties with Kohima completely refutes any simplistic reading of Mr Pawsey as a father figure to the Nagas and whether he acted out of any compassion at all especially in the case of Mari and Dickie.

It is a postcolonial common sensical knowledge that the colonial narratives and their historically controversial legacies are responsible for many of the generalizations, primitivization, and romanticization of the natives.[2] However, *Mari* also serves as an important post-colonial Indigenous voice on the Second World War by foregrounding the lives and experiences of the Angami Nagas. In her introduction to *Decolonizing Methodologies* (1999), Linda Smith writes:

> In positioning myself as an indigenous woman, I am claiming a genealogical, cultural and political set of experiences... I believe that our survival as peoples has come from our knowledge of our contexts, our environment, not from some active beneficence of our Earth Mother. We had to know to survive. We had to work out ways of knowing, we had to predict, to learn and reflect, we had to preserve and protect, we had to defend and attack, we had to be mobile, we had to have social systems which enabled us to do these things (12-13).

The Indigeneity of *Mari* lies in its depiction of the Angami Naga cultural worldview and beliefs from a cultural insider's perspective. The opening chapter gives us a peek into the life of Mari's family when her aunt Anyie Kereikieu, a non-Christian, visited their Christian home, bringing stories of the war and genna day. "The genna days were no work-days when it was taboo to work in the fields or woods" (Kire 5). By depicting the coexistence of the non-Christian and the Christian cultural views in the discussion on war, the text highlights the complex cultural worldviews of the pre-Christian Angami, which could otherwise be eclipsed or distorted by a cultural outsider.

After the war ended in June 1994, 'reconstruction' began and continued until 1945, when the war survivors came back to Kohima to restart their lives. During this period, we could see that, despite having lost family members and having their homes burned to ashes, the Angami Nagas drew on their spirit of resilience and survival from their cultural beliefs, which paved the path to a new life. When Mr Pawsey, the Deputy Commissioner, ordered the village lands to be levelled, the village elders objected as the boundary lines between the clans were important to avert any fights over land disputes (Kire 106–107). The short-term vision of the white administrator could not understand the complexities of land and land distribution in the Angami Naga worldview. The ravages of the war did not destroy the Angami spirit. They had to rebuild Kohima and restart their lives with many new challenges after the mourning period was over.

---

[2] For example, Christoph Von Furer-Haimendorf's *The Naked Nagas* (1939) remains one of the worst controversies.

> The Angami spirit was resilient. People observed long months of mourning for their dead but got on with the business of life determinedly [...] But once the period of mourning was over, further grieving was discouraged. 'Don't displease the spirits,' the villagers said. 'If you grieve too much, it will anger the spirits and even greater grief will come to you.' After a great calamity, our people always tried their best to keep their spirits up. That was the way of our people (Kire 107-108).

The strength of the Angami lay in their belief in maintaining a harmonious relationship with 'the spirits', which the war could not destroy. Ultimately the values, beliefs, and cultural ethos of the Nagas gave them a new lease of life. The reconstruction of the Naga community would not have been possible without a strengthening of the cultural fabric, an important function Easterine Kire performs as a cultural historian in *Mari*. Any reading of the text cannot bypass the historical and cultural legitimacy of the text within the context of the Naga worldview.

"*Mari* is not just Mari's story. It is the story of Kohima and its people" (Kire xii). The text reveals the transformation of Kohima before and after the Second World War. Roughly, the first half of the text is devoted to life in pre-war Kohima while the tension of impending war is slowly building up. This period extends from February 1943 until the outbreak of the Battle of Kohima in April 1944. Remarkably, this short period of a little more than a year preceding the war occupies half of the text, foreshadowing the massive devastation the war will bring about in Kohima. Although *Mari's* central action is the Battle of Kohima, the book's emphasis is the spirit of Kohima and its people. The Battle of Kohima, described by military war historians, who have written and talked about its valour, heroism, and sacrifice, merely serves as the backdrop to this history of Kohima town. This is not to say that the text does not delve deep into the details of the war, but Kohima does not simply remain a battlefield for the British and the Japanese forces. This temporal and spatial configuration in the narrative structure can be considered a critical breakthrough.

DOING INDIGENOUS FEMINISM

This brings us to the question of locating *Mari* within the feminist politics of Northeast India. The subject of feminist politics in Nagaland in particular, or the Northeast in general, has been of major critical concern. In "Politics of

Difference in the Northeast: A Feminist Reflection", Papori Bora unmasks the paradox in the mainstream narratives on women in Northeast India: that the supposedly empowered Naga woman vis-à-vis her counterparts from 'mainland' India is also the depoliticized Naga woman whose socio-political ability is severely delimited by the customary laws (246-249). She instead stresses the need for feminist politics in the Northeast that is delinked from the Eurocentric (the exotic, the docile) and nationalist assumptions (the victims and the mothers), which can lead to the emergence of a new feminist subject. She evokes lawyer and writer Nandita Haksar's argument of "reading and understanding their *own* society with a new perspective" (258-259, emphasis added). Here the agency lies with the Indigenous women; their political articulations with a newfound perspective, which is critical of both the colonial and the nationalist narratives. The works of Easterine Kire and particularly *Mari* fit into this critical framework of Indigenous feminism.

In the essay, "Indigenous Feminism: Theorizing Issues", Suzack and Huhndorf write how Indigenous feminism is as much about indigenous culture as it is about Indigenous gender issues (9-12). Given the history of colonization and the ongoing assimilationist process, Indigenous feminism cannot choose to prioritize gender over culture or vice-versa. In other words, the process of decolonizing gender cannot happen without decolonizing culture. In the light of this argument, we can see that Easterine Kire writes about the culture and history of the Naga people rooted in an Indigenous critical consciousness while narrativizing gender issues vis-à-vis war, conflict, or native customs.

Mari opens up new possibilities for interrogating the intersectionality of gender and Indigeneity in the context of Nagaland/Northeast India. The text has been able to construct a new Naga gender subjectivity without relying on the terms set by colonial scholarship or ethno-nationalist politics. This can be read alongside another work by Kire, *A Terrible Matriarchy*, that looks at the misogynistic underpinnings of the Naga customs and traditions through the story of a little girl, Dielieno, set in the insurgency days of the 1960s and 70s. The sexism and patriarchy in Angami society are so deeply entrenched and evasive that careful unmasking and unsettling of the norms and conventions are required as shown by these powerful tales. Apart from countering the colonial stereotypes and the ethno-nationalist appropriations, Kire's writings also deconstruct the image of the empowered/vilified Naga/Northeast women circulated in the popular national consciousness. What we see in her works is a radical attempt to weave new narratives by centralizing Naga women's experiences, desires, and consciousness, be it those of the five-year-old Dielieno or Khrielieviu Mari O'Leary.

WORKS CITED

Angelou, Maya. "Still I Rise" (1984). *Poetry Foundation*. Accessed 2 Sept 2020.

Bora, Papori. "Politics of Difference in the Northeast: A Feminist Reflection." *Northeast India: A Place of Relations*. Cambridge University Press. 2007. 244-261.

Evans, Martin. "Opening up the battlefield: War studies and the cultural turn." *Journal of War and Culture Studies*.1:1, 2007. 45-51.

Fell, Alison. "Gendering the War Story." Journal of War and Culture Studies.1:1, 2007. 53-58.

Fürer-Haimendorf, Christoph Von. *The Naked Nagas*. London: Methuen & Co.,1939.

Hanley, Lynne. Introduction to *Writing War: Fiction, Gender, and Memory*. University of Massachusetts Press, 1991. 3-9.

Khrienuo. "Naga Role in World War II." Journal of North East India Studies. July-Dec 2013.

Kire, Easterine. *Mari*. Delhi: Harper Collins, 2010. *A Terrible Matriarchy*. Delhi: Zubaan, 2007

Lyman, Robert. "War Comes to the Nagas." *Japan's Last Bid for Victory: the Invasion of India 1944*. Pen and Sword Military. 2011.

Sema, Aghatoli and Dayananda Pathak. "Portraying the Contemporary Spirit of War and Violence in Easterine Kire's *Mari*." Smart Moves Journal IJELLH. 7:11, Nov 2019.

Smith, Linda Tuhiwai. Introduction to *Decolonizing Methodologies*. Zed Books & University of Otago Press, 1999. 1-18.

Suzack, Cheryl and Shari M. Huhndorf. "Indigenous Feminism: Theorizing Issues". *Indigenous Women and Feminism: Politics, Activism and Culture*. Ed. Cheryl Suzack, Shari M. Huhndorf et al. Canada: UBC Press, 2010. 1-20.

Wallace, Diana. Introduction to *The Woman's Historical Novel: British Women Writers, 1900-2000*. New York: Palgrave Macmillan, 2005. 1-24.

Section 3

INDIVIDUAL AND SOCIETY: RETHINKING IDENTITIES

12

LISTENING TO LITTLE PEOPLE INSIDE THE BOX: CULTURE, TRADITION AND IDENTITY THROUGH THE REPRESENTATION OF THE RADIO IN EASTERINE KIRE

Rhelo Kenye

INTRODUCTION

A distinguishing feature of Easterine Kire's writings, primarily in the context of her novels on the Nagas, which form the bulk of her works, has been her ability to provide apt representations of the traditional-cultural ethos of the people without evading the reality of the inroads made by 'external' cultures into the Naga milieu over the years. By this, I mean to imply that Kire's focus on Naga culture in her works is not subsumed by a purist position espousing an exclusive notion of Naga tradition and culture isolated in the past. Rather, her narrative knack, evident in all her writings, for detailing the everyday realities of the common folk reflects how she is able to integrate facets of culture that are both quintessentially Naga as well as those that came from 'outside' (primarily through colonial and missionary encounters) and subsequently became an integral part of the people's everyday experiences.

It can be inferred that this integrative feature of her writing is based mainly on the debate around tradition and modernity. From another perspective, some may argue that using this framework to analyze such a feature of her writing can be problematic. This is because, as an author who has written extensively on Naga peoples' history, Kire is not constrained nor confined by the intricacies of the tradition-modernity debate but is mainly concerned with representing peoples' history and experience as it happened. While such a point of view on the 'universality' of literature leaves scope for further discussion, the objective in this essay is to articulate how Kire manages to bring out the nuances, intricacies, and details of the way history happened. Importantly, by situating her works in the axis of the broad categories of tradition and modernity, this chapter will highlight how such 'modern' interventions and their consequent assimilation into the Naga lifeworld allow us to critically revisit existing notions of culture and identity, which are predominantly grounded in what I call a cultural revivalist position. Here, I am referring to the dominant viewpoint held mainly by Nagas, both in academic and public domains, where the need for the revival of tradition and culture is promoted by holding colonization, proselytization, and Westernization as responsible for their destruction. This position is mainly framed by the broad domain of postcolonial studies.

One such important but often overlooked component of 'outside' culture that became part of the Naga way of life, which Kire clearly brings out in her novels, is the radio. In fact, existing literature on Naga society and history across disciplines is marked by an absence of discourse or emphasis on the role and impact of the radio in the Naga milieu. However, in Kire's works, much attention has been given to this electronic communication medium, which remained an almost indelible presence in Naga people's everyday lives until recent times. Radio forms an integral part of the narrative in her novels like *Mari*, *Bitter Wormwood*, and *A Respectable Woman* – novels that are set around crucial historical events like the Second World War, India's independence, and the Naga (armed) national movement. Thus, by locating the role of the radio in the context of the framework drawn here and by analyzing passages from *Bitter Wormwood* and *A Respectable Woman* (henceforth, BW and ARW) where mention is made of the radio, the following sections will critically examine how Kire represents the device as one that brought the world into the homes of the Nagas, as a cultural agent that contributed to the reconfiguration of the traditional-societal character of the Nagas and their self-perception.

LITTLE PEOPLE INSIDE THE BOX: RADIO, CURIOSITY AND CULTURAL CONTACT

Radio is introduced in Kire's works as the main channel through which people were informed about the new political developments that took place beyond the Naga Hills, mostly after the Second World War and during India's independence. However, before we jump into the niceties of how it informed and affected peoples' perception of the political situation and their worldview, it is vital to examine how she appropriately captures and portrays the Nagas and their fascination with seeing and hearing the radio for the first time. In *BW*, where a whole chapter is devoted to the device with the title "The Radio", Kire describes a scene where the son, mother, and grandmother trio of Mose, Vilaü, and Khrienuo are seen discussing the radio after dinner. Their conversation is as follows;

> "Oh, shall we be listening to the little people inside?" Khrienuo asked with a smile.
> When the radio first came to Kohima village, some people said that there were some little people inside the box who sang songs and read the news.
> "Yes, and we could try singing in it ourselves," Vilaü added with a smile.
> "Mother and Grandmother, surely you don't believe that anymore?" Mose asked with a little surprise.
> "Sure I do," his grandmother continued, "why don't we open it? Just to make sure, you know?" (37)

Sheer curiosity coupled with unfamiliarity with the gadget is observed in these lines, particularly in the case of Vilaü and Khrienuo. Kire goes on to describe how "Vilaü was just as excited as her son" (37) when they brought home a new radio, and when they first listened to it, Vilaü would go on to say, "What a marvellous thing it is!" (38). In *ARW* as well, where she writes about memories of the war and life after the war in Kohima through conversations between the mother-daughter duo of Khonuo and Kevinuo, mention is made of the radio as well. In one of their conversations, Khonuo recounts, "Before the war, our headmaster Mr Supplee used to listen to the radio a lot. It made us curious to listen to the news from outside. I bought a transistor radio with my first salary, and your grandfather and I would listen to the news at night" (55). Here, we notice that Khonuo's curiosity and desire to listen to news through the device leads her to buy one with her first salary. Thus, what do these descriptions of the characters' fascination with the radio entail? What connotation(s) does it bear? Does it, in some ways, underscore the larger notion of cultural imperialism in which the radio was treated and used as its tool? Did their reception of an instrument from 'outside' come into confrontation with 'tradition'? To put it crudely, from the viewpoint of the ardent critics of colonization and Westernization, do these narratives hint at and reinforce the idea of Nagas as 'noble savages', who in their 'ignorance', embraced this object from an 'outside' culture?

Whereas these passages need to be read in the wider context of the stories the respective novels tell, these conjectural questions are raised to probe further in relation to the broader question of culture and identity framed above. From a certain perspective, the characters' curiosity about the radio does convey the idea that it was part of a process in which the Nagas, conditioned by existing socio-political realities, inevitably assimilated cultures and practices brought about by colonial and missionary encounters. By the 1940s, as observed in Kire's novels, we can infer that Naga society had substantially transitioned from its prior-independent village republic(s) setup to what can be broadly put as a more mobilized and 'modernized' community under the structure of a modern nation-state through colonial administration. Therefore, in such a milieu, it is plausible to assume that these women's acceptance of the new medium of information and communication would not have been very difficult.

However, are we supposed to limit our interpretation of such an encounter to the framework of what can be called colonial history? This question and those mentioned above arise under the premise that postcolonial studies comprise the arena within which the subjects of culture, tradition, modernity, and identity in the Naga milieu should be currently perceived and discussed. However, the radio appeared through and during the latter part of the colonial period, and it can also be suggested that Vilaü's fascination with and Khonuo's curiosity about the radio were aroused simply because the instrument and its technology were something new to them. The way Kire narrates their curious encounter with the new gadget shows that the whole process was not regulated or forced upon them by any external pressure, nor were they indifferent to its entry into their everyday life and domestic spaces because it came from outside. That is to hypothetically state that even if the radio had entered the Naga Hills after the colonial powers had left or if it had entered through other channels, it would still have garnered their curiosity due to its novelty. Therefore, along these lines, the point I am making here is that critical reading of an experience such as this in the larger milieu of analyzing culture and identity need not be solely confined within the bounds of postcolonial framework and criticism.

Also, if we were to employ a postcolonial stance on the reaction of these women to the radio, it would have been read as an example of the part of the process of imperialist cultural project where 'ignorance' manifested by the 'native' is used by the colonial power to gradually take over the colonized and their culture. However, if we restrict the reading of Naga history or literature to such a singular position, I would argue that it only and paradoxically reinforces the idea of seeing the 'native' as helpless 'noble savages', who, in their ignorance, gave in to the culture of the colonizers. Attributing traits of 'innocence' and ignorance to these women somehow reduces them, or the Nagas then in general, to people incapable of making their own choices. Thus, Vilaü's, Khrienuo's, Khonuo's, or even Mose's inquisitiveness about and eventual use of the radio need not be seen as some passive form of giving in to an evangelical or imperialist cultural project but can also be understood as an active and organic form of engagement – as we shall observe throughout this chapter – by the common folk with another culture in an everyday context. Kire's articulate and nuanced accounts, evoking older memories and peoples' memories of the more recent past, can be seen as demonstrating cultural contact and not just cultural ascendancy by an external force. It is vital that such differences between contact and control should be identified.

BRINGING THE OUTSIDE WORLD INTO THE NAGA HOME: RADIO, HISTORY AND THE MAKING OF NAGA IDENTITY

As mentioned earlier, the portrayal of the radio in Kire's works is primarily built around the historical facet of how it informed or, rather, introduced the characters to what was happening beyond the Naga Hills during and mainly after the Second World War. In the novels featured here, she does not use the radio as a subsidiary presence to supplement the plot(s) and main themes. Instead, her use of the communication medium in the novels is deliberate. In a certain sense, radio, as described within the larger narrative of her works, is an everyday object that shaped and changed the Nagas' perception of the world and themselves. The following sentences from ARW capture the essence of how radio impacted the Nagas: "We were curious about what was going on beyond our hills. Much of my knowledge about the outside world came via that little radio that we used to listen to every evening" (55-56). These words were said by Khonuo to her daughter Kevinuo, the novel's narrator. She was describing life in Kohima town after the war. Prior to these lines, as cited earlier, Khonuo tells her daughter about how Mr Supplee, the headmaster at her school, used to listen to the radio a lot and how it influenced and made the students curious to listen to the news from outside.

In these lines, we also see the facet of curiosity at play, but what is important to draw from here is that it was the radio that gave Khonuo knowledge of what was going on beyond the Naga Hills. As evident as it appears, the radio significantly affected how Khonuo and her contemporaries gradually integrated new knowledge systems with pre-existing traditional worldviews, mores, and values. It reconfigured their perceptions towards their very sense of the self and existence in relation to other events and people, and thereby also manifested the process of cultural contact that has been explained earlier. Although there are no specific descriptions in the novel about what or how the radio informed Khonuo, her father, and others, one can infer that they mainly received news about political developments and the new nation-states being formed after the Second World War.

In *BW*, we find a more detailed account of the manner in which the radio brought the world into characters' homes. The following conversation between Mose, his mother Vilaü, and grandmother Khrienuo demonstrates how the gadget informed three generations of a family simultaneously about the political state of affairs outside the Naga Hills.

> A man's voice said something loudly in English. "What is he saying, son?" asked Vilaü.
> "Wait, let me listen," said Mose, and he put up the volume higher and stood listening very carefully.
> "The departing British government has left behind two new nations, India and Burma. Partition is the new word that has been formed by the collapse of the British South Asian empire. India and Pakistan are being divided into two separate nations..." the man's voice on the radio.
> Mose could not understand all of what the man said, but what he could, he explained carefully to his mother. (38)

While this passage is self-explanatory, one must delve deeper into, imagine, and locate it in its historical context to understand its full meaning and significance. That is, it must be recognized that such preliminary encounter(s) with the outside world for these characters and many others through the aural-virtual medium of the radio were vital in broadening their horizons beyond their immediate and neighbouring communities and therefore, in shaping initial perceptions of their collective being in relation to others outside their pre-existing lifeworld and worldviews. The sessions of listening to the radio to learn about the outside world can be treated as 'performances' where the protagonists' awareness about other peoples and nations was framed and manifested. Words like 'India', 'Pakistan', 'Burma', 'new nations', and even 'partition' cited in the passage convey that the radio was instrumental in informing Khrienuo, Vilaü, Mose, and others about the existence of the idea and category of nation.

Further, news on the radio about the British leaving behind the nations of India and Burma, as well as news on the partition of India and Pakistan, can be seen as having underlying implications and historical relevance to Indo-Naga political history – the major theme around which the narrative of the novel is woven. By this, I mean to imply that this news about political unrest and partition, in its historical actuality, took place in tandem with the Naga struggle for independence. The eventual decision of Mose and his friend Neituo to join the Naga underground movement, as depicted in the novel, can be said to have been significantly informed and conditioned by the volatile state of political affairs they heard about on the radio. In a certain sense, it can be surmised that the news bears a prophetic tone, a precursor to the sequence of political events of violence and suffering of people that followed in the wake of the Naga struggle for independence against the Indian state, events described in the novel in fair detail. A particular section in the book where radio is described as the source of news on the assassination of Gandhi can also be read in the context of this discussion. The passage reads:

> On the 30th January, [the year was 1948], when Mose turned on the radio, he immediately raised his hand, indicating that everyone should be quiet... After the long broadcast, readings from the Hindu scriptures accompanied by the harmonium could be heard on the radio.
> Mose sat down and stated, "Gandhi was shot dead today!" (47)

Kire states that the school reopened a week after Gandhi's assassination, and the headmaster talked briefly about Gandhi.

> Before he died, this great man met a group of Nagas. He asked how he could help them. The men said they wanted independence from India. Gandhi told them that they had every right to it. This was truly a great man that understood the rights of all human beings. Gandhi's death is a loss not only to India but to the Nagas and to the whole world (48).

While I shall not dwell on the passage per se, it is crucial to note here that through the description of an event such as this, Kire has been able to represent and locate the radio in the history of the Indo-Naga political conflict as well. This account, narrated in the initial part of *BW* can be seen as an antecedent to the political conflict and history portrayed in the rest of the novel. Mose's tone, when he said that Gandhi was shot dead, can be read as an emotional expression of sadness and even regret, not only for the fact of the leader's death but also because the Nagas were pinning their hope for independence on Gandhi, as can be validated in the description made by the school headmaster in the latter passage. In short, we observe the radio not only as a 'modern' object that entered the everyday life and culture of the Naga people but also as a critical historical agent that played its role in the intricate web of political developments during the period.

Thus, the radio in the Naga milieu was not just a gadget that performed the mundane task of disseminating news; the ramifications of its use were far greater in terms of how, as the first major medium of communication, it reconfigured the structures of the Naga lifeworld alongside current developments. Radio provided the first real opening for the Nagas to the reality of a global world, thereby disseminating a more collective sense of multicultural orientation among the Nagas for the first time. It had an active presence in people's daily lives during a critical period of Naga history. Given the historical events around which the narrative of the radio is built, it can be said that the radio and its messages gave the Nagas a sense of history and historicity.

Easterine Kire's contribution to the reading of Naga history and society through her precise and contextualized depiction of the radio is laudable. Khonuo's references to the use of the radio before the war, as well as the narrative around the radio, go in tandem with the post-war rebuilding of Kohima town, and this demonstrates Kire's way of giving her readers a sense of history. It is suggestive of an alternative and, perhaps, more intimate way of looking at history through the retelling of memories.

RADIO, EDUCATION, AND THE ENGLISH LANGUAGE

Characters like Mose in BW and Khonuo and her father in ARW could comprehend and disseminate what was being shared on the radio because they understood English. Their knowledge of English was, in turn, an outcome of the (Western) education they had received. The following passage from ARW shows how the practice of listening to the radio was inherently linked to education. "In those days, if you went to people's houses in the evening after dinner, you would find the family sitting together, listening to the radio. It was the result of education and the very real fact that the war had opened up the world for us" (55). This was said by Khonuo to her daughter Kevinuo. It can also be observed that she was talking about people, houses, and families, and not just particular individuals. This passage reinforces that listening to the radio, and even, therefore, the pursuit of education, took place at a collective or societal level. Here, it is important to probe deeper into how the network between radio, education, and the English language manifested to affect pre-existing structures and notions of society and identity in the Naga milieu.

In the social and political history of Nagas as a people, language in the form of English played a pivotal role in the consolidation of a public sphere through which the idea of a collective identity was forged.[1] It is beyond the scope of this essay to dwell at length on the history and politics of the English language, but it needs to be mentioned here that, through educational institutions and other organizations like the Naga Club or the Naga National Council, which used English in their official circulations or statements, the language played a key role in mobilizing the linguistically heterogeneous tribes who eventually forged their political identity as Nagas. Thus, it is in such a historical milieu that we need to locate and understand how English as a homogenizing factor of modern Naga identity was significantly, although not entirely, disseminated through the medium of the radio. Not that they were deliberately aware of it, but through their daily practice of listening to the radio and to a new common language, people were engaged in a process of shared performance of imagining and forging collective consciousness and identity. Khonuo's account of families listening to the radio in the evening after dinner can therefore be seen as a depiction of such collective performances.

In *BW*, following their question on how big America was, after hearing about elections in America from the radio, the three continued with their conversation. Using maps, Mose compares and explains to his mother and grandmother the sizes of states and countries.

---

[1] Riku Khutso, in his MPhil dissertation submitted to the Department of History, University of Hyderabad, titled "English Language and the Formation of Public Sphere in the Colonial Naga Hills:1870s - 1950s" (2013), has critically studied the spread of the English language through missionary education and colonial intervention, and its subsequent and popular use by the early leaders of frontal Naga organizations like the Naga Club and the Naga National Council (NNC) to propagate their cause. Khutso argues that these historical processes helped create a public sphere for the linguistically diverse Naga society, through which Naga identity formation was consolidated.

"Grandmother, look at this portion which says Uttar Pradesh. If you tried, you could fit in Kohima a hundred times over into Uttar Pradesh. Does that tell you how big India is? How big the rest of the world is?

"Yha!" Khrienuo exclaimed in awe, "I would never have thought of that. How clever you are my child, it was a good thing to send you to school. Your mother and I are getting educated well, you should tell your teacher that." (39)

Here, we see the dynamics between radio and education at play. The passage gives a precise description of the device as a medium of education. The radio did not only augment the process of Naga identity formation at the political scale but, through its role in 'educating' the people, it contributed to a significant reorientation of their socio-cultural identity in relation to their everyday contact and existence with new cultures, brought about by their experience with colonial and missionary encounters. In line with the earlier observation about how such experiences reconfigured the Nagas' understanding of themselves, we can observe in this passage an actual process of how the characters – mainly Vilaü and Khrienuo, who did not go to school – got first-hand experience of looking at a map and being 'educated' about nations and states, thereby plausibly shaping their imagination about nations as well as the world. The coming together of three generations – son, mother, and grandmother in front of the radio for information and knowledge – also depicts the device as a common educational platform. Khrienuo's remark to her grandson about sending him to school being a good thing also reflects the partial transition taking place in their everyday life, from one under traditional systems and institutions to one under a syncretic and 'modern' setup of Naga culture and society.

PERFORMING NEW RITES: RADIO AND THE EVERYDAY LIFE

Analysis of the representation of the radio in Kire's work cannot be complete without considering how the device is linked to and located in the everyday – one of the most significant features of her writings. In a way, we can already perceive this facet of the everyday at play in the study thus far. However, by amalgamating the themes that have been discussed and by examining a few more passages from the selected novels, this section will seek to provide a more comprehensive view of how and why the everyday practice of listening to the radio, as depicted in these works, became a critical process in the complex and gradual reconfiguration of culture, meaning-making, and identity in the Naga milieu.

The word 'ritual' used in *BW*, in describing how Mose, Vilaü, and Khrienuo used to listen to the radio, offers an interesting perspective on how the practice of listening to the device is represented. The passage where the word is used reads: "The radio became a part of their evening ritual. After their supper, they turned on the radio for news at six pm. Khrienuo joined them as often as she could, quietly listening with the other two" (39). The perspective is that the act of listening to a 'modern' object – a modern practice in that sense – is superimposed on the larger framework of an indigenous Naga traditional ethos through the use of the word 'ritual.' Ritual, as a sequence of activities performed in certain prescriptive norms, carries traditional and religious connotations. Thus, it goes without saying that for a predominantly (evolving) traditional society like that of the Nagas, such a word or notion conveys a prominent and recurrent presence. Here, one cannot be sure whether this is why the author has used the word. However, in the larger context within which this essay is grounded, it is fair to suggest that the act of listening to the radio as a ritual gives new meaning to our understanding of concepts like tradition and culture in the Naga milieu where the same word as a religious or traditional practice was an integral part of peoples' lives in the pre-colonial, pre-Christian era.

By using this word, I hold that Kire has been able to fuse a narrative to portray a reality where tradition and modernity inevitably come together. Furthermore, her choice of word underscores her awareness of the changing and fluid façade of culture and tradition. Therefore, along these lines, it can be contended that a revivalist position that holds on to a 'pure' and rigid notion of culture and tradition as a way of life frozen in time is a stance that is invalid in the evolving reality of culture and everyday life. In her work, Easterine Kire, through the detailed depiction of everyday life and moments such as the one cited here, has been able to capture the nuances and intricacies of such realities.

Also, a comparison worth drawing with regard to the notion of cultural contact around the subject of the radio and the everyday, as depicted in the works of Kire, is the tradition of storytelling. In *ARW*, we observe that a good part of the novel is written in such a way that Khonuo narrates stories of the past – the war, her childhood, growing up, and the changes that Kohima went through – to her daughter. In the text, we observe the Naga oral culture of storytelling at play. Moreover, in *BW*, we notice that, after purchasing a radio, Mose translates the news to his mother and grandmother. In both the novels, set around the same time, we observe that Khonuo's stories of the past and Mose's translations of the news happen daily. Thus, although the essence and temporal, cultural context in the performance of both practices vary, we notice that both manifest in the characters' everyday lives. Also, in both cases, there is the practice of telling involved. Notwithstanding the question of consistency in the comparison that has been made, it can be reiterated that Kire's narratives around the radio represent the subtleties of the interaction and merger of cultures and practices and how they characterize the everyday history of Nagas and their society.

Further, in depicting the everyday practice of listening to the radio, Kire represents a changing reality that was immediate and recurrent in peoples' lives in the period around which the novels were set. This observation is made by locating the idea of the everyday in relation to the question of whether tradition, as perceived in the Naga milieu, can be seen as an everyday reality and practice or as one that belonged to the past. While the word 'tradition' is a comprehensive term, it is plausible to suggest that its broad implication in the Naga milieu, as in any other traditional society, has been primarily in terms of values, behaviour, customs, and practices passed down from and rooted in the past. Thus, the manifestation of certain values or, in particular, practices of tradition, as understood in this sense, may not have remained as recurrent or dominant as the daily practice of listening to the radio was during that period. For instance, it is evident that, by then, the contentious practice of headhunting had already receded into the past.[2] It may be added that the entry of the device into the domestic spaces of the characters also reinforces the idea of proximity or immediacy that is discussed here. Unlike certain traditional events like festivals or practices that have to be performed in public domains, radio and the practice of listening to it took place within the more immediate domestic domain of people's homes. Thus, in descriptions like "In those days, if you went to people's houses in the evening after dinner, you would find the family sitting together, listening to the radio (55)", and, in the example cited earlier, we observe how Kire has been able to capture and represent the subtleties of such changes through her focus on the everyday.

With the changing realities brought about in the socio-political spheres through colonial and missionary encounters, it is only pertinent to recognize that the everyday culture and tradition of the people became reconfigured through interventions such as the radio. Kire's awareness of this changing facet of culture, as reflected in her writings, is observed in an interview with Veio Pou for *Scroll* where she states her perception of culture, "For me, my culture is what I know, what I grew up imbibing from what I was taught,

---

[2] For more on the subject, one can refer to Venusa Tinyi's article "The Headhunting Culture of the Nagas: Reinterpreting the Self". In it, he has attempted to provide a better understanding of the term and its practice from the perspective of a native.

what I saw around me, and what I lived and experienced". All that she saw, lived, and experienced is entrenched in this idea of transition.

RADIO AND ITS ROLE IN NAGA HISTORY: TOWARD RETHINKING TRADITION AND IDENTITY

In examining the representation of the radio in the selected novels, analyses across sections of this chapter have emphasized the critical reading of tradition in relation to questions of culture and identity in the evolving history of Naga society. I have not dwelled on the conceptual niceties and intricacies of the rather loaded term 'tradition' per se, but my aim has been to critically revisit and problematize what I have earlier called a revivalist notion of tradition – the predominant position in both academic and public discourse today. By this, I mean that existing critiques on the entry of British Colonial rule and American Baptist missionaries into the Naga hills have treated these historical events as intrusions that have destroyed Naga culture and tradition. Moreover, in the same direction, it can be observed that attempts are being made both in academic and public spheres to inculcate awareness and action on the need to revive tradition, cultures, mores, and values of the past among present-day Nagas. While one cannot deny the degree of impact that these attempts, as well as Westernization and proselytization, has left on the Nagas, there is a need to examine whether such revivalist stance of a 'pure' tradition rooted in the past is still feasible in a contemporary reality where fusions and interactions between cultures, societies, and their practices have become inevitable.

Thus, can the push for the revival of tradition drawn from the past remain isolated from a multicultural present? Locating Kire's narrative around the radio as an everyday reality of people's lives in this framework, this chapter contends that such a view is not viable. It needs to be categorically stated here that a challenge to the current critique of Westernization and proselytization does not mean that this chapter argues in complete favour of these two historical impacts as determining factors, nor is it a contestation to the trend of "corrective anthropology" described by Wouters and Heneise, in which Naga scholars in recent years have sought to rectify what has been written about the Nagas by colonial administrators and anthropologists (4). The telling impact of these events on Naga tradition and society is accepted, and it does not render the notion of tradition, as espoused here, irrelevant. However, in broad terms, when the claim for a unique Naga history and political identity is made while holding on to a purist-revivalist stance, there is a difficult discrepancy and disjuncture between the positions of political and traditional claims to identity. Asserting the latter would, in significant ways, mean reinforcing a time-bound notion of identity rooted in the past, a collective identity confined to and defined by the clan or the village republic, thereby invalidating the more recent construct and category of identity called 'the Nagas'. This is a conundrum that cultural revivalists are faced with when they hold Westernization or proselytization entirely accountable for the destruction of Naga culture and tradition.

Kire's ability to portray the realities of 'modern' cultural interventions such as the radio, while also maintaining the essence of the rich traditional cultural ethos of the Nagas across her works, implies that there is a way through which notions of tradition and identity can be reconfigured without losing the essence of Naga traditional life. In this chapter, I have chosen not to dwell on it given that the emphasis was on the radio, but those who have read her books will concur that themes catering to Naga tradition and culture occur throughout her works. For instance, the title of the novel *Bitter Wormwood*, the book on which this chapter has comprehensively focused, refers to a herb traditionally believed to keep bad spirits away. In *A Respectable Woman*, a brief conversation between Khonuo and her son Ato around the subject of house inheritance after a person's death (45-46) can be seen as an example of the presence or inclusion of Naga traditional themes in her novel. It goes without saying that Kire's other notable works like *When the River Sleeps*, *Sun of the Thundercloud*, and *Spirit Nights*, among others, capture and underscore this reality and the tenacity of the rich cultural tradition of the Nagas as a people.

Easterine Kire's work traverses both modern and traditional milieus and sensibilities to demonstrate the inevitable reality that culture is fluid. In an interview with *The Hindu*, on her 2019 book *Walking the Roadless Road: Exploring the tribes of Nagaland*, and in answer to a query on whether she mourned the loss of traditional culture, Kire replied, "As I grow older, I see the inevitability of change. I believe we can decide how much change will be allowed. Some things should not be replaced, however. For example, we customarily accept that children are to take care of aged parents." This view of hers is a reiteration of the integrative facet of her writing, with regards to culture and tradition, mentioned at the beginning of this chapter. The discrepancy between tradition and everyday life is, in a sense, dealt with through the integrative or syncretic approach of her writing; syncretic not in terms of an effortless assimilation into or fusion with other modes and practices of culture, but one where the essence of the rich Naga traditional past is sustained in tandem with changes and realities effected by a global cultural present.

In a sense, the field of Naga studies is predominantly characterized by a valid need to document, retell, assert, and reclaim culture, identity, and tradition; however, there is a concurrent need to locate and critically engage with the history and role of an 'external' domain like mass media in understanding Naga culture and society, and radio is one example. Apart from the role of print, discourse on the significant effects of the earlier forms of mass media and communication is almost absent as an integral part of a broader study of literary cultures. Drawing primarily from India's post-independence context, Jasmine Yimchunger has observed that "the relationship between Indian media and its more than 100 ethnic minority groups is under-researched" (23). A related work and one of the few catering to this theme in the Northeast region is Joy L.K. Pachuau and Willem van Schendel's *The Camera as Witness: A Social History of Mizoram, Northeast India*. In Kire's representation of the radio as a device that reconfigured the everyday lives of the Naga people and their perception of the self in relation to others through it, she has identified a significant but often overlooked component of material culture and history in the Naga context. The historically grounded depiction of the radio in her works necessitates a more detailed and critical reading of the device in contemporary discourses on Naga culture, society, history, and identity. The current chapter can be seen as a preliminary attempt in that direction. Her ability to capture the experiential relationship between the people and a device like the radio attests to the fact that through her writing, she has been able to keep and tell her people's history, many noteworthy parts of which often go untold in conventional forms of reading and doing history.

WORKS CITED

Khutso, Riku. *English Language and the Formation of Public Sphere in the Colonial Naga Hills: 1870s -1950s*. 2013. University of Hyderabad, MPhil thesis.

Kire, Easterine. *A Respectable Woman*. Zubaan, 2019.

—. *Bitter Wormwood*. Zubaan, 2011.

—. "'I believe we can decide how much change will be allowed": Easterine Kire.' Interview by

Sudipta Datta. *The Hindu*, 29 June 2019, https://www.thehindu.com/books/i-believe-we-can-decide-how-much-change-will-be-allowed-easterine-kire/article28196694.ece. Accessed 11 Oct. 2020.

—. "'Years of listening to stories grows a wealth of knowledge within your spirit": Easterine Kire.'

13

CRITICAL INSIGHTS ON THE TREATMENT OF DEATH IN EASTERINE KIRE'S *A TERRIBLE MATRIARCHY*

Adenuo Shirat Luikham

HAMLET. But that the dread of something after death,
The undiscovered country from whose bourn
No traveler returns, puzzles the will.... (*Hamlet* 1.3.72-88)

In one of Shakespeare's greatest tragedies, *Hamlet*, the young prince ponders on death, referring to it as a country whose mysteries remain undisclosed and from where no traveller returns. These lines embody the enduring preoccupation with a subject that is accepted as an inevitability and yet arouses an unquenchable curiosity. Speculations on death and the beyond can only be experienced through witnessing others on their journeys or through the medium of fiction. According to the German literary critic Walter Benjamin, the answers we seek in fiction become our only means of knowing the death experience denied to us in real life (Hakola and Kivistö).

The confrontation with this reality and the need to make sense of the frailty of our existence become the driving forces for using death in literature at a philosophical level. However, what about the treatment of death and its usage in fiction; what purposes could they have? Death in literature can happen at multiple levels, and physical and psychological deaths help us to imagine death from different perspectives (Hakola and Kivistö). Aristotle, in *Poetics*, recognized the value of literature for humanity when he said that the "object of art is an imitation of life", and he further perceived the value of tragedy – specifically in the imitation of death and dying in art – which enables a cleansing of the soul through *Catharsis* (purification of strong or repressed emotions). The Greek tragedians Sophocles, Aeschylus, and Euripides wrote death-driven plays and used death as a theme to elicit an emotional response in their audiences. For the ancient classical masters, the critical value of death as a theme in literature was to produce a response engaging the emotions that would lead to spiritual cleansing. Some genres of literature, such as elegies and threnodies, dwell specifically on the loss of a beloved or even use descriptions of loss to offer comfort in times of grief. For some writers, death is seen as a release from earthly struggles and pain and can even be welcomed as a life freed from tribulations. Mark Twain, in *Letters from The Earth* (1962), succinctly captures this thought:

> Life was not a valuable gift, but death was. Life was a fever-dream made up of joys embittered by sorrows, pleasure poisoned by pain; a dream that was a nightmare-confusion of spasmodic and fleeting delights, ecstasies, exultations, happinesses, interspersed with long-drawn miseries, griefs, perils, horrors, disappointments, defeats, humiliations, and despairs — the heaviest curse devisable by divine ingenuity; but death was sweet, death was gentle, death was kind; death healed the bruised spirit and the broken heart, and gave them rest and forgetfulness; death was man's best friend; when man could endure life no longer, death came and set him free. (Letter x, 17)

Death in literature also has a moral purpose, for it carries with it the spirit of instruction and judgement, which the classicists insisted on when creating their literary works. Although Plato was a moral philosopher who, in his theory of *mimesis*, viewed the arts as an "imitation of an imitation" and therefore removed from reality and responsible for moral degradation, he was still able to see the value of literature (specifically poetry) as a platform on which writers should aim to present admirable qualities witnessed in great heroes and warriors, and should in its primacy be used in order to contribute to knowledge and refine one's morals (Mambrol).

Therefore, we can see that death has a 'purpose' in literature, and we also find that it functions as a literary device. It is helpful in creating suspense, propelling the plot forward or bringing it to a definitive end. It can also be used in open-ended story-telling, for example, when a character experiences a metaphorical death. Therefore, death as a tool in story-telling is useful and has many facets and purposes. There is, however, the argument that death in literature can exist only as a representation of reality and, therefore, lacks any didactic goals.

Having said that, the representations and treatments of death in literature are as varied as the authors who use them in their work. Therefore, it is of critical importance to study how death is perceived, internalized, and commemorated in the context of different cultures. Easterine Kire's *A Terrible Matriarchy* (hereafter ATM) is a text that exposes to the world the collective consciousness of how death is treated and perceived in the Naga context. In the novel, Kire is directly concerned with the representation of death and its treatment among the Angamis (one of the major Naga tribes). However, since all Naga tribes have a commonality in terms of traditions, customs, rituals and belief systems, the text gives intimate insights into how death is treated and interpreted, especially within the frameworks of the Judeo-Christian religion and traditional beliefs that Nagas incorporate and practice as a part of their identity in contemporary times.

THE TREATMENT OF DEATH IN *ATM*

Kire's ATM is primarily studied for the overarching theme of the domineering grandmother who favours her grandsons and discriminates against her granddaughter Dieleno simply because she has been brought up with the belief that Naga women and men have clearly defined roles to play in a community. While critical studies on the novel have concerned themselves with studying the terrible matriarchal power that the grandmother exercises over her family, especially over the women and the younger male dependents, there is also room for alternative readings. The alternative reading in this paper concerns itself with the treatment of death in the novel. If we read the novel through this lens, the character of the grandmother can also be interpreted as a metaphor (symbolic representation) for the death of Dieleno's aspirations, dreams, and desire for self-actualization. The scope of the paper involves critically examining the following questions: what do we mean by 'treatment of death'? What are some possible interpretations of authorial intention in her treatment of death? And what purpose(s) does it serve?

The treatment of death in literature is multi-faceted. According to the *Cambridge Dictionary*, the word 'treatment' is defined as "the way something [subject matter] is considered or examined". In the *Collins Dictionary*, it is defined as "the manner of handling or dealing with a person or thing, a literary or artistic work". 'Treatment' here can also be seen as an extension of Derrida's concept of 'decentering' – to shift from the established interpretation of *ATM*; to attempt new interrogations and examinations in the reading of the novel. Treatment of death in fiction can be sympathetic or can be used in other ways, for example, as a moral lesson serving as a warning on life choices, a tool to reveal the reasons behind a character's actions, a presentation of religious perspectives, or an illustration of the different stages of grief.

Six deaths are mentioned in *ATM*. In the entirety of the novel, the protagonist experiences loss through the deaths of family members, including her brothers and her grandmother. She also experiences the death of her best friend's father. In the novel, the treatment of death is dualistic in its approach. Firstly, Kire approaches the subject of how death is treated in the Angami culture. Secondly, she offers glimpses of the perception of death in the collective Naga culture and the diverse religious beliefs that are attached to it. Glimpses of funerary rituals, customs, observances, traditions, and burial practices are beautifully interwoven into the story-telling, and as the plot progresses, the reader also learns about the culture of the Nagas regarding traditions and beliefs concerning death. At the same time, her treatment of death is sympathetic because deaths in the novel warn other characters not to choose a life of vice and specifically highlight the fatal consequences of addictions. She is not necessarily a writer who is a moralist but often chooses to give a faithful depiction of the realities of human experiences and, in doing so, speaks to the conscience of the reader. Her treatment of death is also sympathetic in another sense because she uses the death of a pivotal character to explain to the protagonist and the readers why certain events in the novel had to take place. Thus, she uses death to bring closure and show empathy both for the protagonist and the reader.

We first look at how Kire presents and considers death in *ATM* through the cultural lens of the Angami Nagas and their perspective(s) towards death and how it is interpreted within their religious and traditional frameworks. Here, the author's approach towards the subject is shaped by her being situated in the tradition of the Angami Nagas and thereby represents the Angami worldview specific to her experience. Three deaths in the novel – that of Zekuo (Vimenuo's father), Pete (Dielieno's brother) and the grandmother – show valuable insights into how the following are observed in Angami Naga culture: (i) How the dead are mourned and the prominence of women as mourners (ii) Clothing that people wear at the time of the funeral and the mention of shawls of symbolic significance that are used to cover dead bodies (iii) The funerary rites, performed according to the Christian faith, and the burials (iv) How the death and the dead are perceived.

MOURNING AND WOMEN AS MOURNERS:

In the novel, Kire dwells extensively on how the mourning of the dead falls primarily on the shoulders of the women folk. There are some significant examples where women are seen embodying the role of the mourner. Dielieno remarks that "Our women screamed at the death of their loved ones. It was usual to hear mourners scream the name of the deceased when they came to mourn him" (83). Another example is when the lamentations for the dead acquire a chant-like quality, and a lead mourner appears to incite the emotional response in other mourners: "When she began to mourn him loudly, others joined in and the house was full of the sound of wailing again. The women gathered round his body and called his name and some of them beat their cloths on the floor" (85). Physical expressions of grief are described when a dead body is brought into the house; there were women who beat their 'body-cloths' on the floor and even 'stamped the floor' with their feet (283).

Historically, women have been the communicators of mourning and, in the province of the dead, women appear to have been given some distinct responsibilities in attending to this matter. In *Women, Pain and Death*, Evy Johanne Håland writes that: "Women have been traditionally linked to death ... through their prominence in the rituals of mourning, particularly the performance of laments" (4).

Women also take on central responsibilities around the dead involving washing, cooking and feeding. Women can be seen in these mediating roles in *ATM* where the centrality of their responsibilities is highlighted: "There were women helping everywhere. In the kitchen were many neighbour women helping my aunt to cook. Usually, the women made food for the gravediggers and some of the mourners who had come from afar" (Kire 147). However, the practice of these mediating roles is not confined to the Angami Nagas or Nagas in general; such mediating roles can be seen across various religious communities, including Pagan, Jewish, Christian, or Muslim (Håland 9).

CLOTHING AND ITS SIGNIFICANCE:

In *ATM*, special attention is given to the clothing worn by mourners attending the funerals. When Vimenuo's (Dielieno's best friend) father passes away, the community rallies quickly to attend the funeral; Kire carefully takes time to describe the clothing worn by the women and men to attend his funeral.

> We drank tea and I changed into a clean frock and put on my shoes. Neikuo was wearing her black body-cloth. They always did that, the women. If there was a death, they went in their black body-cloths. Hers was completely black with four lines of navy blue on the border. The men also wore black body-cloths with red and green stripes on the border. Their cloths were more colourful than what the old women wore. (83-84)

Kire also brings to light the custom of the Angami Nagas, where body-cloths called *Lohe* in *Tenyidie* (the language of the Angami Naga tribe) are placed over the dead body as a sign of respect and honour. This practice of placing the body-cloth is done during the wake before the funeral formally begins. During Zekuo's wake, Dielieno describes how several body-cloths are placed over him, reaching up to his chest, with the borders having red and green stripes and "patterns down the edge in blue or green or red thread" (87). At the grandmother's wake as well, women continuously streamed in to place new body-cloths (284).

There is also symbolic significance in placing favourite pieces of clothing in the coffin or choosing personal effects to be buried with the dead body. The grandmother had expressed the wish for some of her body-cloths (for example, one which belonged to her mother) to be placed with her in the coffin, and for Pete's burial, Dielieno goes through the trunk containing some of his clothes and personal items to choose some to be buried with him. On this, Dielieno remarks, "Our people always did that. Sometimes it would be clothes like a favourite shirt or sweater of the dead person. Some wives insisted on burying their husband's favourite things ... But it was the custom to bury the dead with their Bible and a box of their belongings" (148).

FUNERARY RITES AND BURIALS:

The coming of Christian missionaries to the Naga Hills around the second half of the 19th century heralded the beginning of unstoppable changes that impacted the Nagas and their identity formation. Many turned to the Judeo-Christian beliefs that the missionaries introduced; the introduction of the Roman script and the establishment of schools following a Western curriculum meant that the worldview of the Nagas was changed forever (Elizabeth 18). By the 20th century, traditional beliefs and practices were superseded by Christian practices, and only a handful of people practised the old religion, which had animistic roots/shades (Pou 63-64).

Christian rites now observed during funerals and burials supplant older traditional beliefs, allowing a distinctive interplay between indigenous beliefs and Christianity. All the funerals described in *ATM* mirror the reality of how deeply the Christian faith has entrenched its roots in the Naga ethos. In the novel, such practices in the Angami context are specifically shown – the invoking of God's presence by the pastor, the prayers for the departed soul, exhorting the mourners in the remembrance of Christian values towards the bereaved family members, and the singing of familiar funeral hymns (86,146, 285).

The burials follow a similar pattern. The coffin is laid in the grave; the pastor sprinkles soil over it, reads from the Bible, and gives a short prayer. The grave diggers are then instructed to fill in, and once the burial is over, a wooden cross with flowers and wreaths from the funeral is laid on top of the grave (88).

Veio Pou, in *Literary Cultures of India's Northeast: Naga Writings in English* (2015), makes a critical observation on how the coming of Christianity brought a complete overhaul in how Nagas actualized and perceived themselves. Although he does not directly connect it with how Nagas perceived death and performed funeral rites and burials according to Christian beliefs, the encounter with the West meant that there were repercussions (68). The coming of Christianity meant that there were substantial distortions in the Naga traditional belief system, which consequently became heavily infused with Judeo-Christian beliefs and practices.

PERCEPTION OF DEATH AND THE DEAD:

In his book *The Nagas*, Julian Jacobs states, "Nagas have complicated beliefs about the soul" (85). There is a belief in all Naga communities that there is a close link between the living and the dead. The use of the supernatural in fiction for Kire acknowledges the reality of the spiritual world and the proximity in which the dead and the living co-exist (Elizabeth 32).

For the Angamis, the creator god is called *Kepenuopfü*. With the coming of Christianity, the name of this supreme deity became explicitly associated with the Christian God – Jehovah. Even though deaths in the novel are given Christian funerals, there is still the idea that the spirit of a person who died due to reckless behaviour is restless and lingers on in the land of the living. By contrast, in other deaths, where the person is acknowledged as a 'good Christian', the spirit is believed to enter heaven directly. This juxtaposition of beliefs about the death of a 'good' person and a 'bad' person gives us an idea of the interweaving of traditional beliefs, retained in the collective consciousness of a people and then synthesized into the framework of an adopted religious belief (Christianity).

For instance, Vimenuo's father, who was known as a drunk and died due to his own reckless behaviour, is not given a peaceful conclusion. Instead, his 'unhappy' spirit appears at his favourite haunts and villagers are unsettled by the sightings of his spirit. Interesting to note is the stark difference in the attitudes of the grandmother, who is Christian and the old woman, who was known to practice the old beliefs. While the grandmother is uncharitable toward Zekuo, referring to him as "that man" and saying that "he didn't deserve a Christian burial", the old woman, who finds the spirit of the man at her hearth, speaks directly to him, telling him that "yours is a different road now".

The old woman, directly addressing the spirit of the departed, gives valuable insight into the pre-Christian beliefs of the Nagas concerning death and the dead. To the men who admonish her for speaking harshly to Zekuo's spirit, she retorts by saying:

> He is no longer a man, don't you see? He is a spirit and that is the way to speak to the spirits of the dead who are not at rest but try to return to the world of the living. They haunt the places they always frequented when they were alive and they seek out the people that were their constant companions because those are the ones who feel sentimental about them and help them to return. But he is dead, he is no longer the Zekuo who was our friend. (91)

The old woman also performs a ritual that requires her to physically strike a *dao* (traditional machete) at different places on her wooden door to stop the spirit from re-entering her house. The old woman performing this ritual was just as powerful as the pastor's prayer because it convinced the villagers that she had done a good job of sending off Zekuo's spirit (91-93).

For the Angamis, the supernatural world and the dead appearing to the living can be perceived in two ways. The first view is that the "unquiet" spirits of the departed linger because of remorse for a life cut short and the unwillingness to accept the finitude of their lives. Appearances of the unquiet spirits in the novel are explained by the sentimental feelings of the deceased's constant companions, who act as portals for the spirit to keep returning. Therefore, the spirit has to be addressed directly, as the old woman did. In the same category are those that die "so early that they keep returning to the place they were last alive on earth" (294).

The second perception involves those that come to say "farewell" to beloved family members and even to offer comfort to the living by showing them that they are happy. An instance of this is when Dielieno's mother describes seeing Pete appear in front of her as she wept at his grave. He smiled and held out his hands and spoke to her, "Mother, He is looking after me, I am not there in the grave there, I am in another place where He is." I saw that he was holding the hand of a man who stood by him, a tall man with a very kind face who kept looking at me with a smile" (296). Another example of this perception is when Dielieno, unsettled by seeing the spirit of the dead grandmother, is comforted by her mother with the words:

> But we also say that our loved ones return not as unquiet spirit but to say farewell in a manner that we would instantly recognize. It is in familiar noises that we associate with them.... If the living ones are very grieved over their going, the dead show themselves to them to comfort them and assure them that they are happy where they are. In our ignorance, we assume that they might still be suffering some earthly pain in the after-world.... So we are granted the grace to see these things ... we should accept it as privileges that are granted to certain special people. (295-296)

THE PURPOSE(S) OF DEATH IN *ATM*:

In the novel, death is approached sympathetically, which serves the dual purpose of warning and bringing closure. Kire calls attention to social ills that negatively impact Nagas today; problems such as alcoholism and wayward living are highlighted. Many characters meet untimely ends due to their overindulgence in such vices, and their behaviours are censured by the community they live in.

Alcohol abuse takes prominence and is shown as the reason for ruptures in relationships between family and friends. The problem of alcoholism in Naga society is realistically depicted by Kire and the reality was that "Many men died in the drinking houses" (125). The drinking houses are described as cesspits where unruly characters would converge and these meetings often ended in violent brawls (82). For the protagonist, the encounter with this social evil is very close to home as she experiences it first-hand with her brother, who eventually succumbs to the disease. It is the cause of death for Zekuo, Sonhie, Rocky, and Vini.

While authorial intentions are subject to personal interpretations, giving a realistic depiction of human experiences in fiction carries the possibility of sparking discussions on certain issues. Kire, as mentioned previously, may not be a moralist in her presentation of the social evils in her stories. However, by studying her characters, readers can appreciate the moral value and purpose of literature. Of course, the art-morality relation is complex and gives rise to critical debates, but the 'tragic' elements in the story-telling undoubtedly allow a catharsis. The tragic happenings in the novel can be justifiably interpreted as epitomizing what Aristotle put forward in his treatise on the art of poetry and the function of tragedy. Pity and fear are aroused by the deaths in *ATM*, allowing a purge of those emotions. Besides, apart from this focus on the psychological cleansing of emotions, the inevitable spirit of instruction prevails through this function of tragedy. In the essay "Literature and Morality", tragic elements in story-telling are said to possess a humanizing potential through which "settled notions of blame and responsibility" are shattered, and one can identify with the suffering of others. Thus, the fates of the characters in the novel whose experiences of death bring out this humanizing quality (Asim Karim et al. 188).

In putting the spotlight on addictions, Kire also shows the psychological trauma that families undergo when the disease of addiction begins to take hold of every aspect of the alcoholic's life. The painful and traumatic last moments spent in the hospital, where family members must wait out the inevitability of the death of a loved one, are articulated with compassion and sympathy. Kire posits the possible reason for the widespread abuse of alcoholism in Naga society when Vini responses to the pleas of family members to give up on drunkenness, he replies:

> "Do you want to know why I drink? Why all of us drink and brawl? It's because life here in Kohima is so meaningless.... Well, they were arguing about politics and the other chap said that it was no use fighting for independence because, in any case, the Naga cause was a dead cause.... Do you know how frustrating it is to be a Naga and live with the fear of being shot all the time? Do you know what it does to your insides when you hear about the people tortured and killed by the army and you can't do anything about it? (247)

While Vini and his cohort are viewed as social pariahs in the community, his plight also sheds light on the nationalist movements in the state and the deadly consequences of conflicts caused by the struggle to attain political autonomy by the Nagas. This opens up a Pandora's box on how some social evils may be rooted in the complexities of the rapid changes that Nagas had to undergo in the face of colonial powers and post-colonial powers moving into exercise authority through force. What is critical to note is that Kire emphasizes how one narrative cannot explain the myriad complexities of issues that the Nagas face today.

Death also serves the purpose of bringing closure to the characters in the story. For Dielieno, the complicated relationship that she had with her grandmother is resolved through the dying process, and death brings a new understanding of the harsh way she was treated. Her mother reveals that the grandmother had given preferential treatment to Dielieno's brothers only because she had grown up experiencing lack and had come to understand that for economic security, one had to depend on the men folk. The use of death as a literary device brings resolution for the protagonist and even for the reader. Dielieno poignantly encapsulates this with her words:

> After talking to Mother, I understood the deep sense of insecurity that led Grandmother to hold the worldview she did. I think I mellowed towards her. My fear of her changed to pity.... I was looking at Grandmother in a different light and it also helped me see myself in a better light. I felt a new sense of worth. (276)

The treatment of death in *ATM* is manifold in its approach. The worldview of the Angamis towards death, as seen in the novel, is a complex admixture of traditional beliefs and practices with the Judeo-Christian faith woven into it at a later stage. Kire's depiction and representation of death and its facets is a faithful and realistic portrayal of human experiences that are universal as well as particular to Angami society and the Nagas as a whole. Death in the worldview of the Angamis is not seen as a finitude but a crossing into a realm where at times, the link between these two worlds becomes blurred. In as much as the Nagas today identify themselves with Christianity and practice it over every aspect of their lives, there remains a remnant of the collective consciousness of the past and its beliefs, and this is deftly constructed and presented poignantly in the pleasant narrative style used by Kire. In the novel, Kire's approach towards death is one of awareness of the finitude of life, which helps us dwell on the human condition and structure our lives in a meaningful way (Hakola and Kivistö x). This meaningful way of presenting death also reminds us of the moral value of literature. It is best encapsulated in the words of Sir Philip Sidney, who argued that the value of creative literature lies in the fact that by adding emotional appeal to the finer human qualities, it can do more to make men finer than the philosophers can.

WORKS CITED

Elizabeth, Vizovono. "An Overview of the Development of Literature in Nagaland." *Insider Perspectives: Critical Essays on Literature from Nagaland.* Barkweaver Publications, 2017, p.1.

___. "Nativising our Narrative: Tenyimia Worldview as Reflected in Easterine Kire's A Naga Village Remembered." *Insider Perspectives,* p. 32.

Hakola, Outi and Sari Kivistö, editors. Introduction. *Death in Literature.* Cambridge Scholars Publishing, 2014, pp. vii-x.

Håland, Evy Johanne, editor. Introduction. *Women, Pain and Death: Rituals and Everyday Life on the Margins of Europe and Beyond.* Cambridge Scholars Publishing, 2008, pp. 4-9.

Jacobs, Julian, et.al. *The Nagas: Hill Peoples of Northeast India.* Thames and Hudson, 1990, pp. 83-85.

Karim, Asim, et al. "Literary and Morality." *IJSSE,* vol. 2, no. 2, 2012, p. 188. www. IJSSE.Org. Accessed 29 Aug. 2020.

Kire, Easterine. A Terrible Matriarchy. Zubaan Books, 2007.

Mambrol, Nasrullah. "Literary Criticism of Plato." *Literary Theory and Criticism.* 1 May 2017, www. literariness.org/2017/05/01/literary-criticism-of-plato/. Accessed 26 Aug. 2020.

Pou, KB Veio. *Literary Cultures of India's Northeast: Naga Writings in English.* Heritage Publishing House, 2015, pp. 63-68.

Shakespeare, William. *The Tragedy of Hamlet: Prince of Denmark,* edited by Barbara Mowat and Paul Werstine, Folger Shakespeare Library, p. 129. PDF file.

"Treatment." Cambridge English Dictionary, www.dictionary.cambridge.org/ dictionary/english/treatment. Accessed 27 Aug. 2020.

"Treatment." Collins English Dictionary, www.collinsdictionary.com/dictionary/ english/treatment. Accessed 27 Aug. 2020.

Twain, Mark. 1962. *Letters from The Earth.* Harper and Row, p. 17. PDF file.

14

ORAL-TRADITION, CHRISTIANITY AND NATURE: A STUDY OF EASTERINE KIRE'S NOVELS

Emisen Jamir

ORAL TRADITION AND NAGA LITERATURE: A BRIEF OVERVIEW

For most of their history, the Nagas have relied on oral narratives to preserve social, historical, and religious records. Oral traditions perform the important function of transmitting or transferring knowledge about social customs and practices, historical events and processes, and religious practices and beliefs from one generation to the next. This process is evident in their songs, song-poems, stories, myths, and legends passed down from one generation to the next. The survival of such narratives requires the collective memory and participation of the entire community. This use of the spoken word, not merely as a form of communication but also as a means of transferring ancestral customs and traditions, constitutes a well-structured system that does not require scripts and written literature.

The arrival of the British in Nagaland in 1832, followed by the American missionaries, brought about drastic changes among the Naga tribes. The missionaries set out to 'educate' the Nagas to enable them to read the Bible and sing hymns. According to M. Alemchiba, while Naga literature has grown out of primers, grammar and translation, much of it is still confined to Christian themes (161). The process of conversion and the introduction of Western education soon posed a substantial threat to the Naga oral tradition. The *morungs*, which were the centres of traditional education for young Naga men and women, were slowly abandoned as Western education took precedence. With greater importance being given to the written word, oral narratives were pushed to the periphery. In addition, the Indo-Japanese war of 1944 and the subsequent conflict sparked by the Nagas' demand for independence soon saw an increase in killings and displacement of Naga people from their villages. In 'War and the Silencing of Naga Narratives,' Easterine Kire states, "The peace that is essential to the continuation of oral narratives was lost. The war years also killed many oral narrators, and folk narratives were further silenced in the premature deaths of their carriers" (np). As a result, the oral tradition of the Nagas began to deteriorate.

With the political upheavals and the huge cultural changes resulting from the arrival of the European colonisers, oral tradition lost its tenacious hold on the Naga people, and the oral mode of communication gave way to a scripted medium. The educational institutions, primarily set up to disseminate the teachings of Christianity, grew in importance as more and more people discovered the benefits of learning the English language. Moreover, the educated Nagas used this tool to voice their discontent with the prevailing political system. The violence and trauma encountered by the people can be seen in the literature of the Nagas, which documents various lives caught in the crossfire.

Naga literature is still a relatively new term employed to describe the works of Naga writers who have tried to capture and record the spaces inhabited by the changing Naga society. While much has been written about the history, culture and politics of the Nagas, the writing of poems, novels, and short stories in English by a Naga writer is a recent phenomenon. Easterine Kire is regarded as the first Naga poet and novelist in English. It is through stories and poems that writers such as Easterine Kire, Temsula Ao, Monalisa Changkija, and Nini Lungalung narrate the everyday realities of the Nagas. The rapidity with which the tribal lives have been transformed is explored in Naga literature through poems, novels and short stories. As Veio Pou states, "Stories and poems by these Naga writers are interwoven with the commonalities of simple and ordinary people's lives. By seasoning life experiences with artistic imaginations, their writings become a manifestation of Naganess, being rooted in the Naga existential reality (49).

Easterine Kire is one of the first Naga writers in English. Her book, *A Naga Village Remembered* (2003), subsequently revised to *Sky Is My Father: A*

Naga Village Remembered (2018), is the first novel by a Naga writer in English. Kire's writings explore the lives of the Nagas from the precolonial past to the present, chronicling their history, religion, and evolving cultural practices. This paper examines the impact of Christianity on the Nagas and how it affected their interaction with the natural world. The paper examines the relationship between man and nature as seen in the novels of Easterine Kire and explores the possibility of reconciliation between the two.

IMPACT OF CHRISTIANITY AND WESTERN EDUCATION IN EASTERINE KIRE'S *SKY IS MY FATHER: A NAGA VILLAGE REMEMBERED*

Using Khonoma village as the setting for her novel, Kire describes the precolonial life of the Nagas, their clash with the British colonisers and the changes that swiftly overtook and unsettled their once solid community life. The arrival of the British resulted in numerous changes, the most significant being that of religion. The introduction of Christianity brought about an almost complete change in the way the Nagas navigated their world. The colonisers came not only with Christian notions of salvation but also brought with them their version of civilisation and progress. As such, the Nagas, with their 'pagan' practices, were to be 'civilised'. As stated by the missionary Mary Clark, "The Nagas, once civilised and Christianised, will make a manly, worthy people" (qtd. in Eaton 13).

Before Christianity, the Nagas believed in the existence of a supernatural power(s), for which regular sacrifices had to be performed as a tribute or appeasement. The religion of the Nagas has often been termed animistic. The word 'animism' was first coined by the anthropologist E.B. Tylor (1832–1917). In his book, *Primitive Cultures. The Encyclopedia of Religion and Nature*, he describes animism not as a "type of religion" but as "a theory of religion" (78). The *New World Encyclopedia* defines animism as the "belief in numerous personalised, supernatural beings endowed with reason, intelligence and/or volition, that inhabit both objects and living beings and govern their existences. More simply, it is the belief that 'everything is conscious' or that 'everything has a soul'" (para. 1). The religion of the Nagas has been subject to debate, with some scholars claiming that, given their belief in a Supreme being, one cannot claim the Nagas to be purely animist (Longvah 138). Moreover, over the years, the term animism has come to be seen as derogatory and condescending by indigenous communities across the world since it implies a religion that is inferior to the existing 'sophisticated' and 'structured' religions like that of Christianity. Thus, while the belief in spirits inhabiting both animate and inanimate objects is evidenced among the various Naga tribes, terms such as 'animism' have been set aside to give way to more inclusive terminology such as indigenous religion(s) or in the context of Nagaland, as Naga Indigenous Religions (Shohe 23).

In Easterine Kire's novel, *Sky is My Father: A Naga Village Remembered*, the pastoral life is broken down in the aftermath of a war, with the British seeking to subjugate the warriors of Khonoma. In her introduction to the novel, Kire writes that "the battle turned into a siege of the tough little Angami village for four months. Finally, on 27 March 1880, a verbal treaty between the representatives of the British Government and the elders of Khonoma concluded the conflict" (Kire xiv). The British entry into Khonoma paved the way for the missionaries to bring Christianity into the land. It should, however, be noted that the battle of Khonoma was not the first entry point for the missionaries into the Naga region. The impact of Christianity was already being felt in different parts of the Naga Hills as a result of contact with the missionaries, and thus, with the suppression of Khonoma village, the same process of conversion and assimilation soon began.

The process started with the setting up of educational institutions and medical facilities. For proselytisation to take place, the Nagas must be taught to read and write. Educational institutions, therefore, had to be established. With the establishment of a new Western educational system, the newly converted were forced to abandon the indigenous educational institutions like the *morungs*, causing irrevocable damage to the cultural and traditional values of the Nagas. The missionaries regarded the spiritual practices of the Nagas as pagan and sought to change what they thought were heathen practices (Eaton 13). Certain practices like head-hunting were given up, and the rigid rules imposed by the missionaries greatly affected and changed the ancient traditional practices of the Nagas. According to R.S. Sugirtharajah:

> The growth of Protestant churches in the colonies had a familiar pattern. First, the denunciation of the natives' idolatrous practices, then preaching accompanied by the presentation and dissemination of the Bible as the answer to their miserable state, followed by the establishment of denominational churches and the founding of educational and medical institutions. (52)

In *Sky Is My Father*, educational institutions are established following the arrival of the British. Seeing that the Nagas had to rely on bone-setters, herbalists and chicken sacrificers, Dr Sidney Rivenburg astutely went back to America to study medicine for two years at Baltimore Medical College.

Equipped with a knowledge of modern medicine, Dr Rivenburg soon settled in among the Nagas, who became less wary of a foreigner bent on healing the sick. By building a rapport with them, Rivenburg made inroads into the conversion process. As Kire explains in the novel, "There seemed to be greater acceptance of the white man, now that he could cure ailments with his medicines. Between treating his patients, Rivenburg continued to tell them of Christ's gospel. He felt he was able to make more inroads in this manner" (117).

A similar progression can be seen in Achebe's *Things Fall Apart*. The coming of the missionaries soon results in the establishment of educational institutions and churches in Umofia. One such missionary is Mr Brown, who seems able to find a balance between the converts and the non-converts, unlike his rather orthodox successor Reverend James Smith. Both Dr Rivenburg in *Sky is My Father* and Achebe's Mr Brown use the Christian notion of a Supreme deity who is above all other deities and seeks no sacrifice from the people for appeasement. Like Nyowe, who seeks reason behind the abandoning of twins in the Evil Forest or the killing of Ikemefuna, Vipiano too questions why her sister, who had always adhered strictly to the village laws and customs, should be the recipient of a 'lashu' death. Questions such as these find their answers in the new religion, and Achebe's Nwoye is among the first to convert. While Mr. Brown is a fictional character, Kire's Dr. Rivenburg is a historical figure and was among the first people to translate the scriptures into Angami. Using historical evidence to corroborate her story, Kire attempts to build a narrative that mirrors many other narratives of the colonised. The methods of Dr Rivenburg and Mr Brown reveal the missionaries' important role in changing the thoughts and precepts of the community.

Change in the educational system was one of the major factors that swiftly assimilated the Naga tribes into the coloniser's culture. The traditional education system gave way to a more 'modern' and 'western' oriented system. Used primarily for a fuller immersion of the Nagas into the Christian religion, the use of the Roman script gradually allowed the converts to grasp the colonisers' language. This process of slowly administering the colonial ways to the Nagas is seen in the following lines from *Sky Is My Father*, "Rivenburg's school was unconventional: he wrote primers in Angami using Roman script. So, Sato's first book was in Angami. Later, he progressed to the higher class, where a very popular class was the "Talking class." In this class, Chaha encouraged his pupils to converse in English" (118). The transition from an oral to a written culture was seen as a necessary step not only for the dissemination of the Biblical word but also as an integral step towards 'civilisation'.

With no written literature of their own, a people's history is stored in memories. The collective memory of the community shapes and strengthens their stories. However, the oral cultures of such communities were thought to be primitive and in need of change. In *The Bible and the Third World: Precolonial, Colonial and Postcolonial Encounters*, R.S. Sugirtharajah states that "The assumption of the missionaries was that oral cultures were empty and were waiting to be filled with written texts" (69). He explains how the early missionaries used the colonialist binary paradigm of Christian/savage, civilised/barbaric, orderly/disorderly to define and explain their dominance over the colonised (62). Inculcating European manners with the aid of the Bible was one of the first measures employed for the 'advancement' of the so-called 'uncivilised'. For the converts, accepting Christianity meant accepting and following the rules of the new religion as interpreted by the missionaries. It called not only for forsaking the old religion but also the old laws, which were inherently bound to their social and religious practices. "The second mark of colonial interpretation," according to Sugirtharajah, "was the introduction of the 'other' alien values under the guise of biblicization" (64). This was evidenced not only in the physical manifestation of the Nagas' use of Western clothes but was also seen in the way this 'alien' culture shaped their thinking. J.P. Mills observed these changes and critiqued their transformations in *The Ao Nagas*:

> A Naga who puts on foreign clothes adopts with them a foreign outlook. His old environment is no longer good enough for him, and what appears particularly abhorrent to him is the prospect of a life-long routine of going down a steep hill every morning, doing a day's work in the fields, and coming up a steep hill every evening. The more "civilised" he is, the less he likes work which entails manual labour. (422)

While considering his observation of the changes occurring within the folds of Naga society, it should also be noted that colonial anthropologists like J. P. Mills believed the Nagas needed to be safeguarded from the onslaught of modernity that was rapidly changing the way Nagas viewed themselves and their world. Therefore, they believed in keeping intact the various institutions and practices of the Nagas and preserving them in their current status as 'noble savages', uncorrupted by 'Westernisation' or 'civilisation'.

The missionaries, on the other hand, sought a different approach. By imposing their "own milieu into a totally different environment, they lost sight of the importance of rooting faith in a manner that does not dissociate Nagas from all that is inherently Naga" (Hümtsoe-Nienu 68-69). As a result, the existing religious practices were discarded for the new religion and new modes of living. Through her novel, Kire illustrates the assimilation of the Nagas into the colonial culture, which led to the rapid disintegration of a once compact communal life. This us/them dichotomy not only disrupted the robust village structure but also unsettled the way the Nagas viewed themselves and their environment.

OTHERING NATURE

This 'othering' of the indigenous communities by the colonisers also extended to their treatment of nature. In this context, Val Plumwood explains the idea of 'hyper-separation'. According to Plumwood, "Hyper-separation means defining the dominant identity emphatically against, or in opposition to, the subordinated identity, by excluding their real or supposed qualities. The function of hyper-separation is to mark out the 'other' for separate and inferior treatment" (54). Considering nature as separate from humans blurs the importance of the human-nature relationship. It introduces the idea of humans as existing outside of nature, thereby denying the connection and devaluing the unity of human beings and nature. Nature becomes a "hyper-separate lower order" (*ibid*). The presumed notion that nature and animals lack consciousness excludes them from the 'thinking', 'rational' world of human beings. Human dependence on nature is relegated to the background, creating a place of denial and ultimately positioning itself above the non-human sphere. Drawing parallels between the colonisers' treatment of the indigenous peoples and nature, Plumwood explains how nature and indigenous people are clubbed together on the premise that they are sub-par to the otherwise 'superior' and 'civilised' coloniser. "Differences are judged", she explains, "as grounds of inferiority, not as welcome and intriguing signs of diversity" (58). By creating an us-them/superior-inferior distinction, one becomes desensitised towards the so-called 'other', setting forth a dangerous precedent as evidenced in the treatment of the indigenous communities by the colonisers.

J. Donald Hughes states that the current ecological crisis results from attitudes that view nature as "something to be freely conquered, used, and dominated without calculation of the resultant cost to mankind and the earth" (158). Christianity saw nature as something to be dominated, and in instilling this notion of nature domination, the Nagas' foray into progress and modernisation began. Nature found its place not side-by-side with the human world but was, instead, seen in relation to its usefulness to humans. By distinguishing nature as existing for the benefit of human beings, a hierarchical structure is put into place where humans are above the natural world. This system can be traced back through the Middle Ages to the Greek Neoplatonists, who propounded a strict hierarchical system with God at the highest level, followed by angels or spirits, heavenly bodies, and human beings, with animals, plants, and minerals occupying the lowest rung. Hughes, however, elaborates that "the process of dominating the earth is seen not as a religious crusade following a biblical commandment but a profitable venture seeking economic benefit" (ibid.).

It has been argued that, while modernity fast-forwarded the inevitable destruction of the earth, the different indigenous peoples of the world were also heading in the same direction. In this regard, the agricultural practices of the Nagas, particularly the slash and burn or *jhum* cultivation, have often been criticised. It has been claimed that such practices inevitably lead to the destruction of the environment. However, various circumstances feature in the employment of such agricultural methods. In Temsula Ao's short story "A New Chapter" in *These Hills called Home: Stories from a War Zone*, the people are aware of the destruction wrought about by such agricultural practices; however, the changing times leave them no choice but to cultivate the land instead of allowing the earth to remain fallow and replenish itself for several years. The indigenous knowledge concerning land demonstrates the empathetic nature of the Nagas towards the non-human world. To quote from the text:

> They knew that the job would not be as difficult as in the old days because the scorched earth had not yet had enough time to replenish herself; the vegetation was young and consisted only of tender saplings, which could be cleared without much effort. In the old days, such areas would have been allowed to lie fallow for at least nine or ten years before the cycle was resumed. But the core of the earth had changed forever in the last decade, and they had no choice but to turn to her ravaged body, to hurt her some more and extract whatever she could yield to them from her depleted resources. (121)

In *Bitter Wormwood*, Kire describes the traditional practice of terrace cultivation among the Angami Nagas, "In this area, everyone cultivated terrace fields. It was more laborious than *jhum* fields, the slash-and-burn method. Nevertheless, people preferred terrace fields, which did not damage the soil as *jhumming* did" (33). The understanding of the land and its uses and the reciprocity of the Nagas in caring for the land are underlined by Kire. That being so, despite the damage to the soil by *jhum* cultivation, Ao's take on this practice highlights how the land is left to replenish before it is cultivated again. The land is allowed to heal before it is reused. Such a profound understanding of the land can only corroborate the notion of the Nagas' close relationship with nature. Only because of the various 'upheavals' in the village were the villagers forced to re-cultivate before the land was fully rested.

With the passage of time, this empathy towards nature gradually disconnects. The fear of burying the past is expressed in Kire's *Son of the Thundercloud*, "Our young should not think that there are lands better than this to build a home. They belong here; they must take the place of their ancestors. They feared that if the young were not taught to love the village, it would soon be abandoned. They had seen it happen around them" (12). The rejection of one's customs and traditions brings famine to the land, famine in both the literal and metaphorical sense. While drought kills and destroys villages, it is the more dangerous 'famine' of stories and songs that ultimately ends them. As mentioned before, oral narratives factored greatly in the eventual survival of a village, its customs and traditions, histories and modes of living. Without such narratives, the ancestral knowledge no longer finds a vessel for its survival and eventually perishes. Thus, in Kire's *Son of the Thundercloud*, the destruction of the land goes side by side with the death of the storytellers. In the novel, Mesanuo tells Pele that the 'dark ones' killed the storytellers because they "did not want them to transform people's minds with their stories" (63). Without the storytellers to narrate the stories of the past that are intrinsically connected to nature, man becomes disconnected not only from himself and his fellow beings but from nature as well. Because of the close connection of the Nagas with the natural world, this detachment of humans from nature ultimately creates a feeling of alienation.

A RETURN TO NATURE

While Easterine Kire explores the estrangement brought about by proselytisation and assimilation of the colonial ways, she writes of ways to reconnect with the natural world. In her novel, *When the River Sleeps*, Kire introduces the readers to Vilie, who seeks to reconnect with nature by moving into the forest and away from human settlements. In the novel, Kire presents a world in which inanimate objects are alive and aware. The river in the novel is seen as a living entity that not only sleeps but, when awake, becomes protective of the heart stone that lies beneath it. Not only is the river given living attributes, such as being in a state of slumber, but even the forest is seen as a maternal figure, providing food and shelter for the inhabitants dwelling within her. Vilie isolates himself from constant human contact, only to direct it towards the forest. He finds, in the forest, a wife-mother figure. Kire reaffirms this by stating that "the forest as wife is also nearly synonymous with the forest as mother because she provides him shelter and food".

This notion of nature as a nurturing figure is repeated in Kire's *Son of the Thundercloud*. The river with its life-giving properties is called 'our mother'. In the novel, "No one came back from the river empty-handed. There was food in the river, and so the villagers called it 'our mother'" (54). With the appearance of rain, the river once again flourishes, and the earth comes alive, hungrily swallowing the seeds. When rain falls on the Village of the Weavers, nature responds rapidly by giving 'birth' to trees and rocks. The image of the forest as a mother is aptly applied in the symbolic rebirth of all things animate and inanimate. The village headman's wonder at the sudden appearance of rocks and trees is answered by Mesanuo. She replies, "It is called birthing, headman. The earth has birthed trees, rocks, stones, and grain, just as a mother births her offspring. The trees and the rocks are the sons of the earth. Take care of them, and they will take care of you and your children" (46).

Through Mesanuo, Kire presses forward the importance of realising the balance needed between man and nature. The effect of human actions on nature is seen as a boomerang effect. As Pele looks at the new-born babe, he recalls his mother singing him a lullaby:

> The river runs
> And it runs
> Into the sea
> And the sea runs
> Into the rain
> Where it all comes from. (47)

The song dwells as an instructive medium explaining the origin of rain. Songs and stories acted as instruments of instruction for the pre-Christian Nagas, and the simple lullaby gives an example of how songs and stories passed through generations—in this case, from Pele's mother to him and then to Rhalie—act as reservoirs of knowledge for the younger generation. It is in such song-poems that the intrinsic connection of humankind with nature is implied. There is no othering of nature. Instead, there is respect for the natural world, which is recognised as a nurturer and provider.

The novels of Easterine Kire reveal the internal tensions that arise while navigating between the past and the present. Kire creates a space to reexamine the current scenario where casual disregard for nature has led to an imbalance in the environment. With the advent of globalisation and technological advancement, it has become more important than ever to remember and acknowledge one's history and culture. The ancestral knowledge passed down through oral narratives needs to be documented and disseminated among the people. Values such as respect for nature, as was once practised in the precolonial era, can be revived.

Kire's writings propose a re-visitation of the past in order to reacquaint oneself with the natural world. To achieve this, there is a need to remove the concept of shame towards the precolonial Naga practices. Kire does this by documenting the myths and history of the Nagas and embedding them within her stories. While attempting to address political and social issues, Kire imbues her narrative with the lived realities of the Nagas that are still closely intertwined with the past. It may not be possible to return to a pre-Christian, precolonial state, but neither is it feasible to move forward without an understanding of one's culture in which identities are rooted. A synthesis of the past and the present is, perhaps, the answer to the existing struggle, and it is in works such as those of Easterine Kire that we are presented with the possibility of reconciling the worlds that have shaped the Nagas today.

WORKS CITED

Achebe, Chinua. *Things Fall Apart*. Heinemann, 1986.

Alemchiba, M. *A Brief Historical Account of Nagaland*. Naga Institute of Culture, 1970.

Ao, Temsula. "A New Chapter". *These Hills Called Home: Stories from a War Zone*. Zubaan, 2006, pp. 121-147.

"Animism". *New World Encyclopedia*. 2009, https://www.newworldencyclopedia. org/entry/Animism. Accessed 24 May 2018.

Chidester, David. "Animism". *Encyclopedia of Religion and Nature*. Continuum, 2005, http://www.religionandnature.com/ern/sample/Chidester-Animism. pdf

Eaton, Richard M. "Conversion to Christianity among the Nagas, 1876-1971." *The Indian Economic and Social History Review*, vol.21, no.1, 1984, pp. 1-44.

Hughes, J. Donald. "The Ancient Roots of our Ecological Crisis." *Environmental Ethics: Divergence and Convergence*, edited by G. Richard Botzler, Susan J. Armstrong, 2nd ed., McGraw Hill, 1998, pp. 157-161.

Hmtsoe-Nienu, Eyingbeni. *God of the Tribes*. Clark Theological College, 2014.

Iralu, Easterine. *A Naga Village Remembered*. Ura Academy, 2003.

Kire, Easterine. *Bitter Wormwood*. Zubaan, 2011.

—. *Sky is my Father: A Naga Village Remembered*. Rev. ed., Speaking Tiger, 2018.

—. *Son of the Thundercloud*. Speaking Tiger, 2016.

—. "Re: Some Answers." Received by Emisenla Jamir. 5 Sept 2016.

—. *When the River Sleeps*. Zubaan, 2014.

Longvah, Shonreiphy. "Christian Conversion, the Rise of Naga Consciousness, and Naga Nationalist Politics". *Nagas in the 21ˢᵗ Century*, edited by Jelle J P Wouters, Michael Heneise, The Highlander Books, 2017, pp. 133-149.

Mills, J.P. *The Ao Nagas*. Oxford UP, 1973.

Plumwood, Val. "Decolonizing Relationships with Nature". *Decolonizing Nature Strategies for Conservation in a Post-colonial Era*, edited by William M Adams, Martin Mulligan, Earthscan, 2003, pp. 51-78.

Pou, K B Veio. *Literary Cultures of India's Northeast: Naga Writings in English*. Heritage, 2015.

Shohe, Loina. "Naga Indigenous Religions: Reconstructing its Nomenclatures." *Panjab University Research Journal (Arts)*, vol. XLVII, no. 2, 2020, pp. 10-27.

Sugirtharajah, R.S. *The Bible and the Third World: Precolonial, Colonial and Postcolonial Encounters*. Cambridge UP, 2004.

15

AN ECOCRITICAL STUDY OF EASTERINE KIRE'S *WHEN THE RIVER SLEEPS* AND *SON OF THE THUNDERCLOUD*

Achingliu Kamei

INTRODUCTION

Literature can be a site for dialogue on ecology. As in art and other fields relating to social reality and lived experiences, the relationship between nature and society can also be found in literature. Perspectives gleaned from literature can further our understanding of ecology through ecocriticism and help reveal new viewpoints in literary and cultural studies. With rare exceptions, the earlier Indian English novels were not written through the lens of ecocriticism. However, nature was often used as the backdrop against which the story developed. The writings from the North Eastern States of India are often characterized by the presence of nature, whether as a beautiful landscape for a backdrop or as spirits and souls playing an active role in the artistic creation. The traditional religion of the Nagas encourages deep respect for nature. The writers are acutely aware of their immediate ecological surroundings; "Nature is not just a source of sustenance for most of the NE states, but more of an extension of identity and roots. Thus, harm to Nature immediately affects the question of identity. Nature becomes a space where an individual identifies himself. Through the spirits of trees and rivers and mountains, one can find the ancestral roots" (Anupama 61).

From the seminal work of Rachel Carson's *Silent Spring* to *The Ecocriticism Reader* (Eds. Cheryll Glotfelty and Harold Fromm), the study of the relationship between literature and the physical environment has come a long way. In addition, *The Environmental Imagination* by Lawrence Buell has revived the term 'ecocriticism'. As a theoretical discourse, ecocriticism negotiates between human and nonhuman. To a certain extent, the conceptual gap between nature and culture has been bridged by ecocriticism. Ecocriticism, in conjunction with the discourse on the harmony between nature and humanity, talks about the destruction of nature. This degradation has been brought about by humanity's creative inventions and activities in pursuit of 'progress', ironically leading to nature's elimination from the Earth. Therefore, the 'progress' of humankind must be arrested.

Much can be gained by analyzing a text ecocritically. Nayar agrees with the theory put forward by Cheryll Glotfelty that one needs to recoup professional dignity for what she calls the undervalued genre of nature writing. According to Nayar,

> Ecocriticism is a critical mode that looks at the representation of nature and landscape texts, paying particular attention to attitudes towards "nature" and the rhetoric employed when speaking about it. It aligns itself with ecological activism and social theory with the assumption that the rhetoric of cultural texts reflects and informs material practices towards the environment while seeking to increase awareness about it and linking itself (and literary texts) with other ecological sciences and approaches (242).

Ecocriticism evades a specific definition, yet many scholars have tried to define the term over the years. A series of sixteen position papers, all entitled 'What is ecocriticism', has been published as part of the 1994 WLA meeting in Salt Lake City on *Defining Ecocritical Theory and Practice*.

According to Thomas K Dean,

> Ecocriticism is a study of culture and cultural products (artworks, writings, scientific theories, etc.) that is in some way or other connected with the human relationship to the natural world. First, ecocriticism is a response to the need for a humanistic understanding of our relationships with the natural world in an age of environmental destruction.

Primarily, environmental crises result from humanity's disconnection from the natural world, brought about by increasing technology and particularization; that is, a mentality of specialization that fails to recognize the interconnectedness of all things. In terms of the academy, ecocriticism is thus a response to the scholarly specialization that has gone out of control; ecocriticism seeks to reattach scholars to each other and scholarship to the real concerns of the world (5).

ENVIRONMENTAL CONCERNS IN LITERARY WORKS:

In almost all of Easterine Kire's work, we can detect an urgency to inform her people and her readers of the need to reconnect with nature and to rein in the disastrous path humans have trodden in the name of progress. Easterine Kire is not the only writer from the North East of India to lament the environmental destruction in the region. As Debajyoti Biswas says,

> Some eminent writers from the Northeastern region like Easterine Kire, Temsula Ao, Yeshe Dorjee Thongchi, Monalisha Chankija, Robin S Ngangom, Vanneihtluanga, Kynpham Sing Nongkynrih, and Mamnag Dai, among many others, have, in their ways, endeavoured to negotiate between the nature/culture, anthropocentric/ecocentric dichotomy through their respective works. But the uniqueness of Kire's writing is that she has the artistic capacity to blend myth and folk elements with the global concern about the environmental crisis... (2).

Kire's first novel, A *Naga Village Remembered* (re-issued as *Sky is My Father: A Naga Village Remembered* in 2018) describes the socio-cultural rituals and heroic deeds of a warrior village. It is a historical novel about the real village society of Khonoma, about ordinary people going about their everyday lives. A *Terrible Matriarchy* (2006) records the growth, emotions, and experiences of a girl child, Dielino. It exposes the intricate tribal social fabric through the story of Dielino and her attempts to challenge the patriarchy. Even in a novel like this that deals with themes of gender discrimination and alcoholism, the natural world is never far away - "Vimenuo and I ran home... or went to look for four-leaf clover... In the second week, we found a four-leaf clover for her" (89).

In most of her novels, Kire dexterously blends historical facts and fiction with environmental issues as a core theme. The way she deals with nature in her writing helps realign readers' conception of the natural world. *Mari* tells the displacement story of Kohima and its people during the Second World War. *Bitter Wormwood* describes an insurgency-torn Naga society. *When the River Sleeps* records tribal identity, rituals, beliefs, reverence for the land, and the close-knit nature of the communities. *A Respectable Woman* is a historical novel intertwined with the memories of war and the transformation of Kohima through the stories of two women.

Among the most critical concerns facing our world are the aesthetic and ethical dilemmas posed by the environmental crisis. Ecocriticism encourages the dialogue between literature and nature and highlights how it can transmit values in a world context. There is a strong hint of nostalgia, especially in the poems and short stories of Ao, Dai, and Kire, with nature playing an active role in their work. They address the issues of loss of identity and the disconnectedness of people from nature through metaphors around trees, mountains, rivers, and animals. The overall effect of their perspectives on the peoples' connection with the natural world is to make the readers realize what it was like to dwell in a harmonious relationship with nature, thereby increasing their ecological awareness. The aim is to address the readers' sensitivities about the importance of preserving the intimate, sacred link between nature and themselves. Some of their works are about geography too. Very soon, if we are not careful, there will be nothing left of nature to talk about. The authors also intend to demonstrate through their fictional writing how modernization has put a strain on people's connection to nature. Among the factors leading to the disconnection was the arrival of the British, accompanied by their religion and their Western political philosophy and ideology. Then, industrialization negatively affected the air, water, soil, and habitat. The people from the North East region believe that one's journey is never one's own. In part, it is the continuation of the one before yours. After your journey, the journey will continue. People who belong to a tight community fare much better in a crisis. The West is in such a sorry state because of its sense of individual entitlement.

Kire and Dai personified rivers in their respective works *When the River Sleeps* and *Small Towns and the River*. 'The river has a soul...the river knows/ the immortality of water' (Dai). The river in the poem has a soul and its own will. The world of nature is represented primarily by the river. Whereas human deaths are frequent, the river is immortal. At the same time, while the human world is marked by sadness and stagnancy, the natural world is full of vigour and movement. In the poem 'For my Son', Kire's anguish over the ecologically broken world due to deforestation and pollution can be seen. 'Before you are born/Into an ever-changing world/before the green pines/fall prey to the woodcutter's axe/and stumps stand, glory/remains, / of once beautiful trees; /before the gloriously/setting sun/is veiled in city smog' (Kire). She implies that this utopia will probably not exist by the time the child is born. The natural world will be gone. All that would remain would be the remnants of past glory, not just the glory of green nature, but also the glory of the people's past valour, ethical, and moral standards.

In the poem *An Obscure Place*, Mamang Dai writes of mountains as places that house the people's histories and their stories of hope and fear, and act as omniscient beings. They are refuges of sorts, for they record the histories of the community. 'There are mountains.../We climbed every slope. We slept by the river/But do not speak of victory yet' (Dai, *Poetry at Sangam*). In the poem, she also addresses the destruction of animal life and metaphorically implies the loss of identity. 'See! They have slain the wild cat/and buried the hornbill in her maternal sleep' (*ibid*). Dai's poems, like *Voice of the Mountain* and *Remembrance*, also speak of the destruction of the land, the diminishing closeness of the people with the land, and the deterioration of relationships between people and between the people and nature. The philosophy and belief systems of the people are intrinsically connected with nature and its preservation. The destruction of the forest kills the inhabitants, and the people's identity, too, is jeopardized.

Temsula Ao has often written about her concern about the destruction of the luxuriant forest and the awe-inspiring mountains of the region. The mountains are symbolic of the people's glory in her writings. Thus, the destruction of the mountains leads to the destruction of the people. From an ecological point of view, disturbing the balance of nature by harming the hills and the mountains is fatal for the communities residing in the area. Her concern about humans taking advantage of nature can be seen in the lines of *Prayer of a Monolith*: They chipped and chiseled/They gave me altered proportions./They pulled me to the village/Strapped to a make-shift carriage... /As their new-found trophy (81-83). She is not only concerned about ravaged nature but also about the rapid changes in the indigenous people, which have endangered their values and ethics. Her poems are works of resistance to the policies of change and 'progress' responsible for the destruction of nature—disturbing the ecological balance by destroying the hills, forests, and rivers, which is fatal for people. Her other poems like *Lament for Earth, The Earthquake, Blood of Others, To the Children of the World*, and *Dying* talk about the dangers of destroying nature and warn society and the patriarchy about the fatal outcomes of abusing Earth and women. Her distress over the destruction of the lush forest and mountains is evident in the abovementioned poems. She introspects poignantly in the poems that the people have strayed from their ways and roots and let the mountain shrink down to an ant hill.

Kire combines postcolonial ecocriticism and phytocriticism. In her writing, there seems to be a concerted effort to do away with the colonial stereotyping of her world. The geographical concepts of mountains, hills, and rivers are interlinked with the philosophy of the people. European colonization has wasted and destroyed much of the traditional knowledge by replacing it with Western educational and cultural systems. This substitution of traditional wisdom with a new knowledge system constructed by the colonists has exploited nature to the maximum. Traditional knowledge is founded upon principles that favour connection rather than isolation and protection rather than exploitation. Furthermore, imbibing Western values has led to individualization instead of participation in communal life so that the individual becomes cut off from regard for nature. Kire's attempts to reawaken the ancient knowledge systems are aimed at restoring and redeeming human faith in the natural world because this will foster respect for nature. In her works, nature has played the ultimate role of a provider, protector, nurturer, and giver of life. Mother Nature sustains and provides for humans. Nature's products deemed free and available should not be taken advantage of, like a woman should not be taken for granted or abused. Humans have lived in nature's lap for millions of years while causing minimum damage. Only around the eighteenth century did the mode of production change with the rise of industrialization. Kire's words in *Son of the Thundercloud* speaks this truth; "When people are overtaken by greed, they are going to bring a lot of trouble into their own lives and into the lives of others" (64-65). If humankind's greed is not arrested, the impending doom is apparent.

EASTERINE KIRE'S TWO SEMINAL NOVELS"

The two novels *When the River Sleeps* and *Son of the Thundercloud* are set in the forests of the Nagas. The readers accompany the protagonists Vilie, a lone middle-aged hunter who found a 'home' in the forest, and Pelevotso (Pele), a perpetual traveller, not just spatially but on a journey of discovery of the ways and the world-view of the Nagas and the inter-relations within the different Naga tribes. *When the River Sleeps* (henceforth WRS) depicts for its readers a nation or a land where people lived complex yet systematic lives, diverse yet bound by similar ethics and a fruitful relationship with the environment. The vast expanse of sky, the wilderness, the winding rivers, birds, and fauna all share sacred space in the scheme of things with humans. A similar narrative is seen in the novel *Son of the Thundercloud* (henceforth ST). One can identify a sense of urgency running throughout the novel: a loss of faith and hope that needs to be restored to understand the relationship between man and nature. After the death of Pelevotso's grandfather, his grandmother lived at the edge of the forest: '...she had lived alone, collecting jungle herbs to heal sick and wounded animals and men' (ST 11). Thus, nature provides for all beings.

In WRS, Kire had many 'elements woven into the story: adventure, quest, folktales, magic and ultimately, reality' (Daftuar). To add to this list are the elements of the spiritual world, the supernatural, legend, myth, and friendship. In the interview with Daftuar, Kire talked of her hunter friends and her son being a hunter. The story of the sleeping river and the charmed stone Kire called the 'heart-stone' was a tale told among Naga hunters. The story stayed with her and was later written up as a novel. The river keeps a unique stone in its bed and allows only a select few to wrest it from its hold. This 'heart-stone', which has the power to bring great material fortune, also has healing power. It is to be used for the benefit of humankind and to heal the broken, the disenfranchised, and the marginalized. Ate, a young girl Vilie 'rescued', was healed from the injury suffered at the claws of the weretiger after the heart-stone was placed on her hand. "He felt for Ate's hand and placed the heart-stone in her palm.... Vilie looked down as he felt a small movement at his feet" (WRS 195-196). Ate was brought back to life with the help of nature.

The river is the harbinger of prosperity, but at the same time, it is also 'treacherous'; similarly, prosperity is treacherous because, when it outgrows itself, it becomes difficult to control. Kire relates the idea of prosperity to the river to signify the importance of respecting both these forces. The role of a river as both benefactor and danger can be seen in ST. The river was once a source of life for the village...there was food in the river, so the villagers called it 'our mother'. Then the drought came in...the water dried down... Our mother is dead! She can no longer feed the children. Who shall be our mother when our mother is dead?'...However, now the river was alive again...The older people said to each other, 'Our mother has come back to feed us' (ST 54-55). Kire also portrays the evil side of humankind. Although Rhalietuo, the 'Son of the Thundercloud', successfully kills the tiger, at a later stage, the readers are told that he becomes a victim of conspiracy and jealousy. She asserts that wickedness and cruelty are endemic in humans. Rhalietuo's own kinsman betrayed him (ST 135). Through this, Kire intends to demonstrate how the coming of colonization put a strain on the Nagas' traditional way of life. Among all the changes that came with development was the loss of the oneness of community and culture among the people. Vilie was given food and shelter yet was also blamed for a murder he did not commit.

The hospitable nature of the Naga people is subtly brought out through Vilie's journey. Vilie was given shelter by the villagers at different stages, expecting nothing in return, even though he was a stranger. Courtesy demanded that a guest must be treated well. People invited Vilie to their homes without any requirement for him to provide identification. Subale, one of the women Vilie encountered in the border village, invited him to come and spend the night in her house. She said her husband, the village headman, would be happy to have him (WRS 87). In ST, she writes, "He [Pele] would partake of the hospitality of the starving inhabitants and continue on his journey" (16). Vilie was known for his tenacity and willpower. Helped by a wise older man, he was able to take possession of the stone that he had dreamed about for many nights. The tight bond of community life was still intact, to a certain degree.

Vilie met a young girl named Ate on his way home. She had lived in a village populated only by women considered to have magical powers (kirhupfumia), who were said to bring a curse on anyone just by pointing their fingers at them. However, Ate turned out to be harmless, unlike her older sister, Zote. She was brought back to Vilie's village and found a home with his paternal aunts. Importantly, she was made the custodian of the heart-stone. Vilie returned to his forest home, where he was murdered for the stone. Ate visits Vilie's forest home regularly and claims to feel his presence. This is an exciting narrative in which the female is made the custodian of a powerful force. In the book, Kire makes a point of mentioning the thriving trade between the Naga tribes in the past. "...Back then, we traded with the Angamis and took their daos, spears, and spades... in exchange for our brine salt, pigs, dried fish, and chilli" (WRS 35). Idele, the Zeliang lady, could even speak Angami, Vilie's language. Vilie made sure he does not misuse other's property. The idyllic picture of rural life is tempered by disturbing signs of the evil in man.

The author shows in a very realistic way that not everyone has good intentions. The drunkard Hiesa blamed Vilie for killing Pehu. The village that turned away the women suspected of having magical powers blundered by sending away Ate, a perfectly normal woman. A greedy man murdered the woodcutter family in the forest. Kire paints a picture of a vivid rural life that is as yet untouched by modernity and technology, although, unlike Frederick Clement's version of the pastoral, in which nature is seen as a stable and harmonious entity in the absence of humans, there were dark elements. The pastoral often uses nature as a reflection of human predicaments.

In both novels, nature is shown as a provider. Vilie had lived in the forest for many decades, depending mainly on it for sustenance. Like a woman, the forest provided him with food, shelter, and all kinds of amenities for his survival. Vilie was not the only one for whom the forest provided; the Nepali family, the Zeliang bark weavers, the villagers living on the borders, and even the *kirhupfumia* received support from the environment. Nature also provided a being who would be able to kill the 'tiger' and set the land free. The single drop of rain in the *Son of the Thundercloud* brings to fulfilment the prophecy of the birth of the Son of the Thundercloud. Pele's arrival brings rain, and Mesanuo is mystically impregnated by one raindrop: "When I was bringing in the herbs that I had put out to dry, I heard the rain coming, and before I could reach the house, a drop of rain fell on me... Nothing except for that one drop of rain. I felt the baby grow inside as soon as that drop landed on me" (ST 36-37). Mesanuo means 'the pure one' in the Angami language, and allegorically she is the manifestation of nature's purity. She represents Mother Earth, which needs rain for growth. All that was needed was just one drop of water. Kire has united Mother Earth with a human mother; both have the capacity to give birth and procreate, yet the patriarchal and consumerist society neglects them. The village headman is a typical representation of the biased patriarchal power that sees and understands everything but cannot accept it because he believes nothing could be superior to him.

The Nagas feared and revered the natural world. In an agricultural society, the survival of the villagers depended on the harvest. They worked together as a community. They reaped the Earth's bounty in economical and effective ways. The women folk gathered nettles, a natural material, from the forest for weaving and collected only enough for immediate use. Weaving skills were passed down from generation to generation. Men caught fish from the river, and vegetables were gathered from the forest or cultivated. People lived off the land and were self-sufficient, for they lived frugally. As a rule, nature was not plundered to make profits to amass wealth. The people in Pele's village started to take things easy because of prosperity and paid a heavy price for it. Kire warns people to be wary of the modern materialistic world where just a few people control maximum wealth and power, leaving thousands in the lurch. Vilie's life is used to demonstrate the wisdom of living frugally.

Vilie has made the forest his 'home' for the past twenty-five years. The other inhabitants of the forest who have intentionally made the forest their home, other than Vilie, are a Nepali couple. They worked as woodcutters and lived in the forest, not out of necessity but because they loved it. Once, when Vilie was visiting them, he asked the husband when his son would be going to school; the Nepali replied, 'I will teach him my trade, and he will grow up and earn an honest living. School is not for the likes of us', at which Vilie thought, 'What could school possibly teach him that his parents could not improve upon? They were rich in their knowledge of the ways of the forest, the herbs one could use for food, the animals and birds one could trap, and the bitter herbs to counteract the sting of a poisonous snake' (*WRS* 15).

The Naga people know nature and its produce intimately. They know the medicinal uses of plants and herbs and rely on them to treat ailments such as fever and combat malicious spirits. Indeed, they rely heavily on nature for any treatment. When Vilie was stung by nettle plants, Idele "looked around for an antidote. She plucked the leaves off a small bitter wormwood plant and kneaded it to a pulp in her hand...Vilie kept rubbing the paste into his skin, and that seemed to ease the smarting" (37). She also gave him rock bee honey, which was a 'cure-all' to put on the swelling from the nettle sting. All this indigenous knowledge about plants is lost with the loss of land. Vilie was an expert in using natural materials to treat injuries. The guardian of the forest carefully tended to injured forest dwellers... He was skilled at using splints to set broken bones. He would make pastes of *ciena* for open wounds, and for bigger wounds, he liked to use the pungent 'Japan *nha*' (Crofton weed) and rock bee honey, for the healing is quick, with little scarring (41). In *Son of The Thundercloud*, Kethono also talked about a healthy vegetarian diet; "We don't eat meat...We use mushrooms as meat supplements and find it much healthier" (93). In the past, the seers knew the properties of the herbs. Recent findings showed that processed food is not suitable for health. In the olden times, people who caught fever would be given a drink made of ginseng and the wild sour seed that grew on certain trees. The elders in the villages knew most of the curative herbs and plants, but unfortunately, they all died before they could pass down the knowledge to the next generation.

The wilderness in *When the River Sleeps* represents the 'New World wilderness' (Gerard), a place of retreat that Vilie withdraws to and finds sanctuary in. Wilderness was first a retreat for Vilie and then a sanctuary. He seeks refuge in the *Rarhuria* or 'unclean forest' when his enemies pursue him to kill him. Only when he was at the heart of the rainforest did Vilie feel safe. The wilderness that Vilie retreated to was a space of great significance. A wilderness was not measured just by human aesthetic or material needs; it was a place of 'sanctuary' for Vilie when he most needed it. He remained in the 'unclean forest' until the wound from the bullet had healed. Wilderness even gave him a clear and logical mind to decide on the best course to take after he got better. Instead of running away, he walked towards the village of his enemies to clear his name. Likewise, in *Son of the Thundercloud*, Mesanuo is metaphorically the Mother Earth that replenishes depleted resources for humanity, rain is the giver of life and hope to humankind, and Rhalie is the seed grain that is necessary for every society to survive. Pele is the harbinger of rain and hope.

CONCLUSION:

Naga literature in English has devoted considerable attention to the natural world. Indeed, the Naga people's deep love of nature and engagement with it are seen in the creative fiction dealing with ecological themes. Kire has consistently demonstrated sensitivity toward the nonhuman world in her fiction and poetry. Her works have been celebrated worldwide. When her literature is read from an ecocritical perspective, it reveals a complex dynamic between people and their environment. The Nagas' knowledge of nature and their love for the beauty of the land is one of the most attractive aspects of their writings. However, in their corpus of literature, explicit concerns about environmental degradation are also present. Kire's novels, which deal with the concerns and issues mentioned above, are easily among the world's best ecocritical novels.

Both novels in this study regard nature as empowered and not oppressed. Indeed, nature has the power to grant wishes to the worthy. The river holds the heart-stone, which every hunter covets. The stone can give a person whatever it is empowered to grant the owner. In the forest, the weretiger, the *gwi*, the tragopan, and many others thrived. The *kirhupfumia* thrown out by the villagers were protected and provided for by nature. Vilie also found protection in nature and, in return, protected nature. Vilie's relationship with the forest fully revealed the harmonious relationship between human beings and nature. Vilie was known far and wide as the 'guardian of the forest'. His reputation as an honest forester went before him. That is how he was set free when tried for homicide. '...this man is known to the community here by reputation. He is the guardian of the forest... whereas Hiesa, our clansman, is known to all as a lover of drink and a belligerent, quarrelsome man' (*WRS* 72).

Nature helps Vilie conquer his fear of people and spirits. He fled from the site of a murder out of fear of being implicated and took shelter in the deep jungle. In the calm of the forest, he could process his thoughts and decided to walk to the ancestral village to try to obtain justice. Nature helped him not only to conquer his fear of people but also his fear of spirits. As Vilie reaches the river of his dreams with the help of ..., he realizes that the 'river is a spirit'. Although he steps into the river to obtain the heart-stone, the force of the rushing water that almost strangled him made him realize that his fight was against a spirit. He conquers the fear of this spirit and the spirits of the widows by invoking nature – "Sky is my father, Earth is my mother, stand aside death! Kepenuopfu fights for me, today is my day! I claim the wealth of the river because mine is the greater spirit. To him who has the greater spirit belongs the stone!" (*WRS* 103).

Nature healed not only Vilie but Ate too, and in the same way, that nature had healed her, she was able to heal and nurture life in turn. Her journey through the forest was therapeutic in overcoming her fear of herself. She had lived her entire young life only with the disowned *kirhupfumia*. Her inherent goodness was brought out by Vilie's faith in her, aided by the stone's power. By the end of her journey from her village to Vilie's ancestral village, she was nurtured and transformed back into an ordinary young woman. She even adopted the baby of the murdered woodcutter couple.

Kire has a sense of urgency to teach the next generation how to live off and with nature. Idele taught the younger generation of women how to harvest nettles and weave clothes from them. "...we have time to make nettle-cloth, and we want the young ones to learn it before we all pass away. We have already lost one of our best weavers", the villagers told Vilie (*WRS* 182). The best weaver was Idele, at whose death her society grieved deeply. Her dying meant the loss of a rich storehouse of knowledge. When Vilie met her, she was tutoring a group of young women in harvesting nettles to weave them into clothes. A great melancholy settled on Vilie on learning of her death. Vilie's death was also a significant loss for his immediate community and the entire Naga community. The guardian of the forest, who protected the *gwi* and the tragopan and acted as a bridge of trust between different Naga communities, also took with him precious knowledge of nature when he was believed to have been murdered because of human greed. Many times, he was protected by the forest. It provided for him materially and psychologically. He remained true to the forest until the very end. Indeed, he gave back to nature as much as he had received from her. He passed on to Ate, a fitting successor, the wonderful gift of the river, which was the heart-stone.

The seemingly effortless narrative style of novels like *When the River Sleeps* and *Son of the Thundercloud* could only be achieved by great storytellers like Easterine Kire. Like nature, the heart-stone needs to continue its journey in the hands of ethical people, giving and taking only what is required and never taking advantage of it for material gain. It is only befitting that Ate, the woman who survived the murder of Vilie, is now the custodian of the mighty heart-stone. In *ST* too, Mesanuo survived to carry on after the murder of her son. She named the village Nouzie, which means compassion. Here, Kire gives a strong message that the faithful stewardship of Mother Earth lies in the hands of women.

WORKS CITED

Ao, Temsula. "Blood of Others." *The Oxford Anthology of Writings from North-East India*, edited by Tilottoma Misra, Oxford University Press, 2011, pp. 81–83.

Biswas, Debajyoti. "Confluence of Myth and Reality in Son of the Thunder Cloud," *MZU Journal of Literature and Cultural Studies*, 2018, www.academia. edu/39813898/Confluence_of_Myth_and_Reality_in_Son_of_the_ Thunder_Cloud. Accessed 10 October 2020.

Chingangbam, Anupama. "An Eco-Critical Approach: A Study of Selected North East Indian Poets." *The Criterion: An International Journal in English*, vol. 5, no.2, Apr. 2014 pp. 59-67., www.the-criterion.com/V5/n2/Anupama.pdf . Accessed 17 August 2020

Daftuar, Swati. "No Division between Spiritual and Physical." *The Hindu*, 21 Nov. 2015, www.thehindu.com/features/lit-for-life/swati-daftuar-speaks-to-easterine-kire-about-when-the-river-sleeps/article7903799.ece. Accessed 20 September 2020

Dai, Mamang. "An Obscure Place by Mamang Dai." *Poetry at Sangam*, poetry. sangamhouse.org/2013/07/an-obscure-place-by-mamang-dai/. Accessed 10 August 2020.

Dai, Mamang. "Small Towns and the River (Poem) - Mamang Dai - India - Poetry International." Homepage of Poetryinternationalweb.net, Writers Workshop, Kolkata, 2004, www.poetryinternational.org/pi/poem/17012/auto/0/0/ Mamang-Dai/Small-Towns-and-the-River/en/nocache. Accessed 10 August 2020.

Deane, Phyllis M. *The First Industrial Revolution*. Cambridge University Press, 1979.

Dean, Thomas K. "What Is Eco-Criticism?" Defining Ecocritical Theory and Practice: Sixteen Position Papers from the 1994 Western Literature Association Meeting, Western Literature Association, October 6, 1994, Utah, https:// www.asle.org/wp-content/uploads/ASLE_Primer_DefiningEcocrit.pdf Accessed 10 October 2020.

Garrard, Greg. *Ecocriticism*. 1st ed., Routledge, 2004.

Kire, Easterine. *A Terrible Matriarchy*. Zuban, 2013.

~ *Son of the Thundercloud*. Speaking Tiger Publishing, 2016.

~ *When the River Sleeps*. Zubaan, 2014.

Warren, K.J. "Feminist Theory: Ecofeminist and CULTURAL FEMINIST." *International Encyclopedia of the Social & Behavioral Sciences*, edited by Paul B Bates and Neil J Smelser, 2001, pp. 5495–5499., doi:10.1016/b0-08-043076-7/03949-8 Accessed 15 December 2011

Nayar, Pramod K. *Contemporary Literary and Cultural Theory: From Structuralism to Ecocriticism*. 5th ed., Pearson India Education, 2013.

16

MYTH, REALITY, AND RE-TELLING: A STUDY OF EASTERINE KIRE'S FICTION

Lalthansangi Ralte

INTRODUCTION

Easterine Kire is a poet and novelist who has written extensively on her people, the Nagas. In this chapter, I shall undertake a study of a selection of her works, while, at the same time, focusing mainly on her three novels, *Mari*, *A Respectable Woman*, and *Son of the Thundercloud*. In *Mari*, Kire tells the story of a Naga woman who fell in love with a British soldier during the Battle of Kohima in the Second World War. *A Respectable Woman* tells how "the War" brought the world closer to the Nagas. Amid post-war reconstruction and rehabilitation, these two novels show how the reality of death is brought home to the people of Nagaland. *Son of the Thundercloud* tells the story of a place where there is no concept of time, where spirits mingle with the living. In these three novels, the novelist deals with life, pain caused by death and peace gained with "hope". Easterine Kire writes about the "virgin" soil of the Naga hills and how the land is taken by a "sojourner" from distant lands. The wisdom of ancestors and storytellers is brought to light as they are the ones who have lived longer than others and continue to live on through their stories. Thus, this chapter will focus on the importance of scripting stories and songs and how this task needs to be taken on by the people of the region/state.

The Nagas are a people "without writing" until the latter part of the 19th century. The renowned anthropologist and structuralist Claude Lèvi-Strauss writes about how "myths get thought in man unbeknownst to him" (1). He further writes that myth describes a "lived experience" (1). Lèvi-Strauss believes that one should try to regain that "mythical thought" (4), which has been lost and forgotten in time and become aware of its existence and importance. (3). He reveals how we "usually and wrongly" describe people "without writing" as "primitive" (11). Lèvi-Strauss argues that the "thought" of people without writing is not inferior but "a fundamentally different kind of thought...entirely determined by emotion and mystic representations" (12). These people "without writing" depend on their myths and legends as their source of historical "facts". By writing about the myths and legends of the Nagas, Kire demonstrates that the Nagas weren't a "primitive" people but a people guided by a strong belief system. Lèvi-Strauss is of the opinion that "history" as we write it is practically based upon written documents (33). The important question is – where do myths and legends end, and where does history begin?

Easterine Kire brings to light the taboos and traditions of her people through her writing. Her novel *Son of the Thundercloud* (henceforth *Son*) tells a timeless tale where myths and legends, the "unknown", mingle with "real-life" experiences. The wise grandmother, who is named "the solitary one", insists on giving a significant name to her grandson. She believes that giving a significant name is important as it will make the person live a powerful life. She names her grandson Pelevotso, which means "faithful to the end". Furthermore, she insists that he is made to understand the true meaning of his name and to live a good life. In tribal cultures, elders are respected, and it is believed that disobeying their words often leads to tragedy. In her poem *Genesis*, Easterine Kire writes -

> Kevilesie speaks of a time
> when her hills were untamed
> her soil young and virgin
> and her warriors worthy
> the earth had felt good
> and full and rich and kind to his touch (*Dancing Earth* 139).

Being a Naga of the Angami tribe, Easterine Kire's fiction mainly deals with the culture and tradition of the Angamis. In her book *Walking the Roadless Road Exploring the Tribes of Nagaland*, she writes, "the Angami is deeply aware of the spiritual world around him and accepts its parallel existence with the natural world" (63). In *Son*, Pelevotso was raised in a household that respected the taboos of the community. It was his grandmother who told him to open his heart to the unknown. It is only when disaster happens that one is reminded of the old storyteller who told tales of taboos, traditions, and the spiritual world.

The Angamis have a linguistic taboo where hunters refer to the tiger as "elder brother". After Rhalietuo kills the spirit tiger and returns to his village, he is denied entry at the gate as the villagers knew he had killed their "elder brother" (*Son* 131). Easterine Kire has written stories about a man who became a bear, weretigermen, and people who became one with the spirits of their dead fathers (*The Windhover Collection* 75-80). The short story *The Weretigerman* is about weretigermen, half-man, half-spirit, who die when their "spirit" tigers are killed. In this story, she writes that "the nexus between tiger and man was still attended by the mystery and the awe that shrouds the supernatural" (77).

LIFE, DESTINY, AND DEATH

In the three novels chosen for this study, Easterine Kire writes about the loss of a dear one. Pelevotso, a heartbroken man, who has lost his wife and children to famine, is reminded of having a purpose in life, a destiny. Rhalietuo's dying aunt Kethonuo tells him about mortality, that "it is a good thing that we are made to die" (*Son* 110). Rhalietuo, Son of the Thundercloud, has a destiny, and this destiny is to kill the tiger that killed his father and brothers. The prophecy is that the Son of the Thundercloud, Rhalietuo (redeemer), will kill the tiger and free the people from fear. On their return to the Village of Weavers, the headman of the village told Pele that not everyone hoped that the prophecy would be fulfilled.

In this Christological tale, the prophecies directly talk about what was prophesied about the birth of Christ. In the Bible, after Isaiah, there was no word from God for 700 years. Similarly, in the novel, the sisters were simply living on faith, expecting the prophecy of the Saviour's birth to happen in their time. The headman and his wife believe that Rhalietuo and Pele will be able to kill the tiger but that the death of the tiger will put all of them in danger. They believe that the tiger is protecting their fields, keeping other animals away, and making sure that they have good harvests so that they can sacrifice to him. The hostility of the "real people" (119) is a response to Rhalietuo's goodness. The tiger was not an animal of flesh and blood but a spirit that had spread its influence over the people who believed in its power and offered sacrifices to it. The tiger's power was spread by word of mouth, which frightened the people and made them believe in it even more.

Mary Mead Clark, an American who came to Nagaland with her husband on a mission to convert the natives to Christianity, documented her experiences along with her husband's in *A Corner in India*. In this book, she wrote of the indigenous beliefs of the Nagas as "the old, cruel faith" which was "a religion of fear" (168). She says that Naga animism was mainly occupied with "propitiating spirits through animal sacrifices, *gennas* (a complex term, including the notions of taboo or forbidden things or forbidden days, and the ceremonies connected with them), and other arcane rituals" (Borgohain and Borgohain 88). Similarly, in the prophecy of the Son of the Thundercloud, the fear of the tiger strengthens its existence, making the people question the truth of the prophecy of the Saviour. In the story, the people "allowed the dark ones to enslave their minds and fill them with fear and sorrow and despair until they died" (*Son* 63).

At the launch of her book *A Respectable Woman* in Aizawl on 4th November 2019, Easterine Kire spoke of a tradition of prophecy by non-Christian prophetesses. Dressed all in white, they used to go to different Angami villages. One such prophetess carried a little machete and dramatically delivered her predictions. First, she prophesied that war was coming and, indeed, the Second World War happened in the Naga hills. After that, she prophesied a new war, and the Indo-Naga war happened. Kire mentioned that, even after Christianity, the number of prophets has increased and that there are many centres where "prophecies" are given for people to use as guides in their lives. In *Son of the Thundercloud*, the prophecies received were from the spirit world, given to guide people into their destined futures. And it is very much part of native wisdom to discern prophecy as true or false.

The Mizos also have a tradition of prophecies. In the 1937 September edition of the Mizo newspaper *Mizo leh Vai Chanchinbu*, we find that there was a spiritual revival in the village of Kelkang on the western border of Mizoram. The revivalists prophesied that the world would end in four-months-time and so there was no need to go to school. Mr Pasina, a revivalist, prophesied that God would provide them with threshed rice. He went around shouting that Kelkang would be the spiritual headquarters in Mizoram. He predicted that "rice will rain down from the heavens", and claimed that this prophecy was known throughout the world (Chhawntluanga 31). Later on, many people even said that this particular prophecy must have meant the rice supplied by the government after Mizoram became a Union Territory in 1972.

During the spiritual revival of 1937, there was another prophecy that three men would be imprisoned and that there would be an earthquake the night they were released. On 12th September 1937, three men from Kelkang village were imprisoned under a three-year sentence. In July 1939, there was an earthquake, just one month before their release on 29th August of that year (33). It was also prophesied that the Mizos would experience the wealth of Burma. The revivalists staged a play and prophesied that the Crown would be defeated. Then came the Second World War. The defeat of the Crown could mean the independence of the colonies. There was a prophecy that the chief of Kelkang village would be fined 60 rupees; this prophecy also came true (33). Many plays enacted by the revivalists were also considered to prophecy the "grouping" of villages during *Rambuai* (troubled times), the period of insurgency in Mizoram (34). Accordingly, it is difficult for a people with a tradition of prophecies to abruptly stop believing in them, as there have been many instances where the prophecies came true, thus reinforcing the belief.

In her novels, *Mari* and *A Respectable Woman*, Easterine Kire brings together history, real-life and fiction. *Mari* roughly covers the period from 1943 to 1998. The Battle of Kohima, referred to as "The War", was fought between the British and the Japanese troops from 4th April to 22nd June 1944. The fighting, which continued for roughly two and a half months, took many lives and destroyed many buildings. *Mari* is based on a true story, the story of Khrielieviu Mari O' Leary, the author's mother's eldest sister. In her author's note, Easterine Kire describes how she wrote this novel based on the diary Mari kept during the war years and the stories narrated by her own mother. She also wrote that her people have very little memory of what they were doing before the war years; she even refers to it as "the big bang, the beginning of all life" (viii). The War brought the Nagas face to face with many changes; they even saw aeroplanes, which none of them had expected to see during their lifetime. With war approaching, many new roads were built in Kohima by the beginning of 1942. Many young Naga men left for Tiddim in Burma to work as labourers. In preparation for war, they were employed to dig roads and were paid well for their work. It was March 1943 when the war reached Kohima –

> It began with hordes of refugees that the Japanese invasion had pushed into our lands. They came in wretched bands; starving, diseased dregs of humanity, droves of them dropping down dead by the roadside or in the refugee camps. The Burmese refugees, as we called them, were not ethnically Burmese but largely of Tamilian stock, for many Tamilians had settled in Burma as traders before the war. They carried their belongings with them, in little boxes or bags, and many had bleeding feet as they had walked a very long distance barefoot. (17)

The War brought with it death, starvation, and disease; the Nagas encountered misery and grief of a new order. As war broke out, the more modern Naga men with western hairstyles were given "Naga haircuts". This was done so that they would not be easy targets for the Japanese, who could pick them out and force them to work as spies. Modern clothes and haircuts could be taken as a sign that one was educated and, therefore, could be more "useful" to the enemy as they had more knowledge about the area beyond their village. The fairer men and women were made to smear ash on their faces as fair skin also signified that the person was not an agricultural worker living in the village but a wealthy person from the town. In times of war, the allure of beauty brings with it the threat of danger; the women, especially, had to hide their beauty by smearing ash on their faces and wearing old, faded clothes and waistcloths. There were stories of women raped by the Japanese troops. Before the Japanese came, the Nagas knew very little of this most atrocious crime. The yesteryears, when "the earth had felt good/and full and rich and kind to his touch" (*Dancing Earth* 139) are gone. "Plague, a sojourner" has taken their land and "reaped premature harvests of fields and men" (140). The War introduced the Nagas to the British, Indian, and Gurkha troops. The devastation wrought by guns and bombs left a lasting effect on the people.

In Easterine Kire's novel *Mari*, the protagonist fell in love with Victor, a Staff Sergeant in the British Army, before the war. In March, 1944, Vic started living with Mari's family and moved all of his belongings to their house. The coming of war made it acceptable for them to live together because, in their culture, "Vic coming to live with me made us a married pair" (*Mari* 62). On the night of 3rd April 1944, Mari had to flee with her family as the Japanese troops had reached Kohima. She had to part with Vic, who had to stay on and protect Kohima from the Japanese troops. Mari, her brother, his wife, and a woman named Vikieu and her baby left together. As they were parting with Vic, Vikieu looked at him anxiously and asked Mari to tell him to take good care and drive safely. Vikieu said, "I could see sudden death on his forehead. I can't say how or when, but I could see it very clearly" (71). This alarmed Mari and made her worry for Vic even more. They fled to the village of Chieswema, which was soon occupied by Japanese soldiers, so they had to flee to the forest. Food became scarce, and any procured food was first shared with families and then shared with others only when it was in excess. War hardened the people who had been taught to give the better portions of food to their neighbours; war made them think only of themselves. The sound of distant gunfire and bombs became a part of their lives, and "silence" became abnormal.

One day, as they were fleeing through the woods, a bee kept buzzing in front of Mari's face and would not leave her. She and the others became alarmed as their people were "keenly alive to unusual signs in the natural world…If a bee will not stop bothering a person for a long time, it is because it has a message for the person" (98). Mari, fearing that Vic or her family had been killed, began to weep uncontrollably. When she was unable to control her tears, her sisters, overcome by the uncertainty of life, also began to cry. After the incident with the bee, Mari's mind continued to be occupied with thoughts of Vic and her mother, wondering if they were safe. On 1ˢᵗ May 1944, after safely reaching Jotsoma, Mari was told the terrible news that Vic was killed by a sniper's bullet on 18ᵗʰ April, the same day that the bee kept buzzing near her. In tribal cultures, these "signs" are still revered even though one is unable to explain the origin of such beliefs. The origin of such beliefs is hard to trace because these beliefs have been around for a long time, spanning many generations. The Nagas take their cues from the natural world. If one hears the cry of a migratory bird at night, it means death is coming to your family. If insects, animals, and birds behave in an unnatural manner, it means they have something to convey pertaining to you, as in the case of Mari regarding Vic's death (Easterine Kire at her book launch in Aizawl in 2019). One can say that such beliefs originate and build up from the past experiences of people in the community. Some women have the gift of "reading" people's destinies by looking at them. The woman accompanying Mari on their escape to Chieswema saw in Victor's face that he would die a sudden death. His sudden death happened, reinforcing the belief.

Easterine Kire's *A Respectable Woman* opens in the aftermath of the War. The novel begins –

> It took my mother, Khonuo, exactly forty-five years before she
> could bring herself to talk about the war. She was ten years old
> when the Japanese invaded our hills in 1944. (3)

Memories of war, of an unrecognizable Kohima in the aftermath of the War, are forever etched in the people's hearts. The end of the War was a moment of victory and triumph, but the people were brought back to reality when they were unable to find their homes. In her novel, she writes about the pain of her community, their grief and horror as they mourned loudly the homes and family members they lost to the War. After the War, Kohima was rebuilt; the District Commissioner (DC) and his men set up a table where the people who had lost their homes and households reported themselves, clan by clan.

The suffering undergone by the Nagas during and after the War – the struggle to earn a living and support a family – is shown in *A Respectable Woman*. Khonuo became a widow in 1971 at the very young age of thirty-seven. She went back to her job as a teacher because she had to earn for her family. After the death of her husband, her friends and relatives would send them food to show their sympathy and as "a way to partake in their sorrow" (A *Respectable Woman* 35). Khonuo would tell her daughter Kevinuo about her generation of people and how they were more broad-minded than the present generation. The War had changed people; she said that they had seen the devastation of war, and how one could lose everything one owned overnight. The imminence of death made them value love and generosity above all else. Her brother Amo had a war wound, a splinter that had lodged very close to his heart. Amo refused to marry, knowing that he could die if the splinter punctured his aorta. He died when he was thirty-nine years old. Amo's younger brother Razuo died when he was only seven. Their mother continued to mourn for him, and when Amo died, she was overcome by profound sorrow. It is said that she died of a broken heart because she was so deeply affected by the death of her sons that she lost her will to live. Some of Amo's soldier friends never returned after the War. The families of those soldiers found it difficult to find closure as they could not mourn the bodies of their loved ones. The War brought them closer to all kinds of emotions, bringing along development whereby the gap between the rich and the poor deepened. It even brought "home the reality of death" (54). The sufferings of the people were "experiences of bereavement and loss, social isolation and personal estrangement", which included "feelings of depression, anxiety, guilt, humiliation, boredom and distress" (Nayar 2011, 78).

DEPARTURE OF THE BRITISH

The British left Nagaland in 1947 and left the Naga-inhabited areas divided between India and Burma. Leaders of the Naga National Council (NNC) protested and refused to join the Indian union. This response was countered by the Indian government sending in armed police to suppress the freedom movement. Kethonuo described the acts of violence committed on her people, in which young and old died from starvation and beatings. She said, "We were no longer safe in our own homes...it was like a whole generation of men disappeared because they were all killed, one after the other...Life was so much worse than it was during the Japanese war...British and Indian soldiers came by the thousands, but we never feared them; we knew they were there to protect our lands. But now people had grown to fear the sight of the Indian soldiers" (A *Respectable Woman* 58-59). The Naga men were committed to fighting for their land; before Christianity entered their lands, they would always feel obliged to avenge the killing of a family member. This spirit of avenging the death of a loved one still burnt in the hearts of the Nagas. In expressing the willingness of the Naga men to lay down their lives for their homeland, Kire puts forth the question – "Was it because it was so close to the Japanese war where they had witnessed men laying down their lives to defend Kohima against the invaders?" (62). The unrest made the people more determined to live a normal life in order to survive. Life was harder for the wives of the men who had gone to join the Underground army as they had to singlehandedly take care of their children.

Khonuo had a deep and meaningful relationship with her daughter, and she would tell her about her own grandfather, a famous bone-setter. Her grandfather would never ask for payment and refuse payment, saying that "this is a gift from *Terhuomia* (the spirits)" (49). However, this bone-setting skill was practised only by non-Christians, as the bone-setters would talk to the spirits before attending to their patients. During her growing-up years in the 1970s, Kevinuo heard of various spirit sightings, especially of a warrior spirit who would be seen wearing the traditional attire of a warrior. Atsa Nisou, her grandmother who was not a Christian, told her that she had seen the warrior spirit many times, maybe because he did not like her coming too often to a Christian's house. She furthermore said that spirits are afraid of Christians, which is why they frighten the non-Christians to prevent them from converting to Christianity.

In their book *Scrolls of Strife The endless history of the Nagas*, Homen Borgohain and Pradipta Borgohain write about the "continuing battle" of the Nagas with the Indian government. In *A Respectable Woman*, Kire tells the story of the Nagas right after the Second World War. As time passed, development in and around Kohima led to an increase in travel, further leading to the development of trade and commerce in Nagaland. As there were better opportunities to succeed in the capital town, there was a great influx of population in the 1970s and 1980s. Even during that time, armed conflict and militarization were still ongoing in Nagaland.

In 1975, the government of India imposed President's rule in Nagaland, which resulted in the signing of the Shillong Accord by a section of the Naga National Council (NNC) leaders in November 1975. The Shillong Accord was denounced by leaders like Isak Swu and Thuingaleng Muivah, who aligned with Khaplang, with whom they formed the National Socialist Council of Nagaland (NSCN) in 1980. In 1988, NSCN split into two factions – one led by Khaplang and the other by Swu and Muivah (Srikanth and Thomas, 62-63). Later on, the National Socialist Council of Nagaland (Isak-Muivah) (NSCN-IM) signed a ceasefire agreement with the Indian government in 1997. Even as recently as 2009, these authors write, "the military is still obtrusive enough to add to the overall fear-factor, giving Nagaland an aura of a forbidden land" (Borgohain and Borgohain 175-176).

Dolly Kikon, an anthropologist from Nagaland, has written extensively on conflict and sexual violence in Nagaland. She has termed the Indo-Naga conflict "the longest insurgency in South Asia" (22) in her book *Life and Dignity*. She uses the phrase "culture of impunity" frequently to explain the injustice in the legal system in the state. She writes, "By culture of impunity, I am referring to the established practice of absolving perpetrators and granting them legal impunity under extra-constitutional regulations like the Armed Forces Special Powers Act" (1958) (23-24). The ongoing political unrest in the state brought about frustration in the men who succumbed to drinking and alcohol abuse. *A Respectable Woman* tells the story of the evils of alcoholism and how a sprightly young woman becomes a victim of an abusive drunken husband. Easterine Kire writes, "...the debate drew on the stories of those families where the men were using up their salaries on alcohol and had nothing left to support their families" (102). This was one of the "real" problems faced by many Naga families where stories of wives being severely beaten by their drunken husbands began to surface in many discussions – "...It is not a good system we have of sending girls back to husbands who are abusive. It's as good as sending them back to their deaths". (103) Kevinuo had a heated discussion with her best friend Beinuo regarding marriage and what it would be like to be beaten by their husbands, supposing they had one. Beinuo, without hesitation, said that if her husband beat her, she would beat him right back, adding that he had no right to beat her. The two friends talked of the many things girls had to leave behind to start a family with their husbands. Beinuo even said, "It's almost as though we enter into a life of slavery for the honour of being someone's wife". (105) Beinuo tragically ended up marrying an abusive husband, who was not happy when they had a daughter. When Beinuo shared this with Kevinuo, she said that it was a matter she had to sort out on her own as it was "their" problem. After the death of their infant son, Beinuo's husband, Meselhuo, became more violent, blaming her for the death of their son. Finally, the day came when Beinuo died at the hands of her abusive husband; on her death bed, she told Kevinuo all the abuses she had suffered at the hands of her husband, how she was afraid to tell her because she would insist that she leave him. She also begged her best friend to take care of her daughter Uvi after her death.

In the "real" world, a woman cannot easily leave her husband, no matter how abusive he is. A divorced woman will no longer be a "respectable woman" in society; society will also blame her for the abuses suggesting that she may have challenged her husband to end up being beaten up so severely. Dolly Kikon writes about how Naga women "suffer quietly as they were often held accountable" (Kikon 104) for the abuse they suffer in the hands of their men, even in the hands of their husbands. Abuse within the family is considered an "internal matter" (117) to be dealt with within the family.

In *A Respectable Woman,* no matter how violent and irresponsible her father was, it was impossible for Uvi to be taken care of by Kevinuo. Meselhuo even said that his family was his "property", so he could do whatever he wanted with it. In Angami customary law, if a woman was mistreated by her husband, her brothers had the right to take her away from him. Beinuo's tragedy was that she had no brothers, and her father, the one person who could bring a case against Meselhuo, did not do anything.

Soon after Beinuo's death, Meselhuo died after being severely beaten by the nighttime Central Reserve Police patrol as he and his friend, in their drunken stupor, were throwing stones at the patrol. Kevinuo, more determined than ever to take care of Uvi, thought of ways to adopt her. Her mother told her that it was not "culturally correct" for her to take care of her best friend's daughter as they were not related by blood. Kevinuo needed to have an ancestor who connected her family to Meselhuo's family so that "cultural obligation" could be used as the reason for wanting to adopt Uvi. Her brother Ato said, "If we could find one common ancestor, then I could present myself as a male relative with a responsibility to look after the orphaned child of my kinsman and they would find that harder to refuse". (159) Such is the authority of the men in Naga society where "the metaphor 'being a woman' indicated inadequacy and deficiency, and women were seen as inferior, ignorant, ill-prepared, insufficient, and unacceptable as decision makers" (Kikon 118-119). After finding that they had common ancestors with Meselhuo's family, his mother agreed to Uvi being raised by Kevinuo, an educated single woman and her mother's best friend.

STORIES AND THE STORYTELLER

Storytellers pass on the knowledge system of their people orally from generation to generation. They are the memory-keepers who, in narrating their stories preserve their ancestors' traditions, customs, and knowledge. With the development of print culture, these memories and knowledge systems become inscribed in books for future generations to read and study. It has often been argued that some elements are lost when oral narratives are converted to print. Claude Lèvi-Strauss, discussing myths, writes, "... there are some things we have lost, and we should try perhaps to regain them, because I am not sure that...we can regain these things exactly as if they had never been lost" (Lèvi-Strauss 3). Walter J. Ong writes of oral culture, that they "use stories of human action, to store, organize and communicate much of what they know." (140) Easterine Kire faithfully clings to her people's oral past and her ancestors' wisdom in her works. For her people, there is a mythical story connected to every mountain, river and waterfall, every beast. In *Son of the Thundercloud*, Kire writes of the "way" of her people, their traditions, and the taboos that must be obeyed to avoid misfortune.

In *Son of the Thundercloud*, the names she gives her characters become very relevant as the story progresses. Pelevotso (which means faithful till the end) faces sorrow and betrayal, but after seeing the goodness of Mesanuo and her son Rhalietuo and her sisters Kethonuo and Siedze, hope is revived in his heart. He was faithful to these four people till the end; he knew that his destiny was to be a part of their lives and to help them fulfil their destinies. Mesanuo, the pure one, mysteriously became pregnant with a son when a single raindrop fell on her from the sky. Her destiny was to give birth to a son who would kill the tiger spirit and free his people. Rhalietuo, the redeemer, fulfilled his destiny by killing the tiger spirit and freeing his people from its bad influence. After Mesanuo, previously referred to as "the tiger widow", gave birth to her son, the villagers began to question the credibility of the situation. Some thought it was "just a story" and some even said she must have had a secret lover. They chose to believe what was more plausible.

Mesanuo told Pele about life before the drought and how there were storytellers who spread joy and hope by telling their tales. The storytellers were all killed by the "dark ones" who did not want the people to be transformed by the stories – "without the stories, people believed they were destined to suffer, and they allowed the dark ones to enslave their minds and fill them with fear and sorrow and despair until they died". (63) The "dark ones" could be satanic forces seducing people with their lies, depriving them of hope and letting their minds grow darker and darker. The effect was so strong that people even forgot that they controlled their own destinies. The tiger spirit even succeeded in seducing the villagers so that they worshipped him and made them say that the story of the raindrop son was a lie. They gradually forgot their ancestors' instructions, and the tales of their people were believed to be "just myths". The acceptance of the darkness brought about the drought (lack of rain) and the drought of stories and hope.

Kire highlights the importance of storytellers, especially for a people who had an oral culture till very recently. Through her novel, Kire tells how "prophecies die in the face of unbelief" (117). The world often ridicules the story of the virgin birth of Christ in the same manner that the Village of Weavers begins to doubt the birth of the raindrop son. It is when Pele,

Mesanuo, Rhalie, Kethonuo, and Siedze are on the mountaintop that all the supernatural and spiritual things start to happen. The faith that brings miracles to birth is born up on the mountain, not down in the valley. When Pele reaches the mountaintop, his disbelief is slowly peeled off, even if he is reluctant to believe. The storytellers become responsible to their people as they are the "memory-keepers" of their race. The task of scripting stories and putting them in print becomes very crucial because the process of re-telling often adulterates stories in the same manner that the prophecy of the Son of the Thundercloud has many different versions.

CONCLUSION

Easterine Kire represents "real" events, events beyond one's control, which nevertheless appear "unreal" in some of her works. She writes about real-life horrors, like a husband beating his wife to death, in her book *A Respectable Woman*. A husband who beats his wife without any inhibition traces "the culture of impunity and the liberty of perpetrators" (Kikon) in Nagaland. Regarding the enforcement of law in the land, Kikon writes, "As the guilty stood outside the purview of law, it ushered a culture of impunity among Naga society at large that legitimized everyday violence including domestic and sexual assaults. In some cases, if the survivor seeks to take up the case, the family members blame the victim for shaming the household members and abandons her" (*Life and Dignity* 24).

Kire writes about the suffering of a woman who bears a child without a husband in *Mari*. In *Son of the Thundercloud*, she writes about the responsibility of the storytellers who had the power to transform people. In this novel, she brings forth the true meaning of life through her depiction of myth, the spiritual world, and the real world. Kire writes about the real-life horrors brought about by war and its aftermath, of a people disillusioned by the government and by life. She makes her readers witness to the suffering of her people, the representation of suffering which "gives a voice to those who suffer, while alerting us (those who are witnesses) to the need to alleviate such suffering, recognise the victims and attempt to reorder the conditions in which suffering takes place". (Nayar 2011, 78). Her fiction becomes a testimonial for her people, representing their pain by putting it into print. She breaks new ground by telling the untold stories of her people, including the hidden stories of the sufferings of women, and speaks for them by telling their stories. Thus, through her stories, Kire shows how "the domestic is a part of the public sphere for societies in armed conflict because testimonies of violence and loss are not personal affairs" (Sundar and Kikon 79).

WORKS CITED

Borgohain, Homen and Borgohain, Pradipta. *Scrolls of Strife (The endless history of the Nagas)*. Rupa Publications India Pvt. Ltd., 2011.

Chhawntluanga. *Kelkang Hlimpui 1937*. Synod Publication Board, 1985.

Clark, Mary Mead. *A Corner in India*. Christian Literature Centre, 1978.

Kikon, Dolly. *Life and Dignity*. North Eastern Social Research Centre (NESRC), 2015.

Kikon, Dolly. "Memories of Rape". *Fault Lines of History*. Zubaan, 2016.

Kire, Easterine. *The Windhover Collection*. Steven Herlekar, 2001.

Kire, Easterine. *Mari*. Harper Collins Publishers India, 2010.

Kire, Easterine. *Son of the Thundercloud*. Speaking Tiger, 2016.

Kire, Easterine. *A Respectable Woman*. Zubaan, 2019.

Kire, Easterine. *Walking the Roadless Road Exploring the Tribes of Nagaland*. Aleph Book Company, 2019.

Makthanga. ed. *Mizo leh Vai Chanchinbu*. The Assistant Superintendent, N. Lushai Hills, Aijal. Issue 9, September 1937.

Nayar, Pramod K. *States of Sentiment Exploring the Cultures of Emotion*. Orient Blackswan, 2011.

Ngangom, Robin S. and Nongkynrih, Kynpham S. *Dancing Earth – An Anthology of Poetry from North-East India*. Penguin Books India, 2009.

Ong, Walter J. *Orality and Literacy The Technologizing of the Word*. TJ Press, 1982.

Strauss, Claude Levis. *Myth and Meaning*. Routledge Indian Reprint, 2006.

Srikanth, H. and Thomas, C.J. "Naga Resistance Movement and the Peace Process in Northeast India" in *Peace and Democracy in South Asia*. Volume 1, Issue 2, 2005 accessed on 8/8/2022.

Sundar, Nandini and Kikon, Dolly. "Writing Counter-insurgency, Conflict and Democracy". *Indian Democracy Origins, Trajectories, Contestations*. Pluto Press, 2019.

INDEX